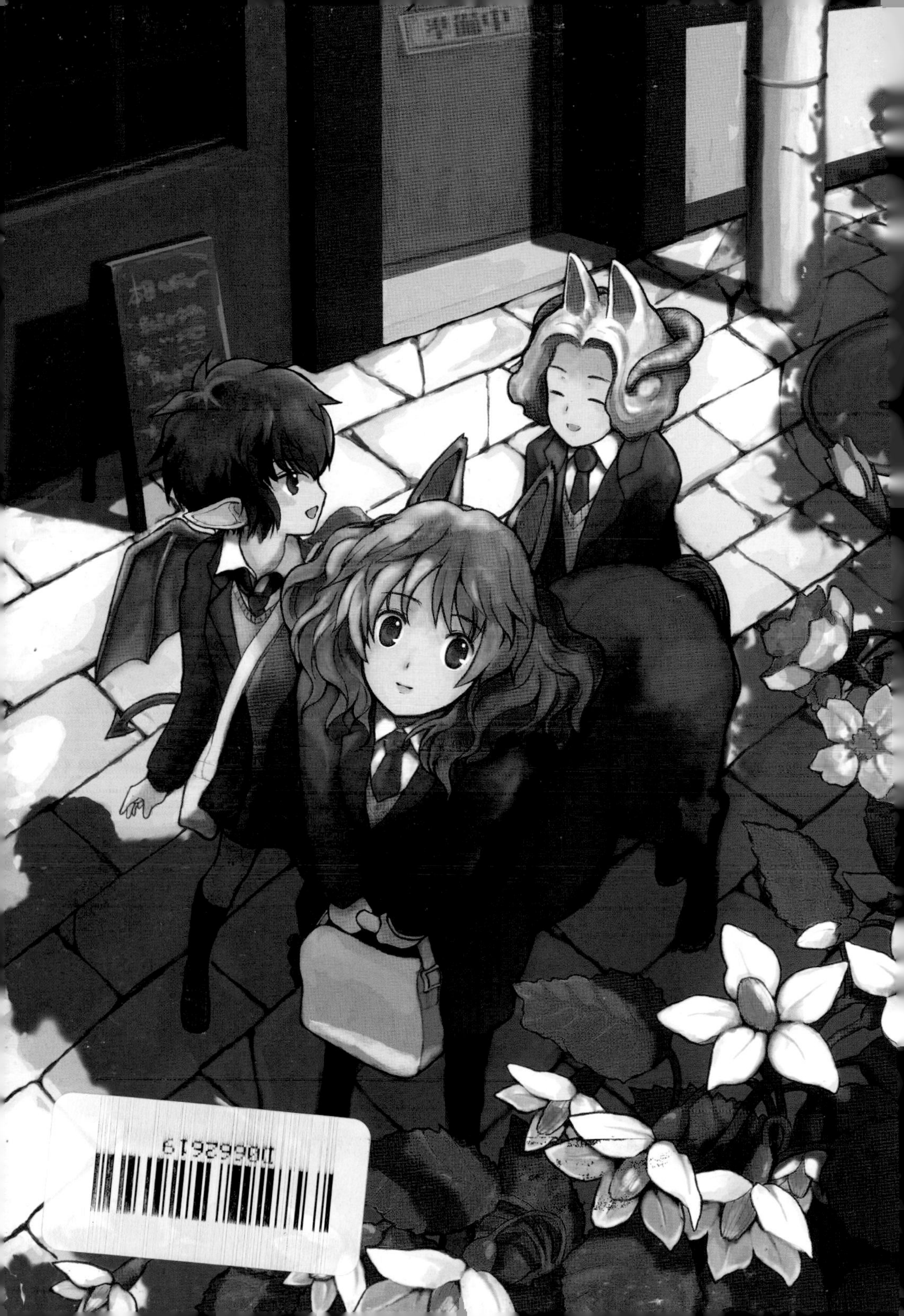

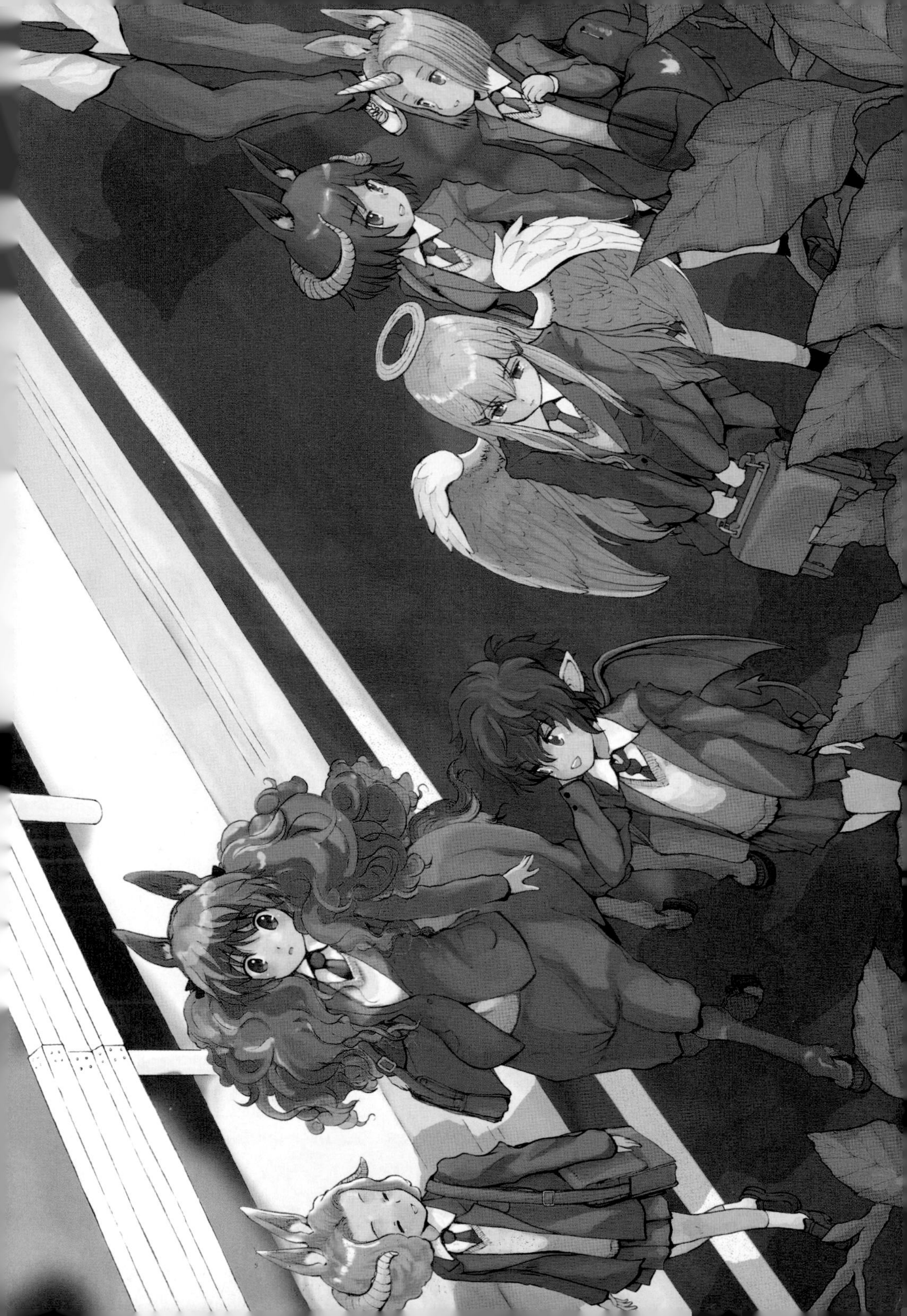

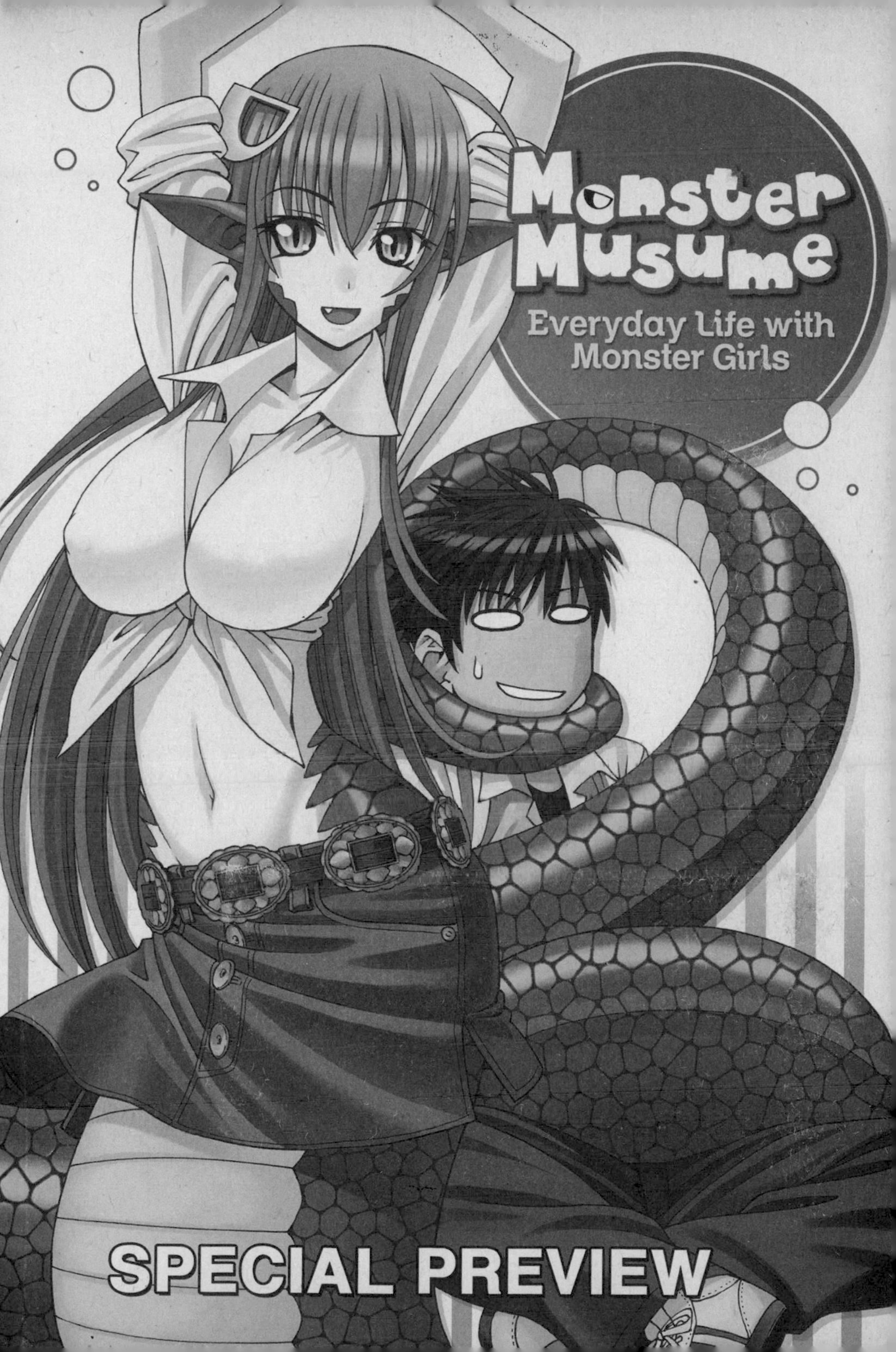
Monster Musume
Everyday Life with Monster Girls
SPECIAL PREVIEW

LEARN ABOUT OUR TOWN!
KANATA CITY'S PAST, PRESENT, AND FUTURE.

The southern region bordered by the Sanzuse River (on the Yamato Kingdom side) is called Konata [此方] and means "this side," while the northern areas beyond the river are known as Kanata [彼方], or "that side." Akenuma no Saku [朱沼柵 (or Red Swamp Line)] is so named due to the red swamps that used to exist in this region. It is also known as the Akenuma Line because forts were built to ward off enemies on the north side. In later times, the Yamato clans continued to expand northward, and Kanata [彼方] became Furukanata [古彼方 (old Kanata)], and the new area was named Imakanata [今彼方 (present Kanata)], and the land beyond it Ima no Hate [今果 (the present end)]**.

The arrival of Buddhism changed the world perspective of Kanata and intermingled with the old ways. The concept of life after death was introduced, and the Sanzuse River became the mythological river the dead must cross before entering the afterlife.

The land of Kanata is known for one other thing. Shu [朱 (crimson red)], in other words, red mercuric sulfide, which is used to create the red pigment known as vermillion, ran through the land. The aristocratic Akaike family mined this vein and used the resulting wealth to raise temples and further develop the land.

As stated above, the city of Kanata was sandwiched between the Yamato Kingdom and the northern indigenous Ezo people. Unfortunately, the lack of written records from the Ezo tribes makes it difficult to discern their cultural history. There are many theories regarding the true nature of the Ezo tribes, some that even go so far to suggest they were an ethnic group of angelfolk. Based on existing artifacts and the historical records of the Yamato Kingdom, the Ezo have been portrayed mainly as hunters and gatherers. One theory suggests that the Yamato Kingdom completely conquered the Ezo people. The current consensus is that the Ezo gradually and peacefully assimilated into Yamato culture.

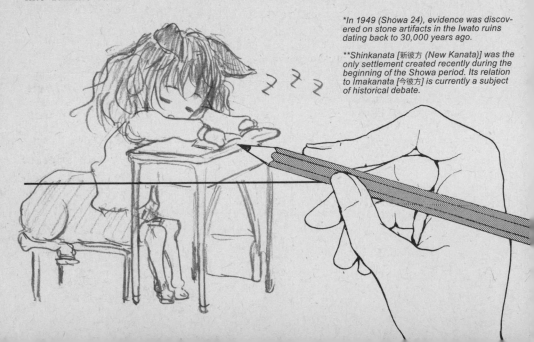

*In 1949 (Showa 24), evidence was discovered on stone artifacts in the Iwato ruins dating back to 30,000 years ago.

**Shinkanata [新彼方 (New Kanata)] was the only settlement created recently during the beginning of the Showa period. Its relation to Imakanata [今彼方] is currently a subject of historical debate.

LEARN ABOUT OUR TOWN! KANATA CITY'S PAST, PRESENT, AND FUTURE.

WHAT KIND OF PLACE IS KANATA CITY?

The place we live, Kanata City, is 72 km southeast of the capital in the flatlands of the Kanto region. We are positioned southwest in the Hidachi Prefecture. The city is 284.07 square meters and the main Sanzuse River runs through the center of the city and separates into the smaller Chino River Tributary. To the north is Mt. Akaba which is 887 meters tall.

NAN-OKU PREFECTURE
TOUNO PREFECTURE
HIDACHI PREFECTURE
KANATA CITY
TOUGO PREFECTURE
KANATA CITY

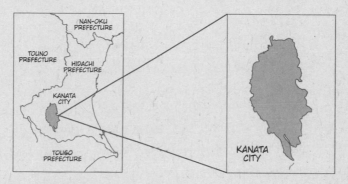

THE START OF KANATA CITY

It is said that people began to inhabit Kanata over 30,000 years ago*. Its name appeared on record during the Kofun period of the 5th century.

The area around Kanata City is called Hidachi, which has become the name of the entire prefecture. There are two main theories as to the origin of the name Hidachi: one is that it derives from the kanji 火起ち, which means "the flames of war," and another from the kanji 火絶ち, which means "the extinguishing of human life." The fact that the ancient Yamato Kingdom used this strategically beneficial flatland region of Kanata as the frontline for many of its wars during the 5th and 6th centuries gives strong support to these two hypotheses. Since history is written by the victors (in this case, the Yamato clans), the lands beyond this strategic line were always considered to have been populated by barbaric savages (ie. the Ezo tribes.) As if to highlight this point, there are ancient regions that surround the city called Konata [此方], Akenuma no Saku [朱沼柵], Furukanata [古彼方], Imakanata [今彼方], and Ima no Hate [今彼方].

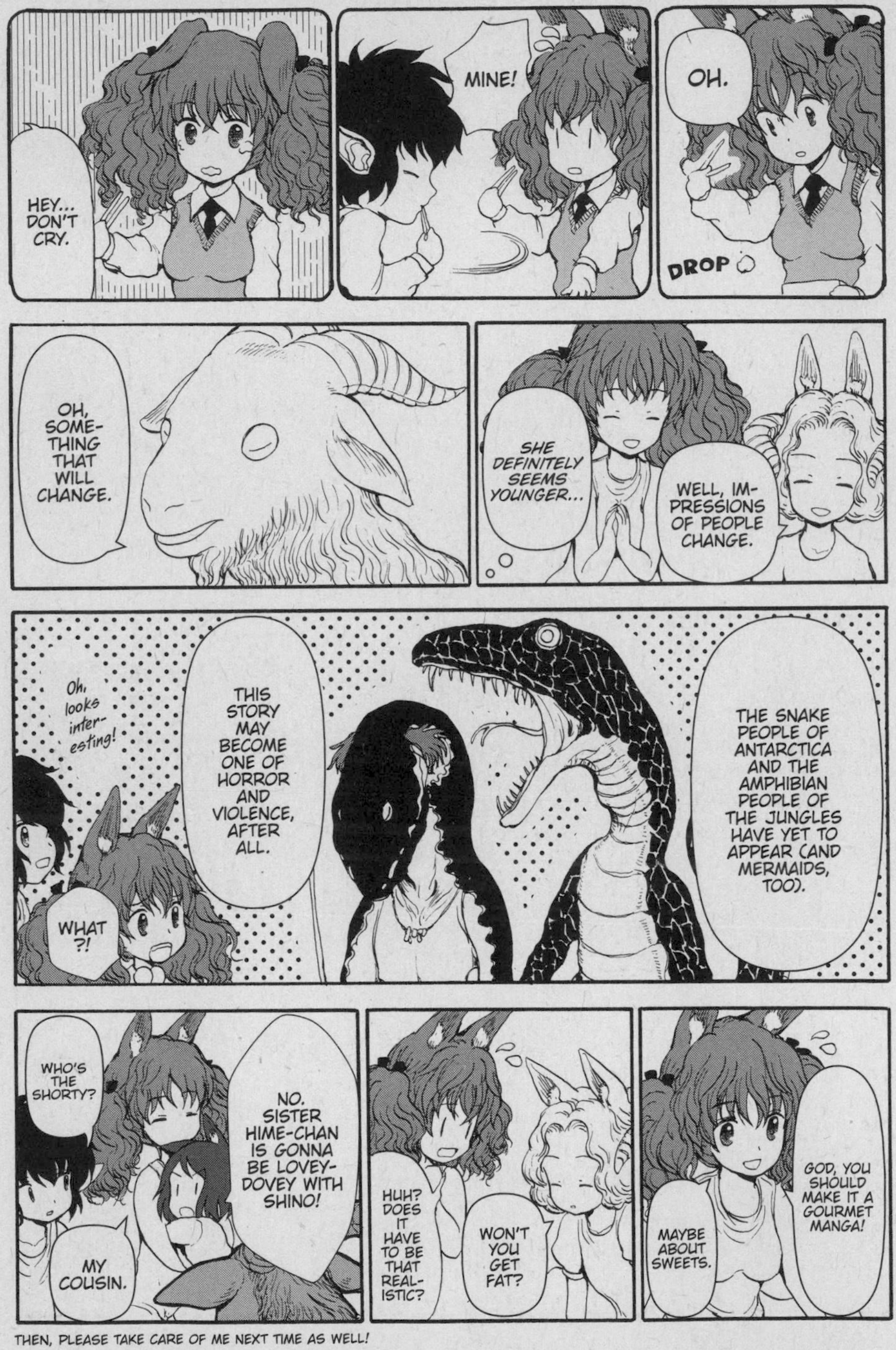
OH.
DROP
MINE!
HEY... DON'T CRY.
SHE DEFINITELY SEEMS YOUNGER...
WELL, IM-PRESSIONS OF PEOPLE CHANGE.
OH, SOME-THING THAT WILL CHANGE.
THE SNAKE PEOPLE OF ANTARCTICA AND THE AMPHIBIAN PEOPLE OF THE JUNGLES HAVE YET TO APPEAR (AND MERMAIDS, TOO).
THIS STORY MAY BECOME ONE OF HORROR AND VIOLENCE, AFTER ALL.
Oh, looks inter-esting!
WHAT?!
GOD, YOU SHOULD MAKE IT A GOURMET MANGA!
MAYBE ABOUT SWEETS.
WON'T YOU GET FAT?
HUH? DOES IT HAVE TO BE THAT REAL-ISTIC?
NO. SISTER HIME-CHAN IS GONNA BE LOVEY-DOVEY WITH SHINO!
WHO'S THE SHORTY?
MY COUSIN.

THEN, PLEASE TAKE CARE OF ME NEXT TIME AS WELL!

AFTERWORD

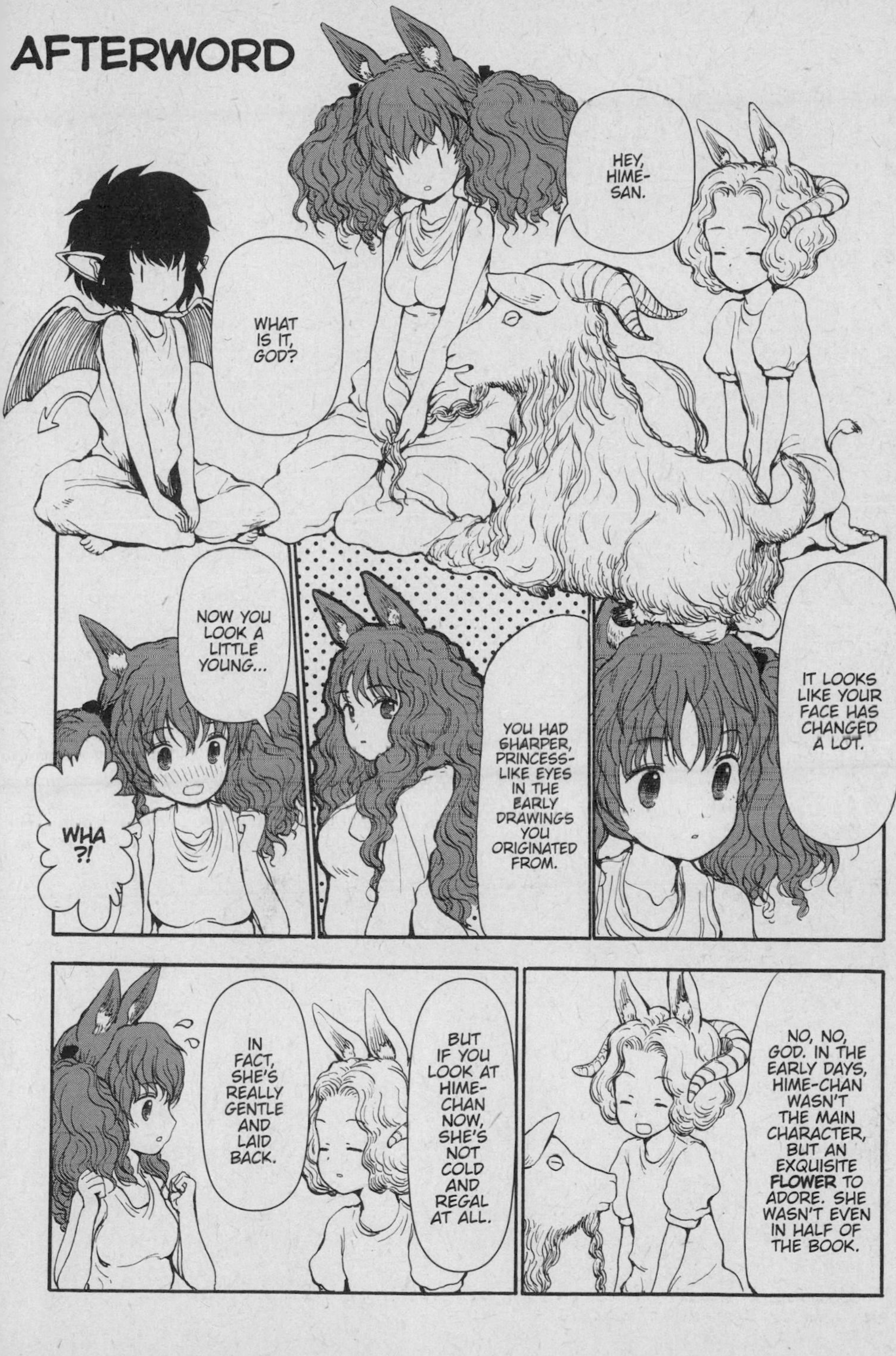
HEY, HIME-SAN.
WHAT IS IT, GOD?
IT LOOKS LIKE YOUR FACE HAS CHANGED A LOT.
YOU HAD SHARPER, PRINCESS-LIKE EYES IN THE EARLY DRAWINGS YOU ORIGINATED FROM.
NOW YOU LOOK A LITTLE YOUNG...
WHA ?!
NO, NO, GOD. IN THE EARLY DAYS, HIME-CHAN WASN'T THE MAIN CHARACTER, BUT AN EXQUISITE **FLOWER** TO ADORE. SHE WASN'T EVEN IN HALF OF THE BOOK.
BUT IF YOU LOOK AT HIME-CHAN NOW, SHE'S NOT COLD AND REGAL AT ALL.
IN FACT, SHE'S REALLY GENTLE AND LAID BACK.

A CentaUr's Life

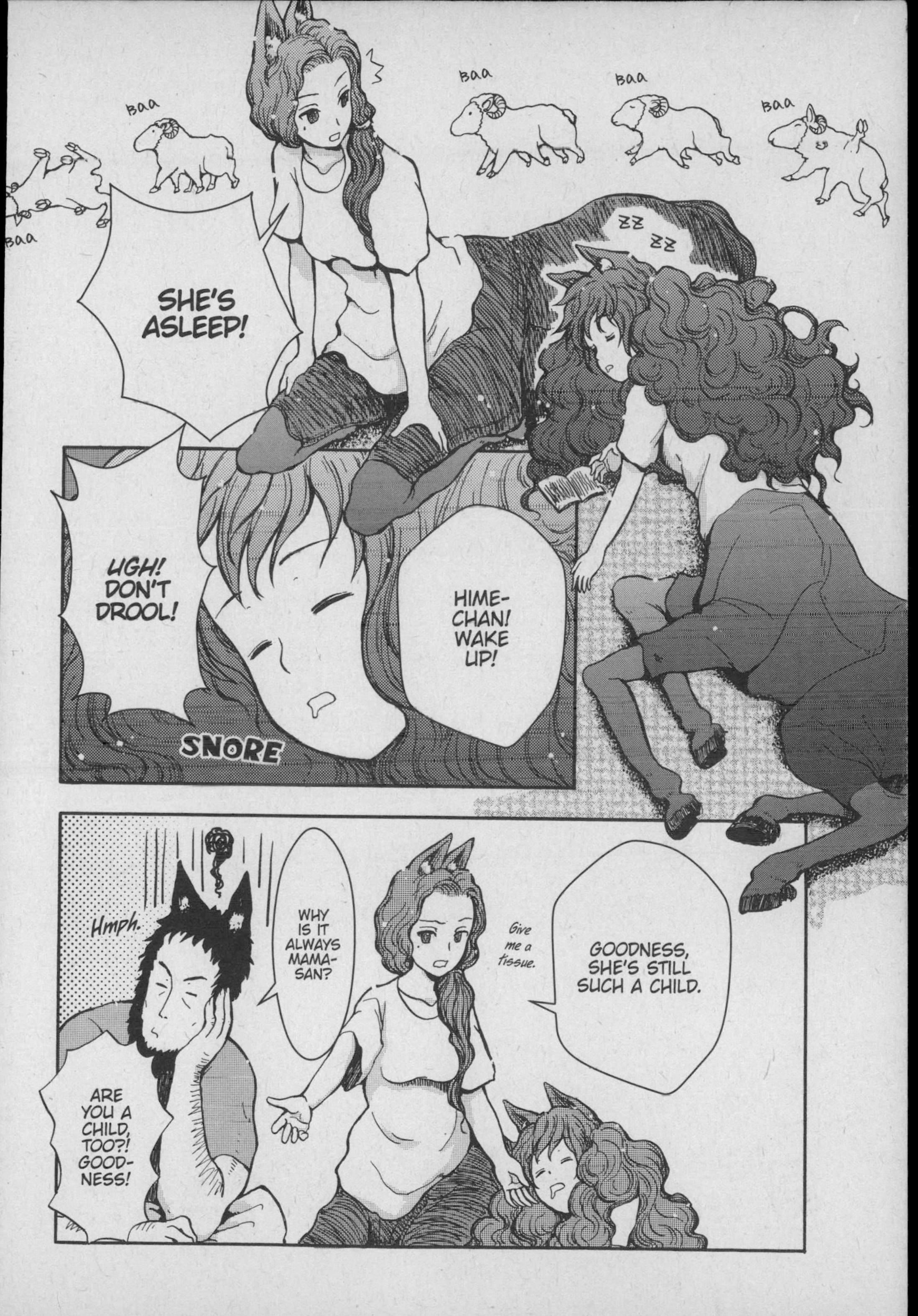
Baa
Baa
Baa
Baa
Baa
SHE'S ASLEEP!
ZZ ZZ
HIME-CHAN! WAKE UP!
UGH! DON'T DROOL!
SNORE
GOODNESS, SHE'S STILL SUCH A CHILD.
Give me a tissue.
WHY IS IT ALWAYS MAMA-SAN?
Hmph.
ARE YOU A CHILD, TOO?! GOODNESS!

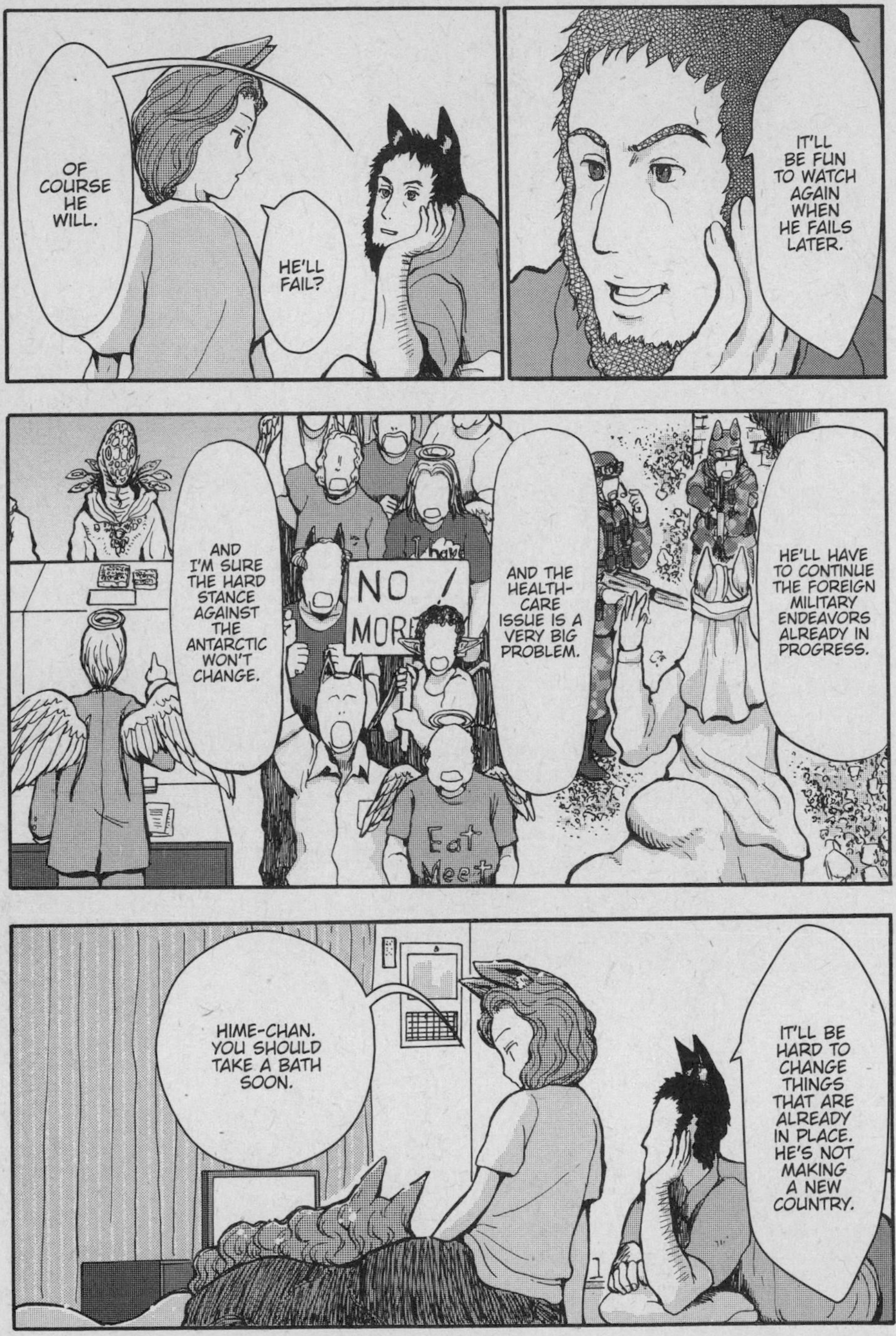
IT'LL BE FUN TO WATCH AGAIN WHEN HE FAILS LATER.
HE'LL FAIL?
OF COURSE HE WILL.
HE'LL HAVE TO CONTINUE THE FOREIGN MILITARY ENDEAVORS ALREADY IN PROGRESS.
AND THE HEALTH-CARE ISSUE IS A VERY BIG PROBLEM.
NO
Eat Meet
AND I'M SURE THE HARD STANCE AGAINST THE ANTARCTIC WON'T CHANGE.
IT'LL BE HARD TO CHANGE THINGS THAT ARE ALREADY IN PLACE. HE'S NOT MAKING A NEW COUNTRY.
HIME-CHAN. YOU SHOULD TAKE A BATH SOON.

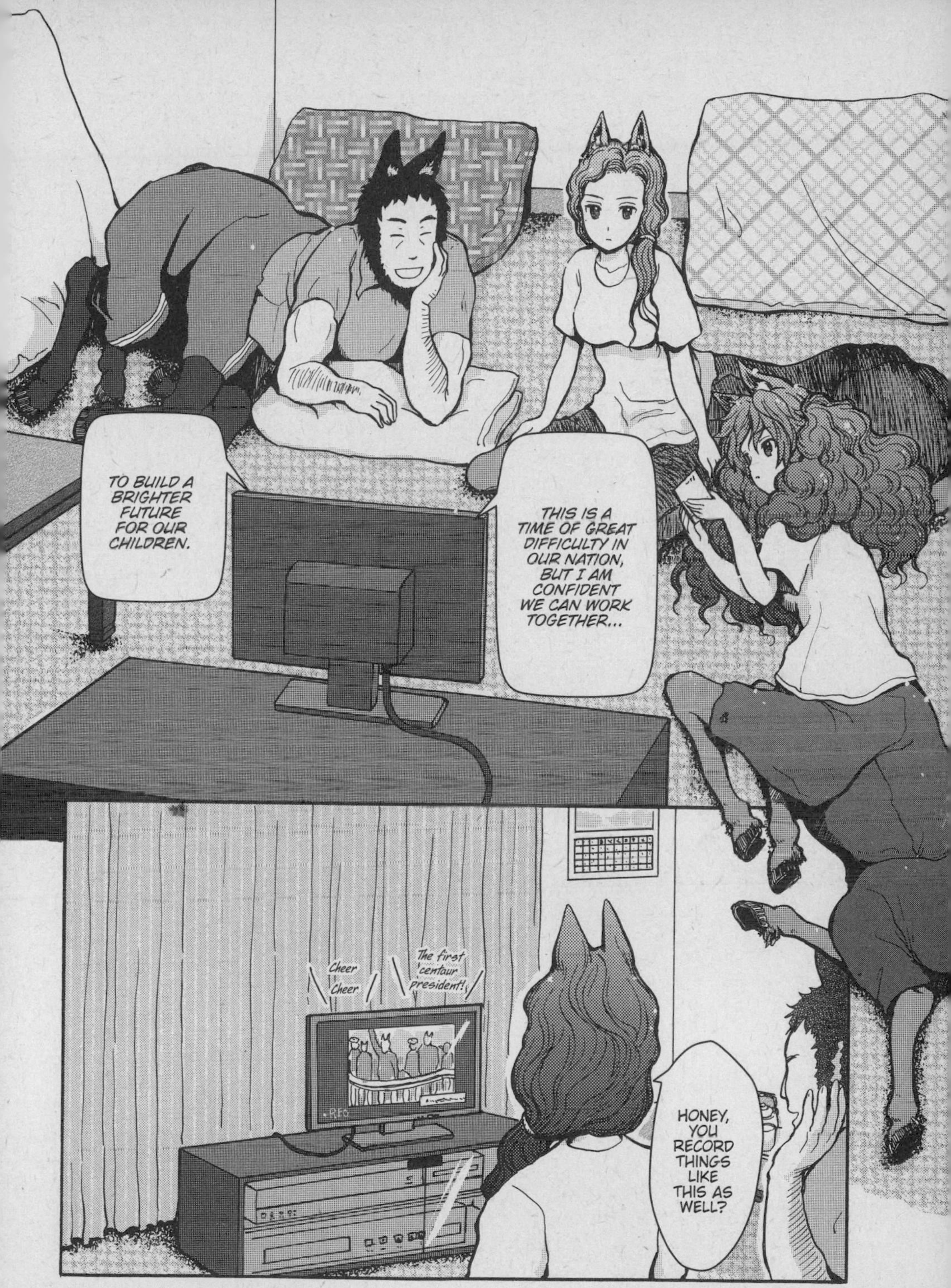
THIS IS A TIME OF GREAT DIFFICULTY IN OUR NATION, BUT I AM CONFIDENT WE CAN WORK TOGETHER...
TO BUILD A BRIGHTER FUTURE FOR OUR CHILDREN.
The first centaur president!
Cheer Cheer
HONEY, YOU RECORD THINGS LIKE THIS AS WELL?

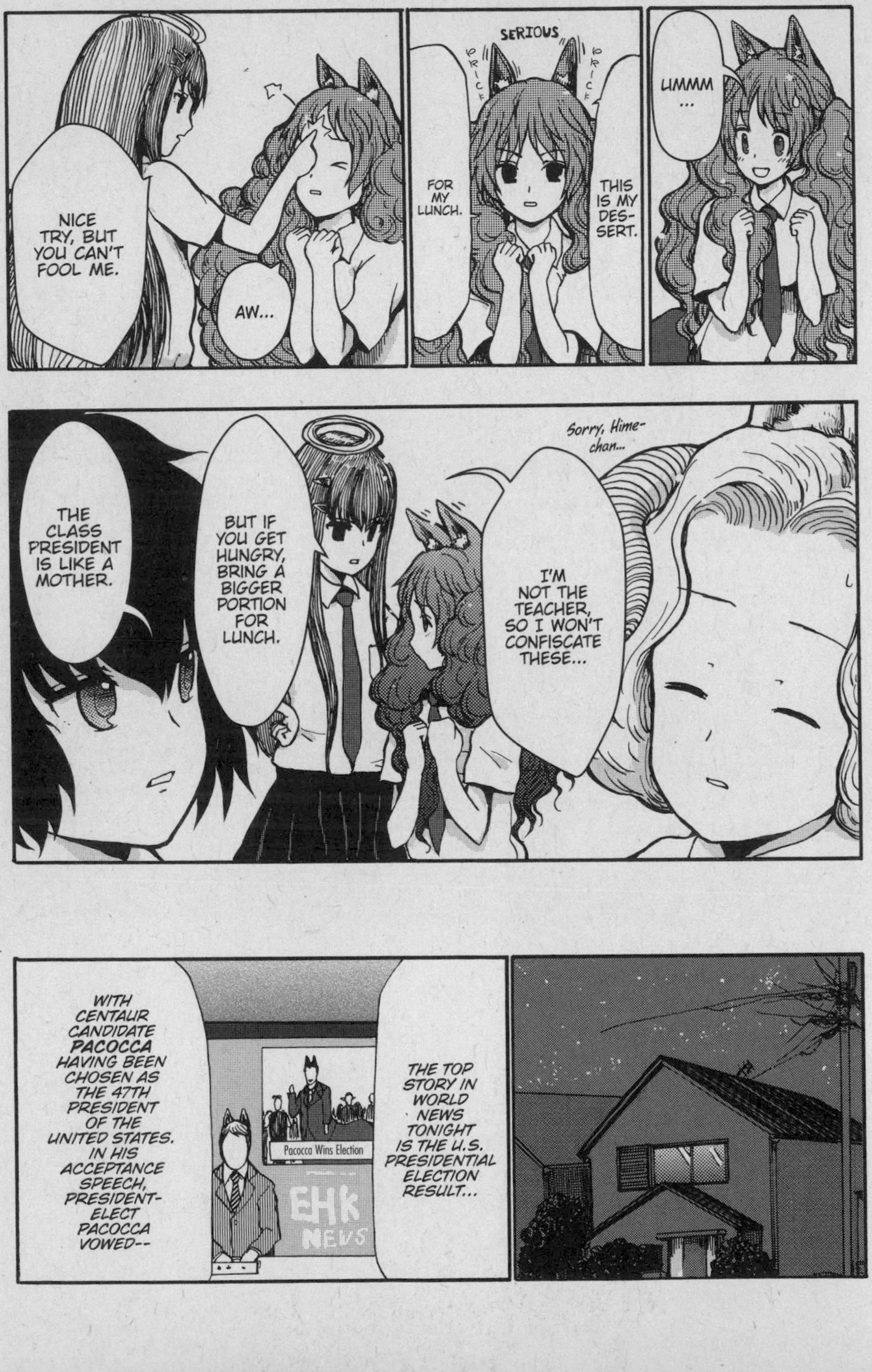
UMMM ...
SERIOUS
PRICK
PRICK
THIS IS MY DESSERT.
FOR MY LUNCH.
NICE TRY, BUT YOU CAN'T FOOL ME.
AW...
Sorry, Hime-chan...
I'M NOT THE TEACHER, SO I WON'T CONFISCATE THESE...
BUT IF YOU GET HUNGRY, BRING A BIGGER PORTION FOR LUNCH.
THE CLASS PRESIDENT IS LIKE A MOTHER.
THE TOP STORY IN WORLD NEWS TONIGHT IS THE U.S. PRESIDENTIAL ELECTION RESULT...
Pacocca Wins Election
EHK NEWS
WITH CENTAUR CANDIDATE PACOCCA HAVING BEEN CHOSEN AS THE 47TH PRESIDENT OF THE UNITED STATES. IN HIS ACCEPTANCE SPEECH, PRESIDENT-ELECT PACOCCA VOWED--

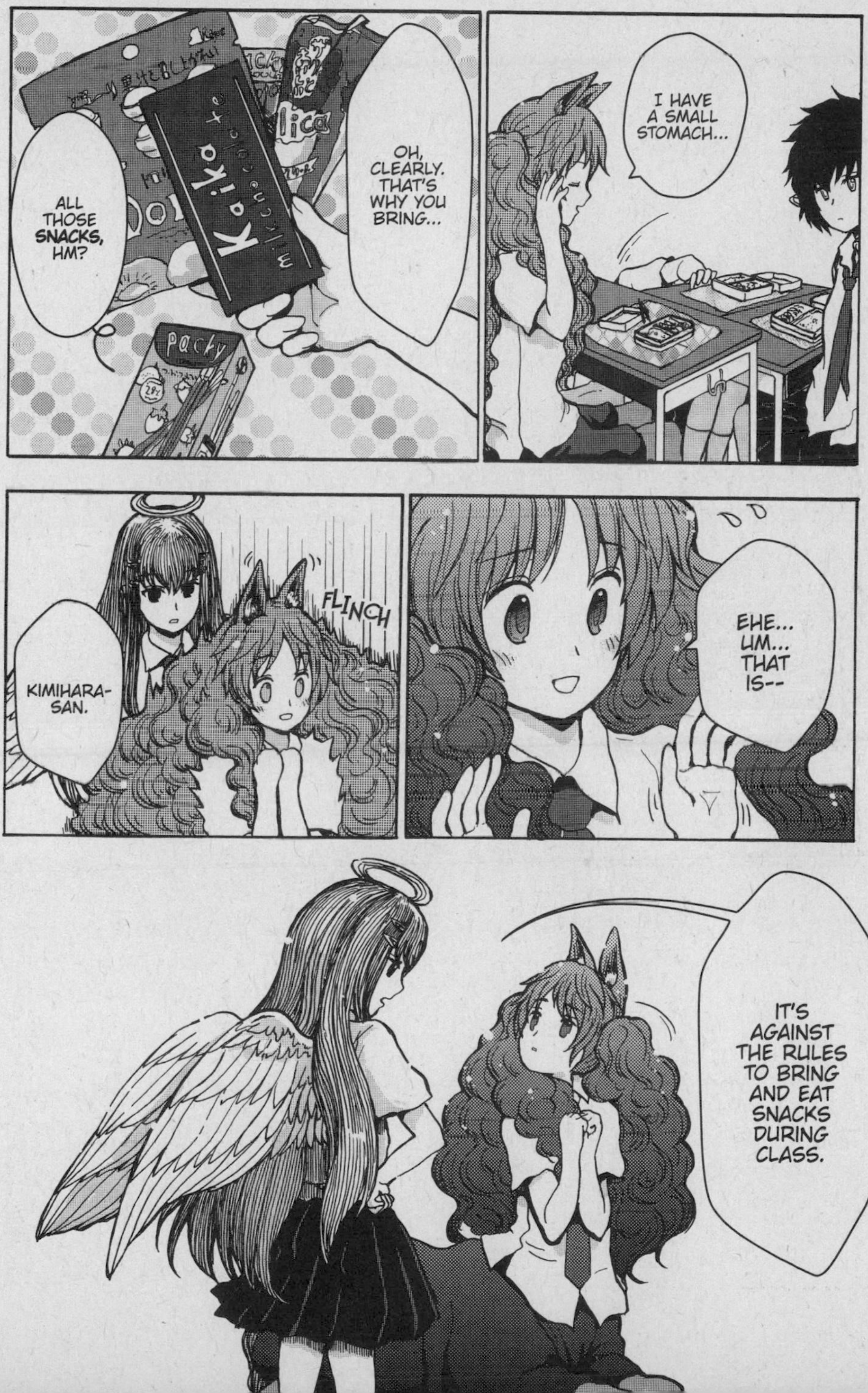
I HAVE A SMALL STOMACH...
OH, CLEARLY. THAT'S WHY YOU BRING...
ALL THOSE SNACKS, HM?
EHE... UM... THAT IS--
FLINCH
KIMIHARA-SAN.
IT'S AGAINST THE RULES TO BRING AND EAT SNACKS DURING CLASS.

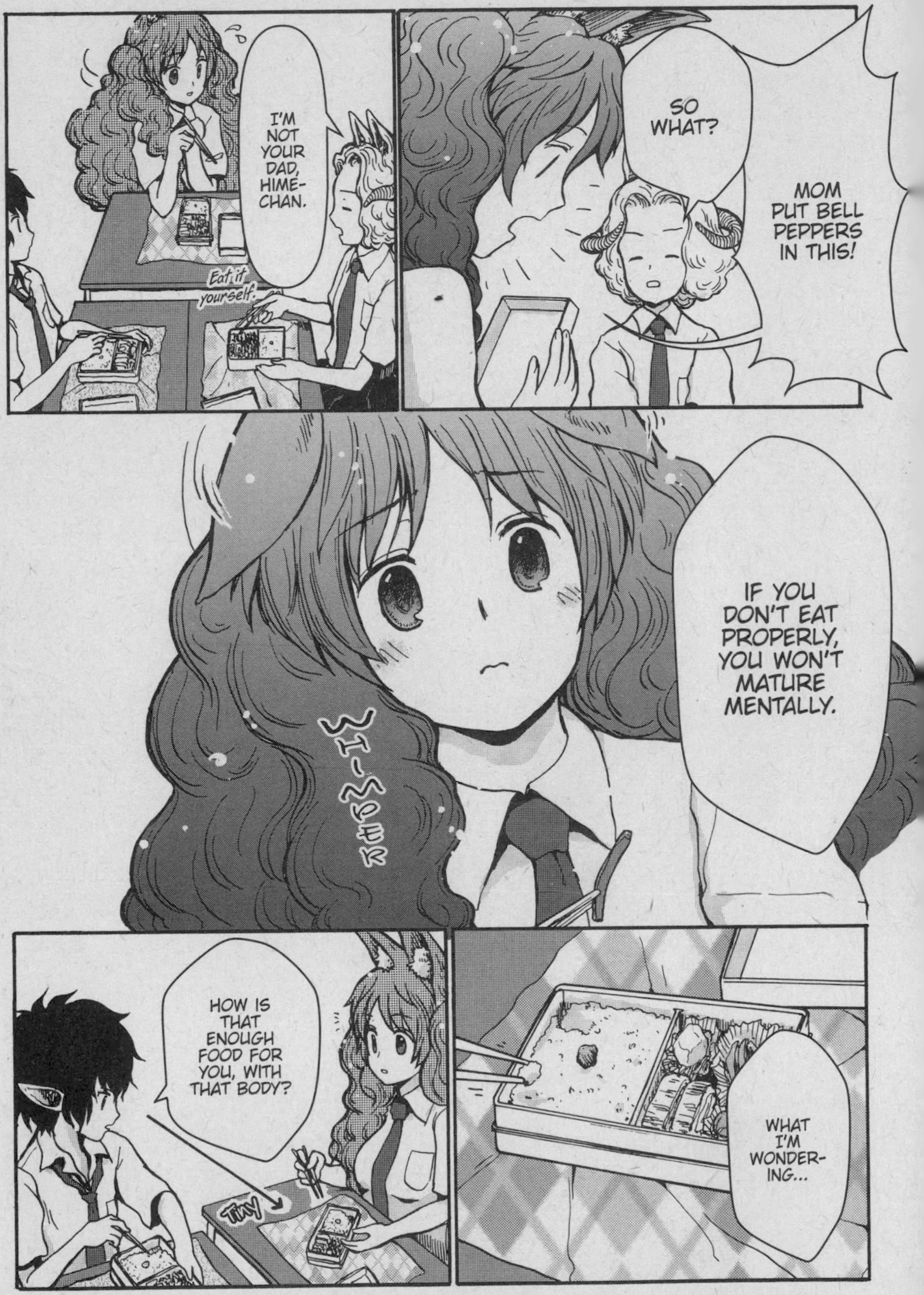
MOM PUT BELL PEPPERS IN THIS!
SO WHAT?
I'M NOT YOUR DAD, HIME-CHAN.
Eat it yourself.
IF YOU DON'T EAT PROPERLY, YOU WON'T MATURE MENTALLY.
WHIMPER
WHAT I'M WONDERING...
HOW IS THAT ENOUGH FOOD FOR YOU, WITH THAT BODY?
TINY

Oh!
IF SHE MESSES UP AGAIN...
I'LL NEVER HEAR THE END OF IT FROM MY FATHER-IN-LAW.
Anyone can make a mistake.
NAG
NAG
DROOOP
THIS IS SUCH AN OUTDATED TRADITION. WHY DOES SHE NEED TO BE ABLE TO DRAW A BOW?
GRUMBLE
GRUMBLE
AND HE ALWAYS SAYS "THE KIMIHARA FAMILY" THIS AND "TRADITION" THAT, OVER AND OVER.
PEOPLE ALL ORIGINATED FROM AFRICAN MONKEYS!
BING
BONG
BEEENG
BOOONG
OH!

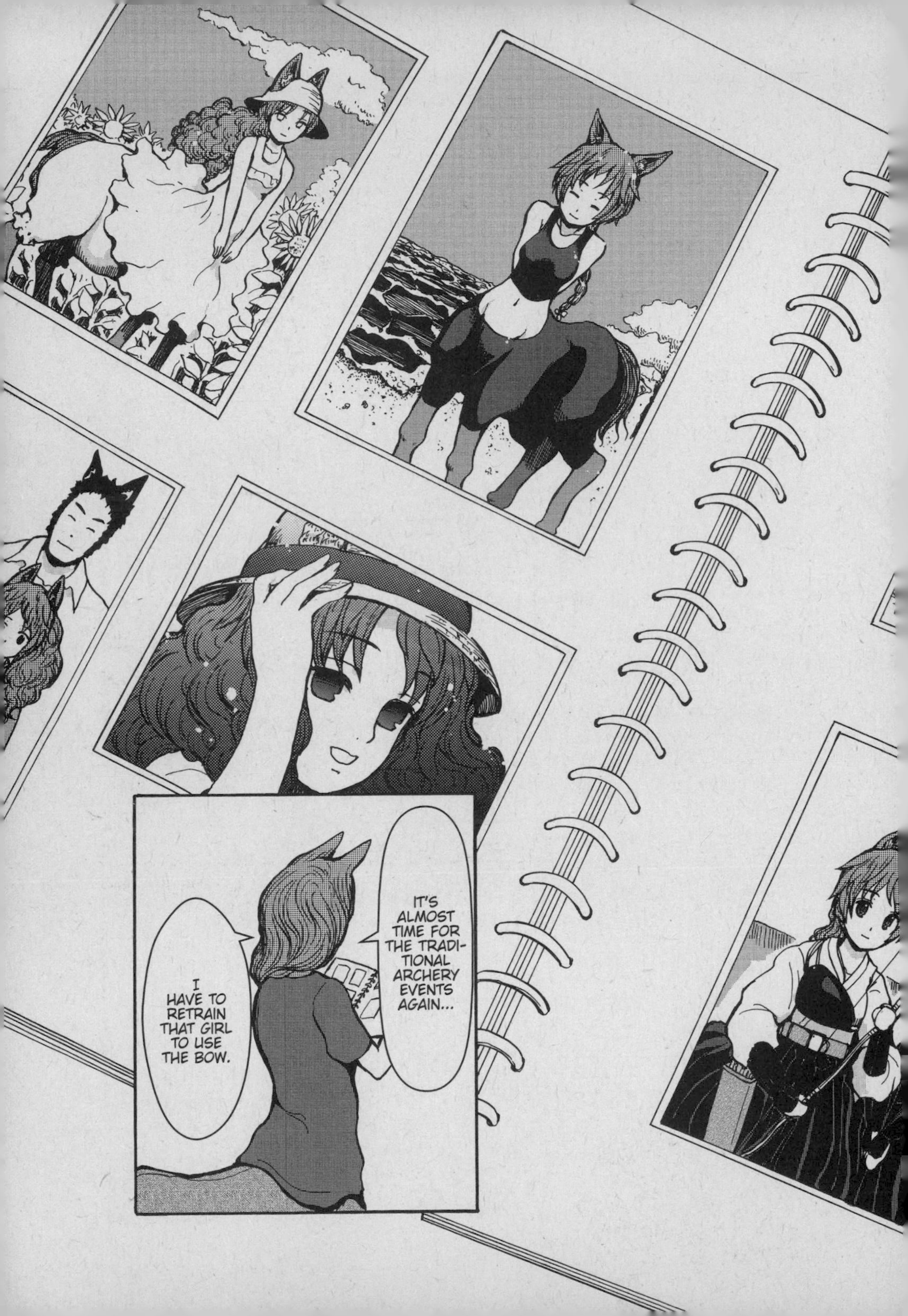
IT'S ALMOST TIME FOR THE TRADI- TIONAL ARCHERY EVENTS AGAIN...
I HAVE TO RETRAIN THAT GIRL TO USE THE BOW.

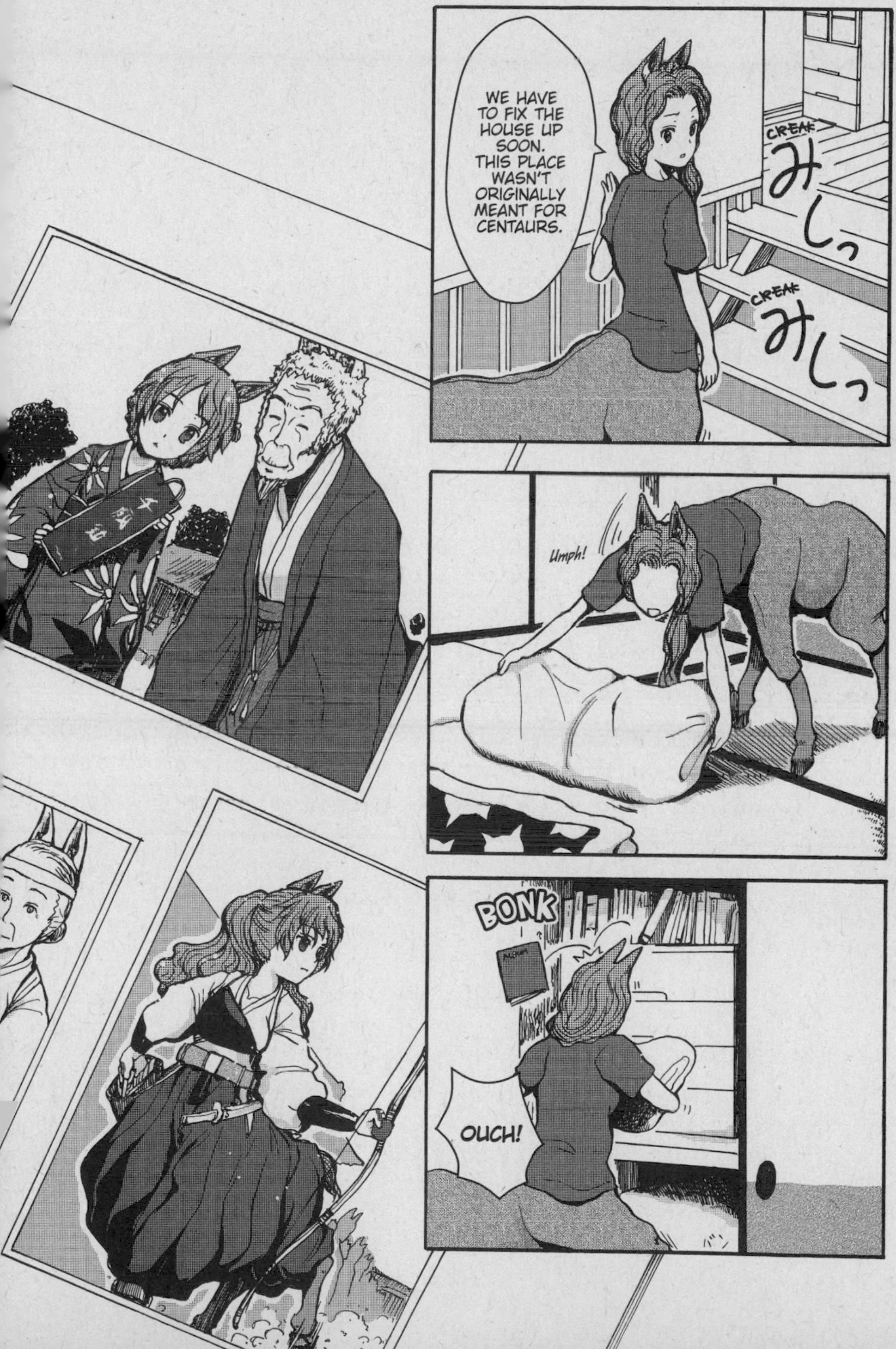
WE HAVE TO FIX THE HOUSE UP SOON. THIS PLACE WASN'T ORIGINALLY MEANT FOR CENTAURS.
CREAK
みしっ
CREAK
みしっ
Umph!
BONK
OUCH!

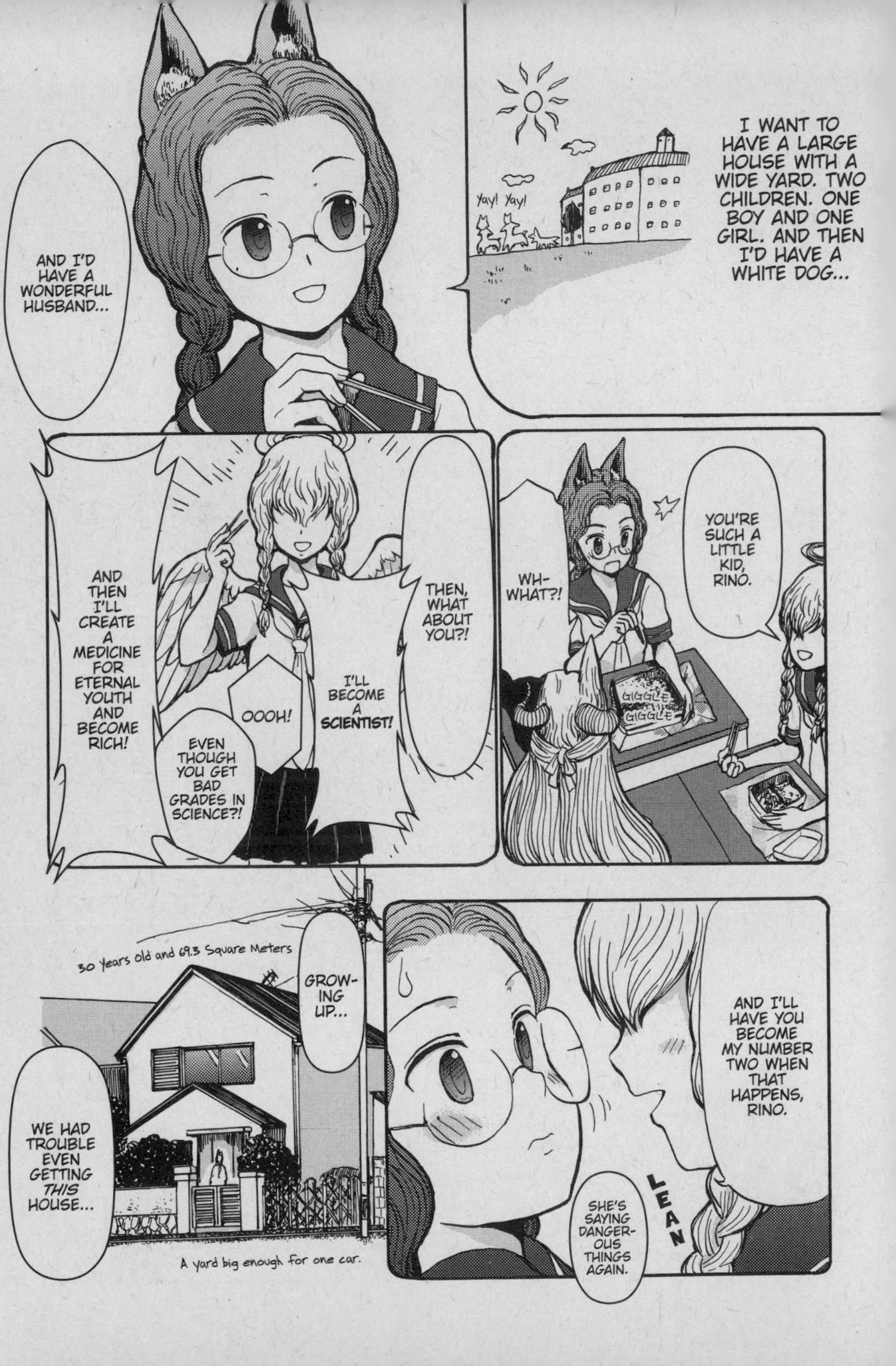
I WANT TO HAVE A LARGE HOUSE WITH A WIDE YARD. TWO CHILDREN. ONE BOY AND ONE GIRL. AND THEN I'D HAVE A WHITE DOG...
Yay! Yay!
AND I'D HAVE A WONDERFUL HUSBAND...
YOU'RE SUCH A LITTLE KID, RINO.
WH-WHAT?!
GIGGLE GIGGLE
THEN, WHAT ABOUT YOU?!
I'LL BECOME A **SCIENTIST!**
OOOH!
EVEN THOUGH YOU GET BAD GRADES IN SCIENCE?!
AND THEN I'LL CREATE A MEDICINE FOR ETERNAL YOUTH AND BECOME RICH!
AND I'LL HAVE YOU BECOME MY NUMBER TWO WHEN THAT HAPPENS, RINO.
LEAN
SHE'S SAYING DANGER-OUS THINGS AGAIN.
GROW-ING UP...
30 Years old and 69.3 Square Meters
WE HAD TROUBLE EVEN GETTING *THIS* HOUSE...
A yard big enough for one car.

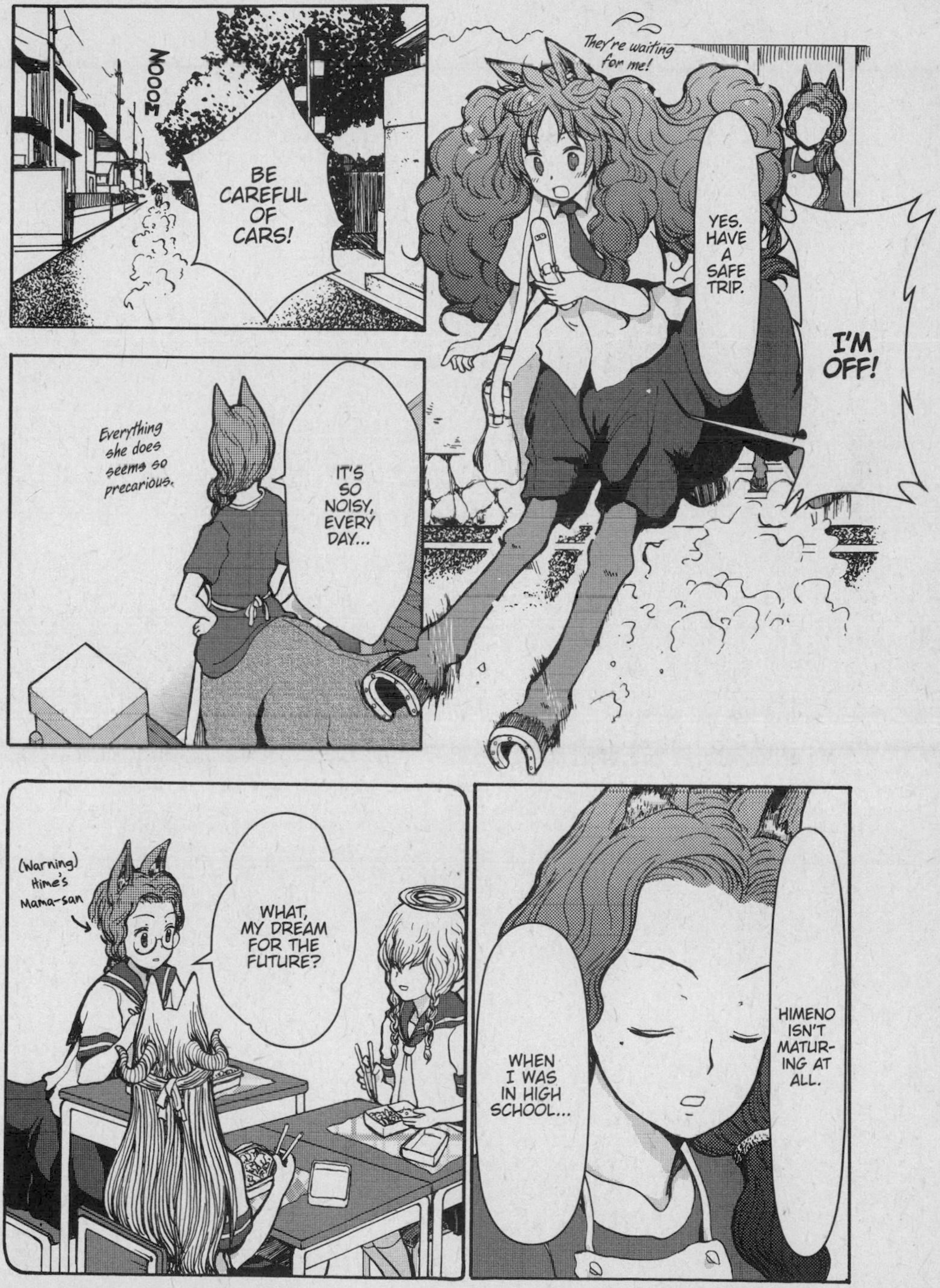
They're waiting for me!
YES. HAVE A SAFE TRIP.
I'M OFF!
NOOOM
BE CAREFUL OF CARS!
IT'S SO NOISY, EVERY DAY...
Everything she does seems so precarious.
HIMENO ISN'T MATURING AT ALL.
WHEN I WAS IN HIGH SCHOOL...
WHAT, MY DREAM FOR THE FUTURE?
(Warning) Hime's Mama-san

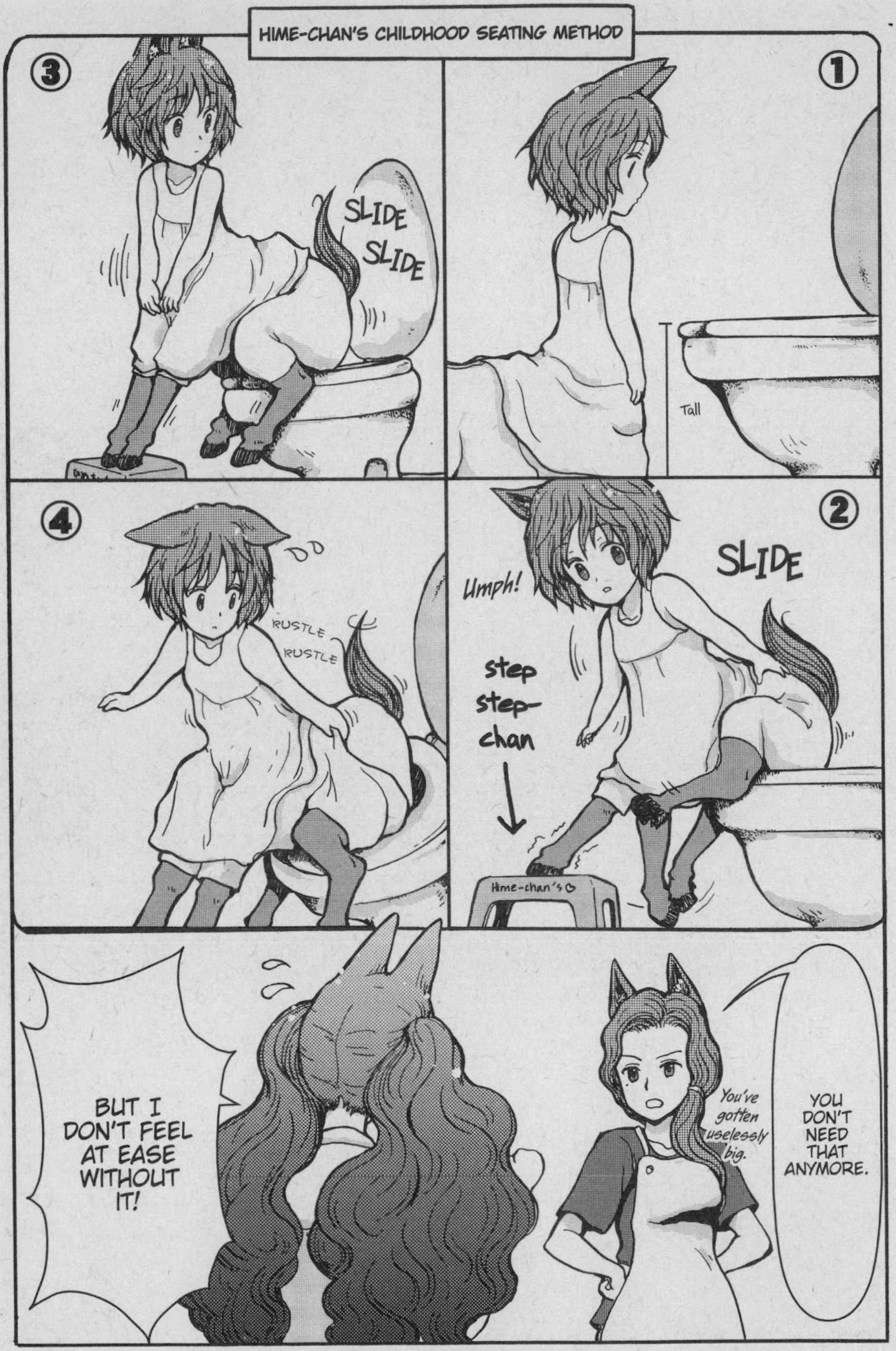
HIME-CHAN'S CHILDHOOD SEATING METHOD
1
Tall
2
SLIDE
Umph!
step step-chan
Hime-chan's
3
SLIDE SLIDE
4
RUSTLE RUSTLE
YOU DON'T NEED THAT ANYMORE.
You've gotten uselessly big.
BUT I DON'T FEEL AT EASE WITHOUT IT!

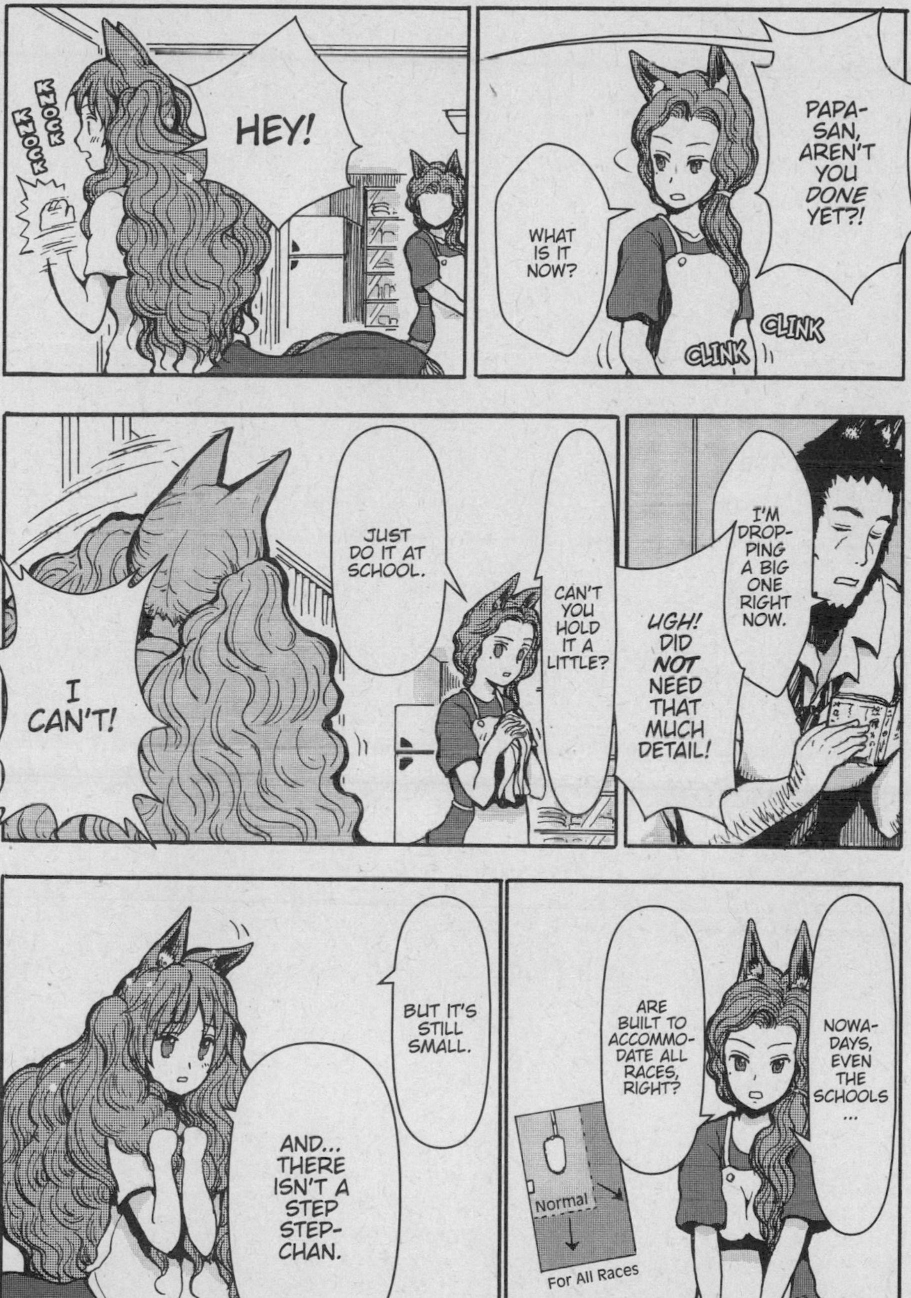
PAPA-SAN, AREN'T YOU DONE YET?!
WHAT IS IT NOW?
CLINK
CLINK
HEY!
KNOCK KNOCK
I'M DROPPING A BIG ONE RIGHT NOW.
UGH! DID *NOT* NEED THAT MUCH DETAIL!
CAN'T YOU HOLD IT A LITTLE?
JUST DO IT AT SCHOOL.
I CAN'T!
NOWADAYS, EVEN THE SCHOOLS...
ARE BUILT TO ACCOMMODATE ALL RACES, RIGHT?
Normal
For All Races
BUT IT'S STILL SMALL.
AND... THERE ISN'T A STEP STEP-CHAN.

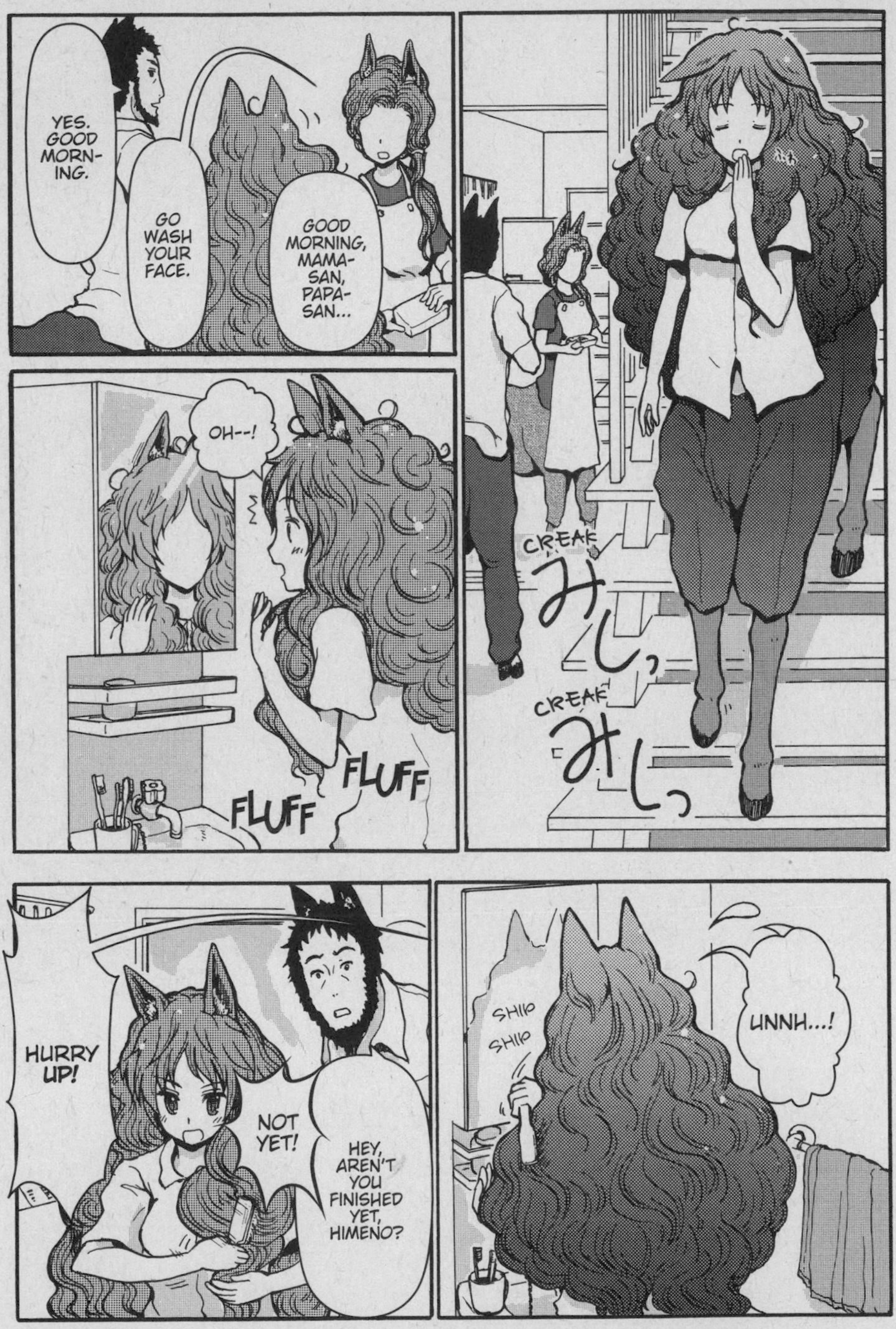
CREAK
みしっ
CREAK
みしっ
GOOD MORNING, MAMA-SAN, PAPA-SAN...
GO WASH YOUR FACE.
YES. GOOD MORNING.
OH--!
FLUFF
FLUFF
UNNH...!
SHIP
SHIP
HEY, AREN'T YOU FINISHED YET, HIMENO?
NOT YET!
HURRY UP!

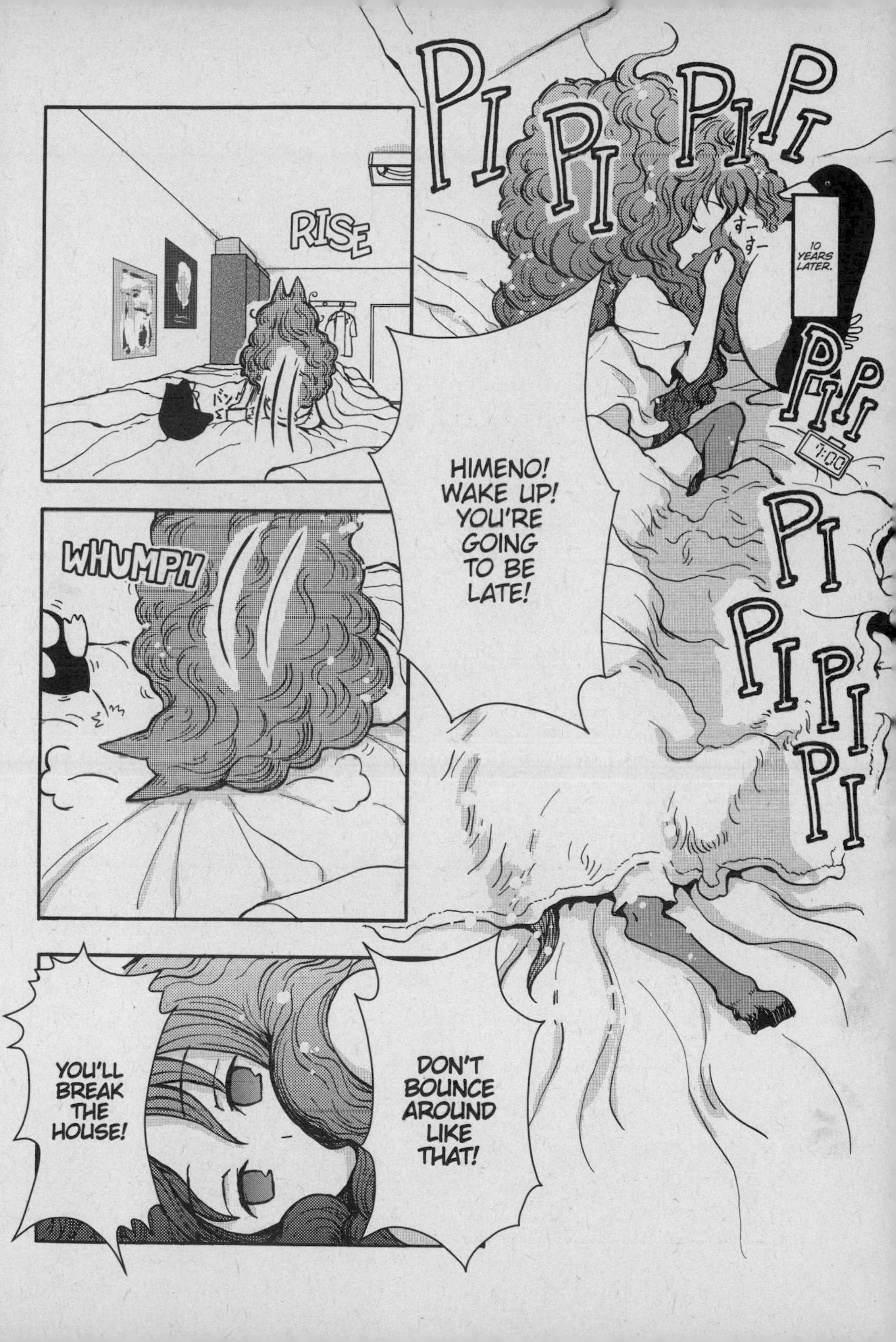
PI PI PI PI
すーすー
10 YEARS LATER.
PI PI PI
PI PI PI PI PI
HIMENO! WAKE UP! YOU'RE GOING TO BE LATE!
RISE
WHUMPH
DON'T BOUNCE AROUND LIKE THAT!
YOU'LL BREAK THE HOUSE!

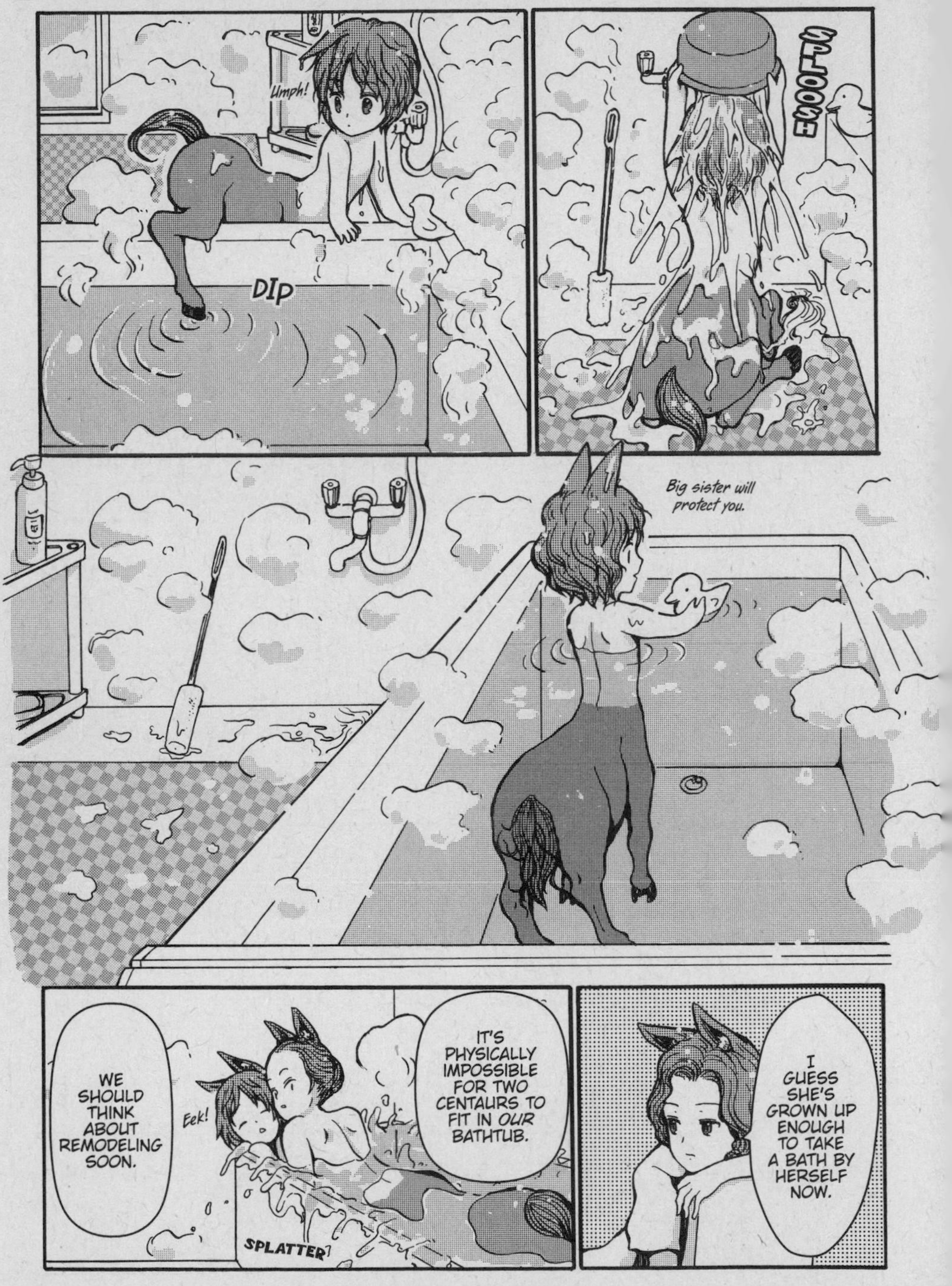
SPLOOSH
Umph!
DIP
Big sister will protect you.
I GUESS SHE'S GROWN UP ENOUGH TO TAKE A BATH BY HERSELF NOW.
IT'S PHYSICALLY IMPOSSIBLE FOR TWO CENTAURS TO FIT IN *OUR* BATHTUB.
Eek!
WE SHOULD THINK ABOUT REMODELING SOON.
SPLATTER

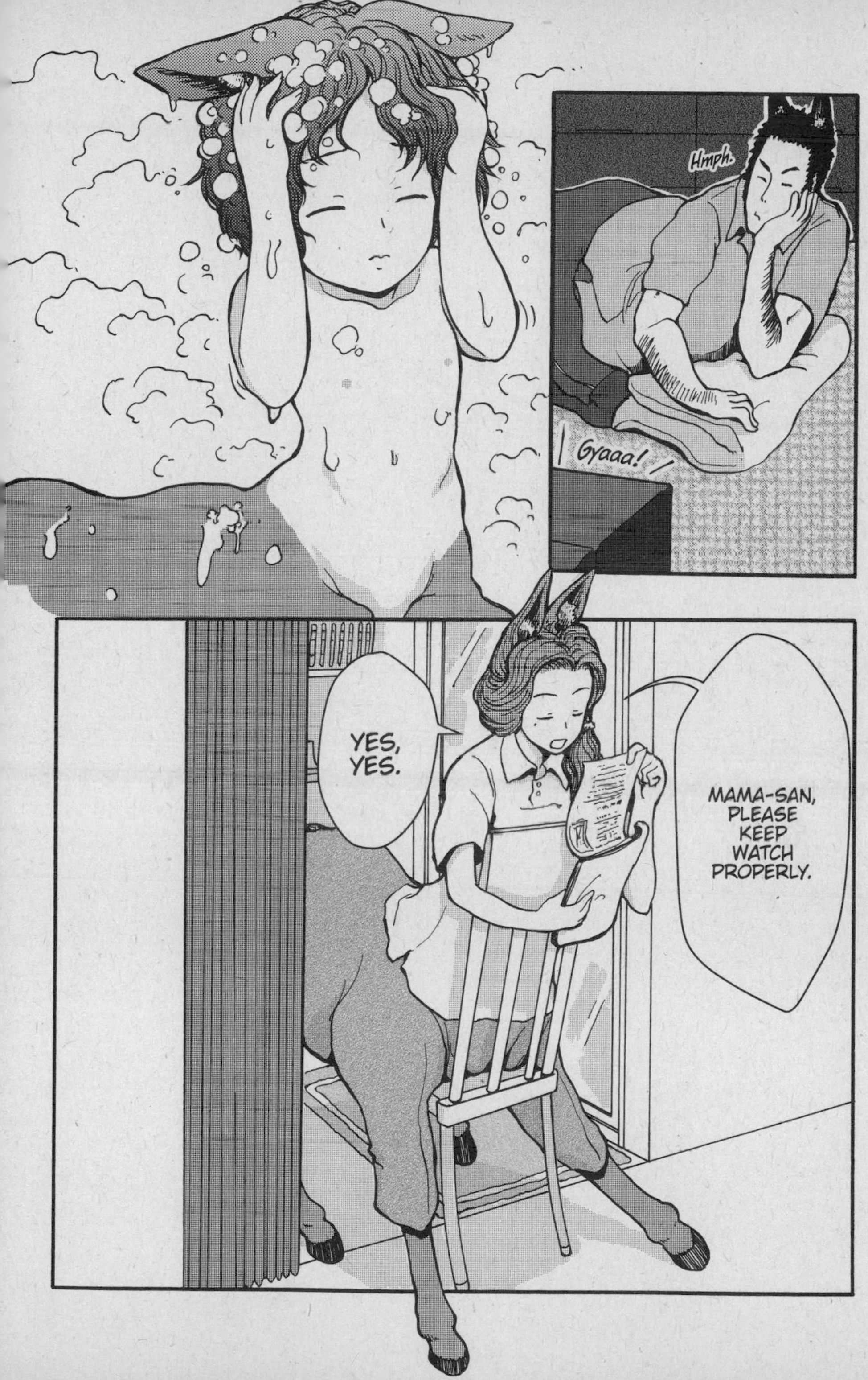
Hmph.
Gyaaa!
MAMA-SAN, PLEASE KEEP WATCH PROPERLY.
YES, YES.

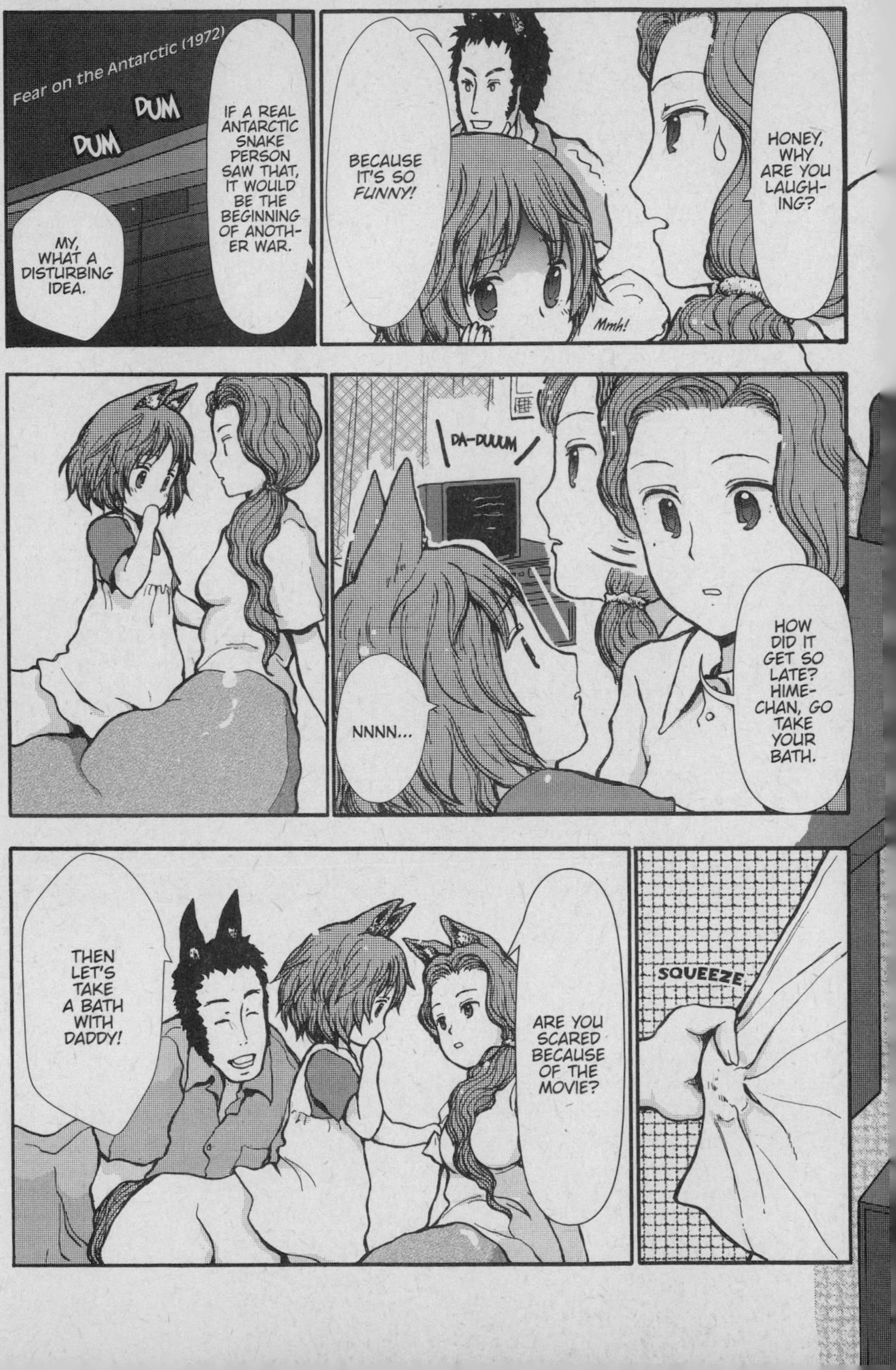
HONEY, WHY ARE YOU LAUGHING?
BECAUSE IT'S SO FUNNY!
Mmh!
Fear on the Antarctic (1972)
DUM
DUM
IF A REAL ANTARCTIC SNAKE PERSON SAW THAT, IT WOULD BE THE BEGINNING OF ANOTHER WAR.
MY, WHAT A DISTURBING IDEA.
DA-DUUUM
HOW DID IT GET SO LATE? HIME-CHAN, GO TAKE YOUR BATH.
NNNN...
SQUEEZE
ARE YOU SCARED BECAUSE OF THE MOVIE?
THEN LET'S TAKE A BATH WITH DADDY!

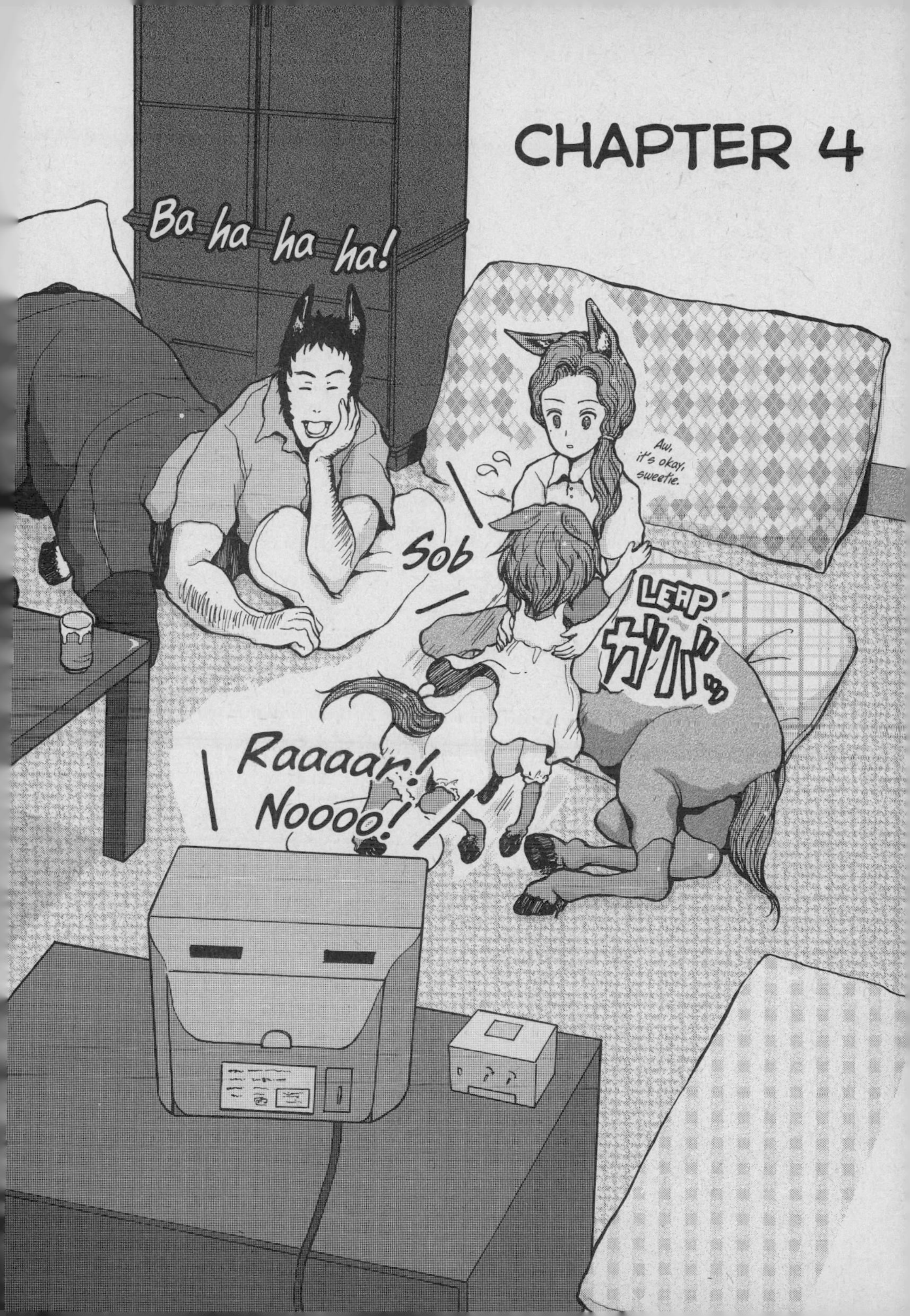
CHAPTER 4
Aw, it's okay, sweetie.
LEAP
ガバッ
Sob
Ba ha ha ha!
Raaaar! Noooo!

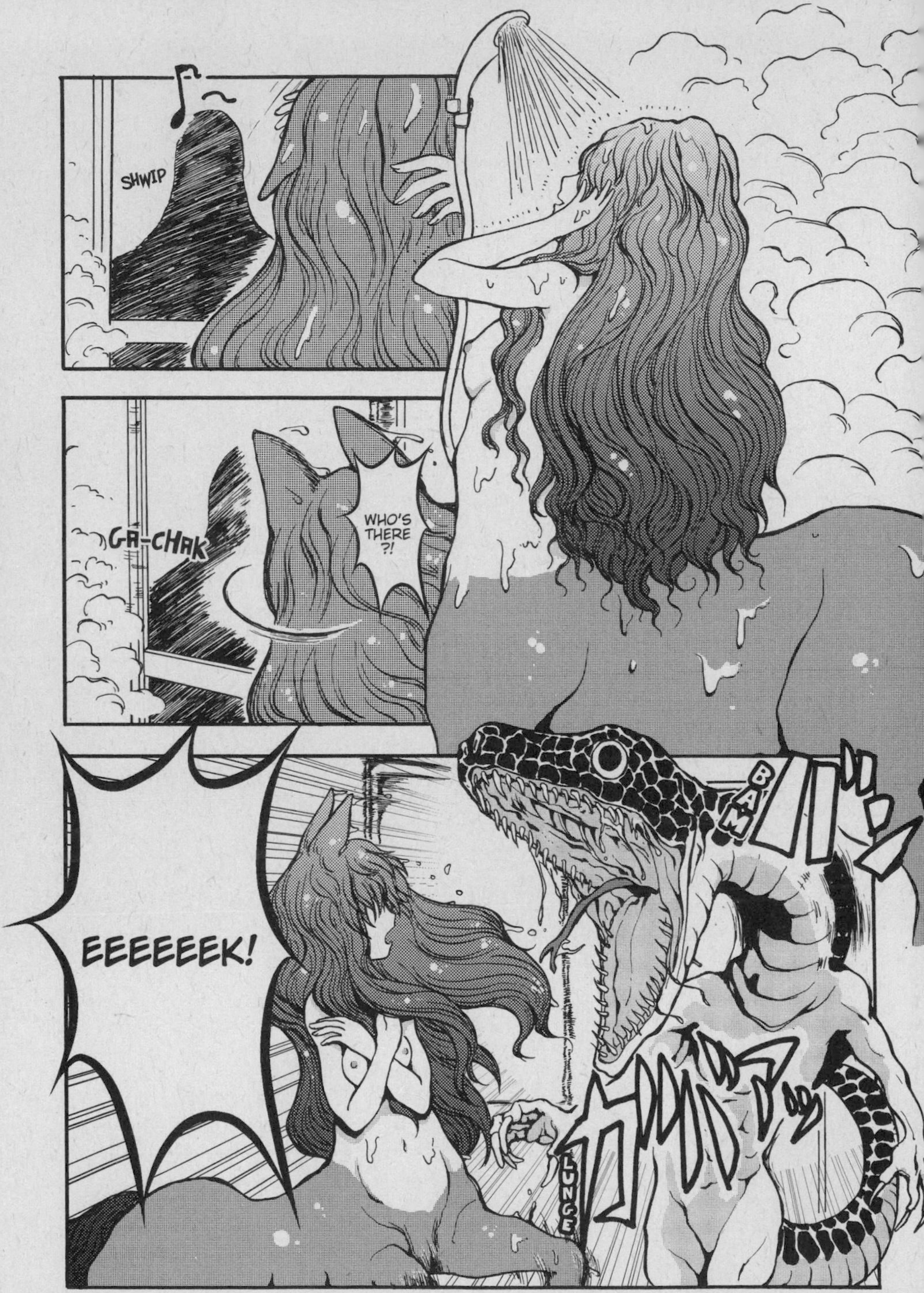
SHWIP
GA-CHAK
WHO'S THERE ?!
BAM
EEEEEEK!
LUNGE

A CENTAUR'S UNDERGARMENTS

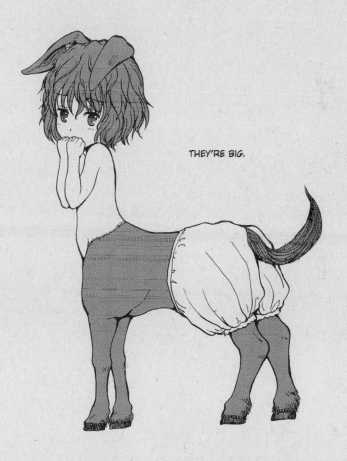

THEY'RE BIG.

A Centaur's Life

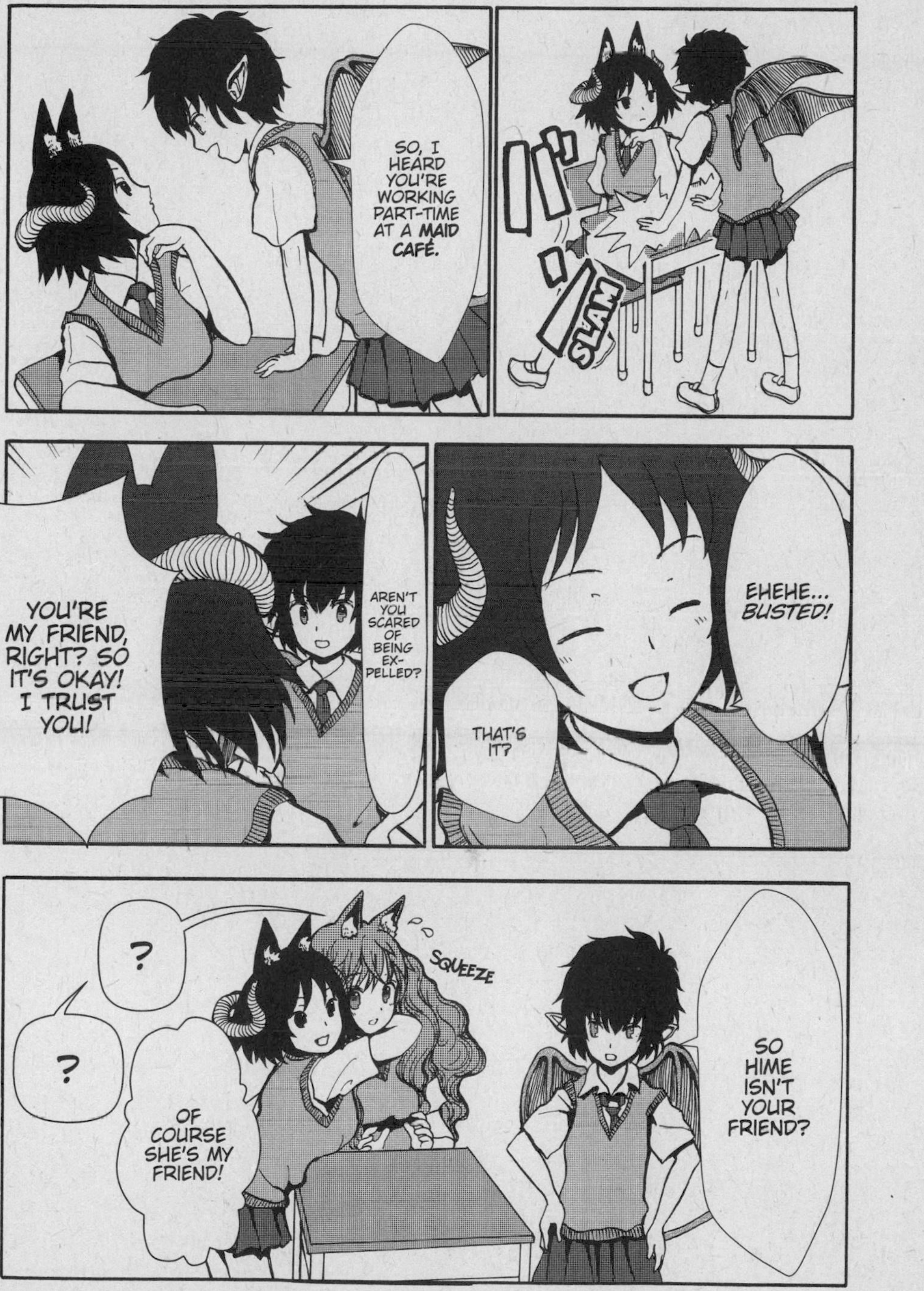
SLAM
SO, I HEARD YOU'RE WORKING PART-TIME AT A MAID CAFÉ.
EHEHE... BUSTED!
THAT'S IT?
AREN'T YOU SCARED OF BEING EX-PELLED?
YOU'RE MY FRIEND, RIGHT? SO IT'S OKAY! I TRUST YOU!
SO HIME ISN'T YOUR FRIEND?
SQUEEZE
OF COURSE SHE'S MY FRIEND!
?
?

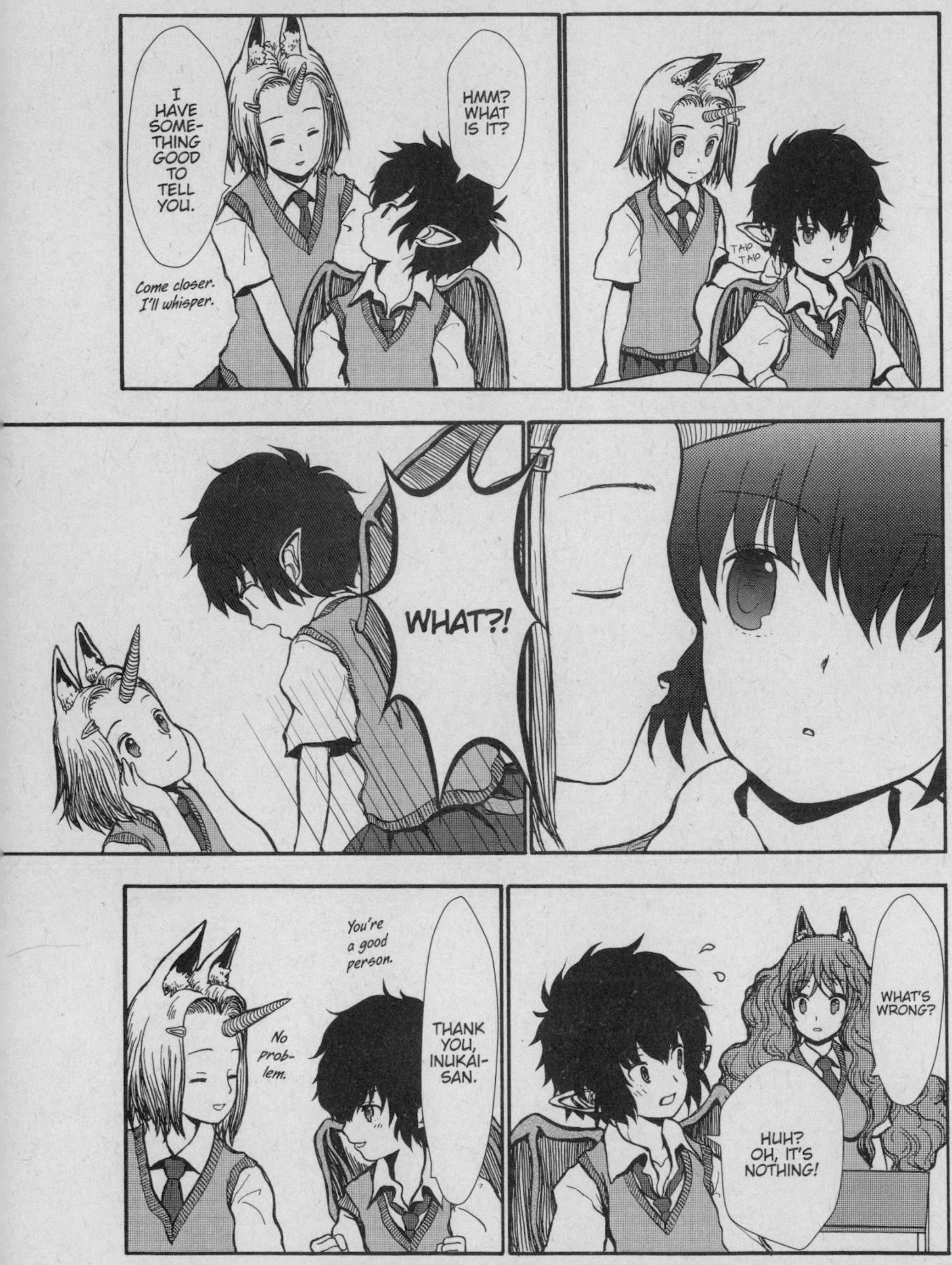
TAP TAP
HMM? WHAT IS IT?
I HAVE SOMETHING GOOD TO TELL YOU.
Come closer. I'll whisper.
WHAT?!
WHAT'S WRONG?
HUH? OH, IT'S NOTHING!
THANK YOU, INUKAI-SAN.
You're a good person.
No problem.

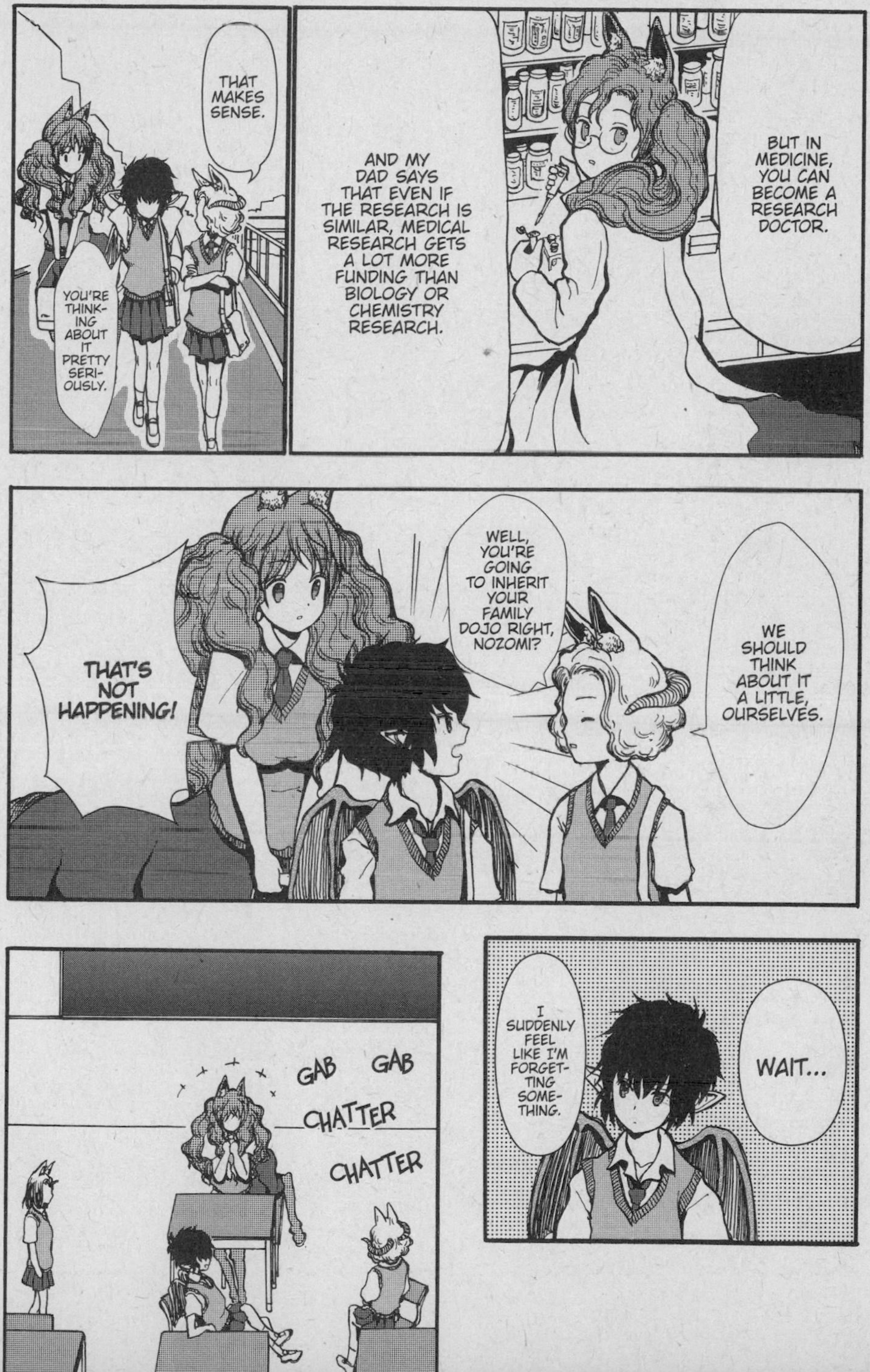
BUT IN MEDICINE, YOU CAN BECOME A RESEARCH DOCTOR.
AND MY DAD SAYS THAT EVEN IF THE RESEARCH IS SIMILAR, MEDICAL RESEARCH GETS A LOT MORE FUNDING THAN BIOLOGY OR CHEMISTRY RESEARCH.
THAT MAKES SENSE.
YOU'RE THINKING ABOUT IT PRETTY SERIOUSLY.
WE SHOULD THINK ABOUT IT A LITTLE, OURSELVES.
WELL, YOU'RE GOING TO INHERIT YOUR FAMILY DOJO RIGHT, NOZOMI?
THAT'S NOT HAPPENING!
WAIT...
I SUDDENLY FEEL LIKE I'M FORGETTING SOMETHING.
GAB GAB
CHATTER
CHATTER

MAYBE IT WOULD BE BETTER TO BECOME A VETERINARIAN?
Please hold him down.
BUT THE IDEA OF BEING BITTEN IS A LITTLE SCARY.
I'VE ONLY EVER HAD FISH...
HOW ABOUT A FISH STAND? ONE THAT SELLS TROPICAL FISH.
A FISH STAND IS A PLACE YOU *EAT* FISH, DUMMY.
TROPICAL FISH ARE HARD TO RAISE. YOU HAVE TO WORRY ABOUT NITROGEN, PH, AND TEMPERATURE LEVELS.
Green Water
THE GOLDFISH I WON AT THE GOLDFISH STAND IS STILL ALIVE, EVEN THOUGH I DON'T CLEAN HIS BOWL AT ALL.
THAT'S FINE HOW IT IS.
THE ALGAE GETS RID OF THE CARBON DIOXIDE THROUGH PHOTOSYNTHESIS AND BREAKS DOWN WASTE. IT BECOMES GOOD FOOD, TOO.
Light
+
CO_2
O_2
NH_4^+
HNO_2
HNO_3
N_2
THE PROBLEM IS WHEN PEOPLE KEEP THE BOWL CLEAN BECAUSE OF HOW IT LOOKS.
OH! YOU ALREADY SOUND LIKE A PROFESSOR.
YOU'RE TOO NICE!

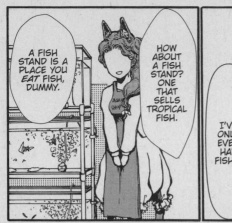

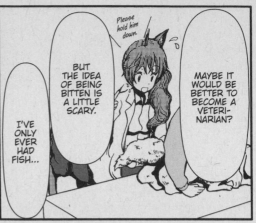

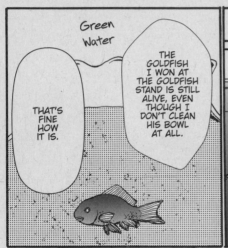

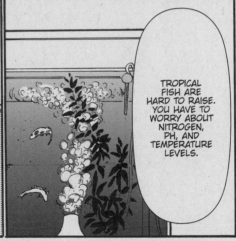

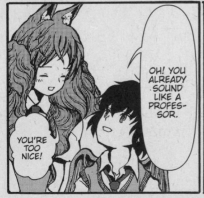

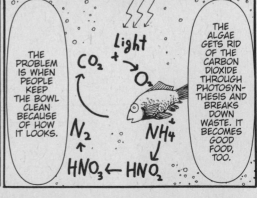

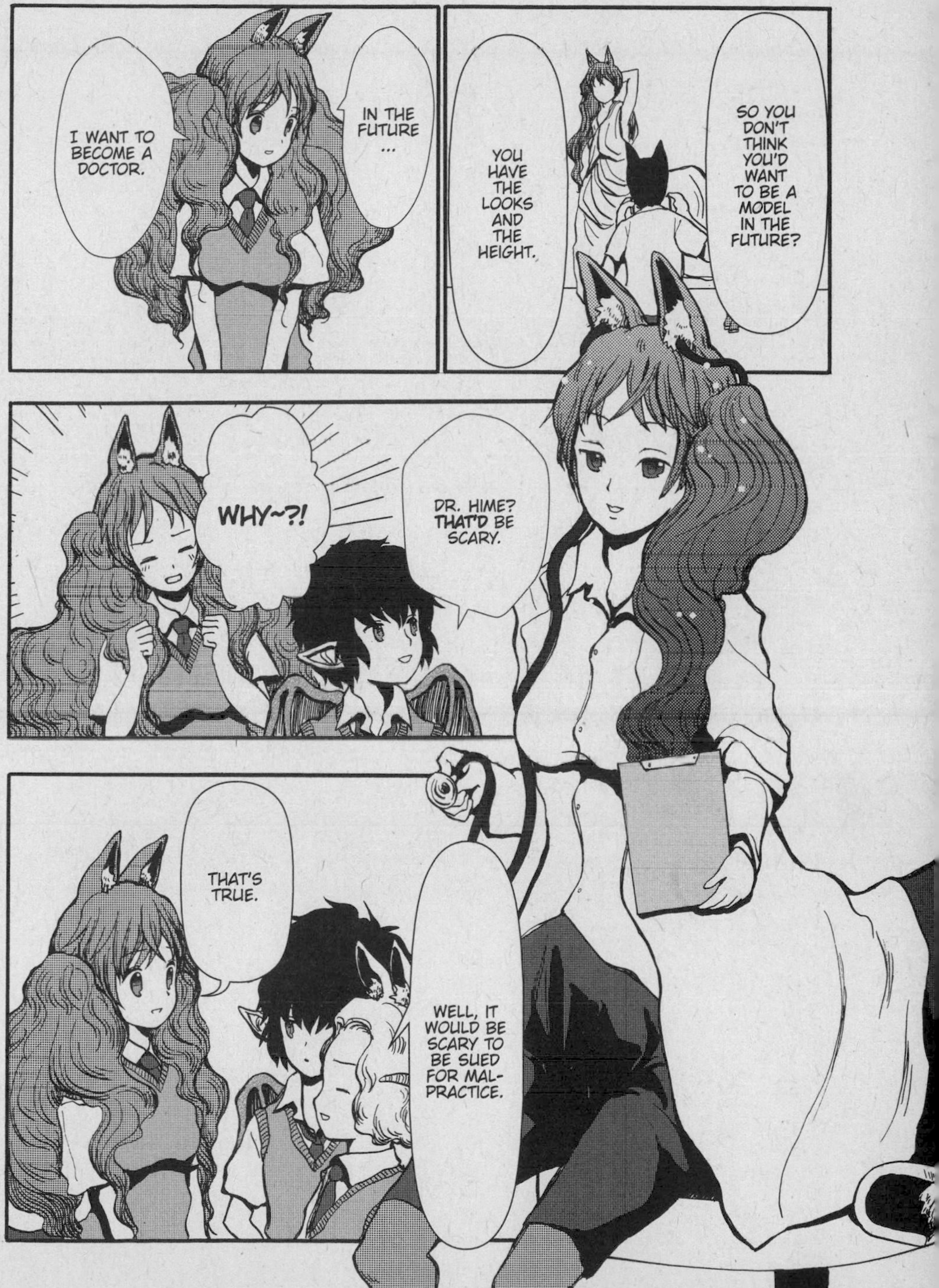
SO YOU DON'T THINK YOU'D WANT TO BE A MODEL IN THE FUTURE?
YOU HAVE THE LOOKS AND THE HEIGHT.
IN THE FUTURE ...
I WANT TO BECOME A DOCTOR.
DR. HIME? THAT'D BE SCARY.
WHY~?!
WELL, IT WOULD BE SCARY TO BE SUED FOR MAL-PRACTICE.
THAT'S TRUE.

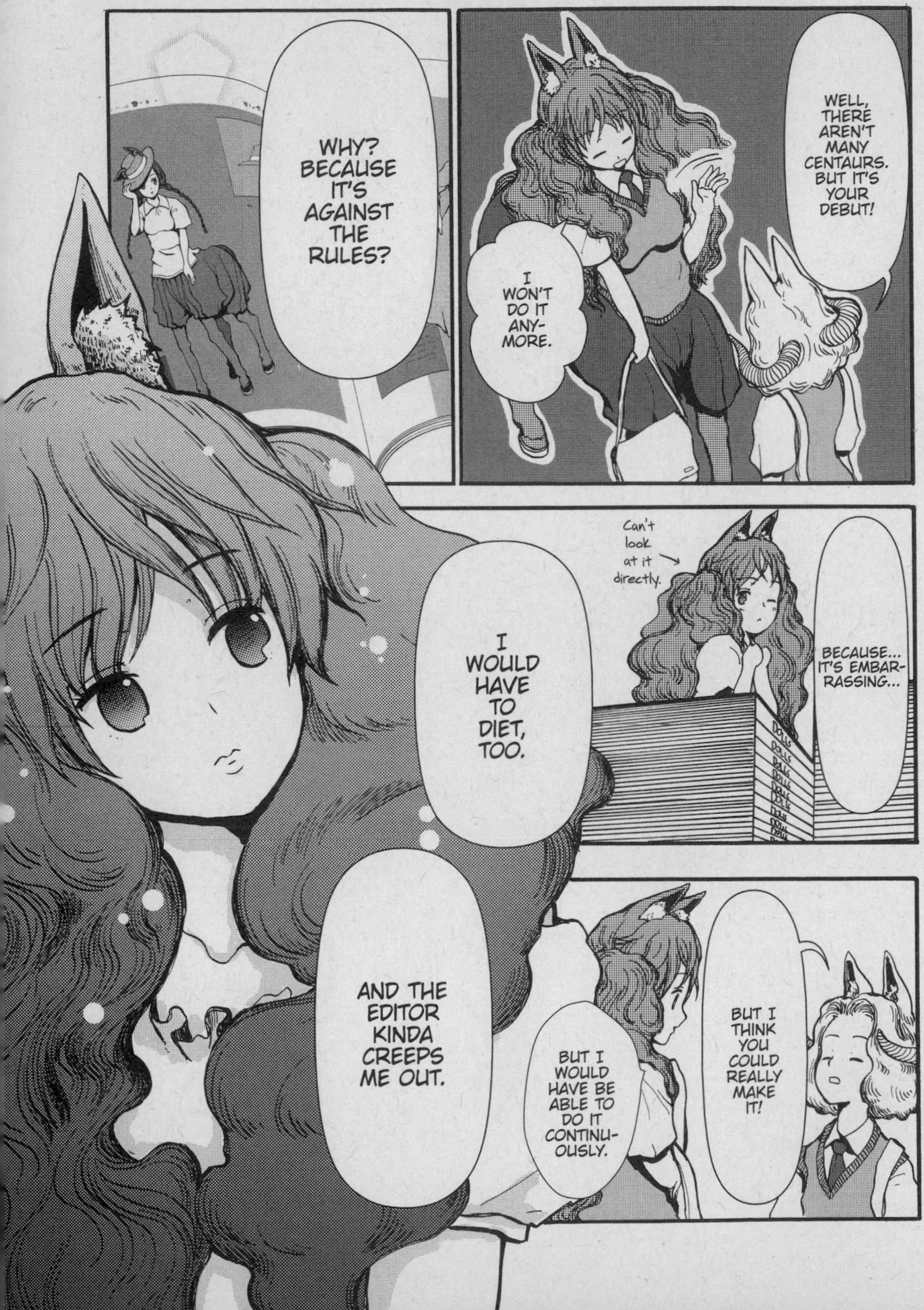
WELL, THERE AREN'T MANY CENTAURS. BUT IT'S YOUR DEBUT!
I WON'T DO IT ANY-MORE.
WHY? BECAUSE IT'S AGAINST THE RULES?
BECAUSE... IT'S EMBAR-RASSING...
Can't look at it directly.
BUT I THINK YOU COULD REALLY MAKE IT!
BUT I WOULD HAVE BE ABLE TO DO IT CONTINU-OUSLY.
I WOULD HAVE TO DIET, TOO.
AND THE EDITOR KINDA CREEPS ME OUT.

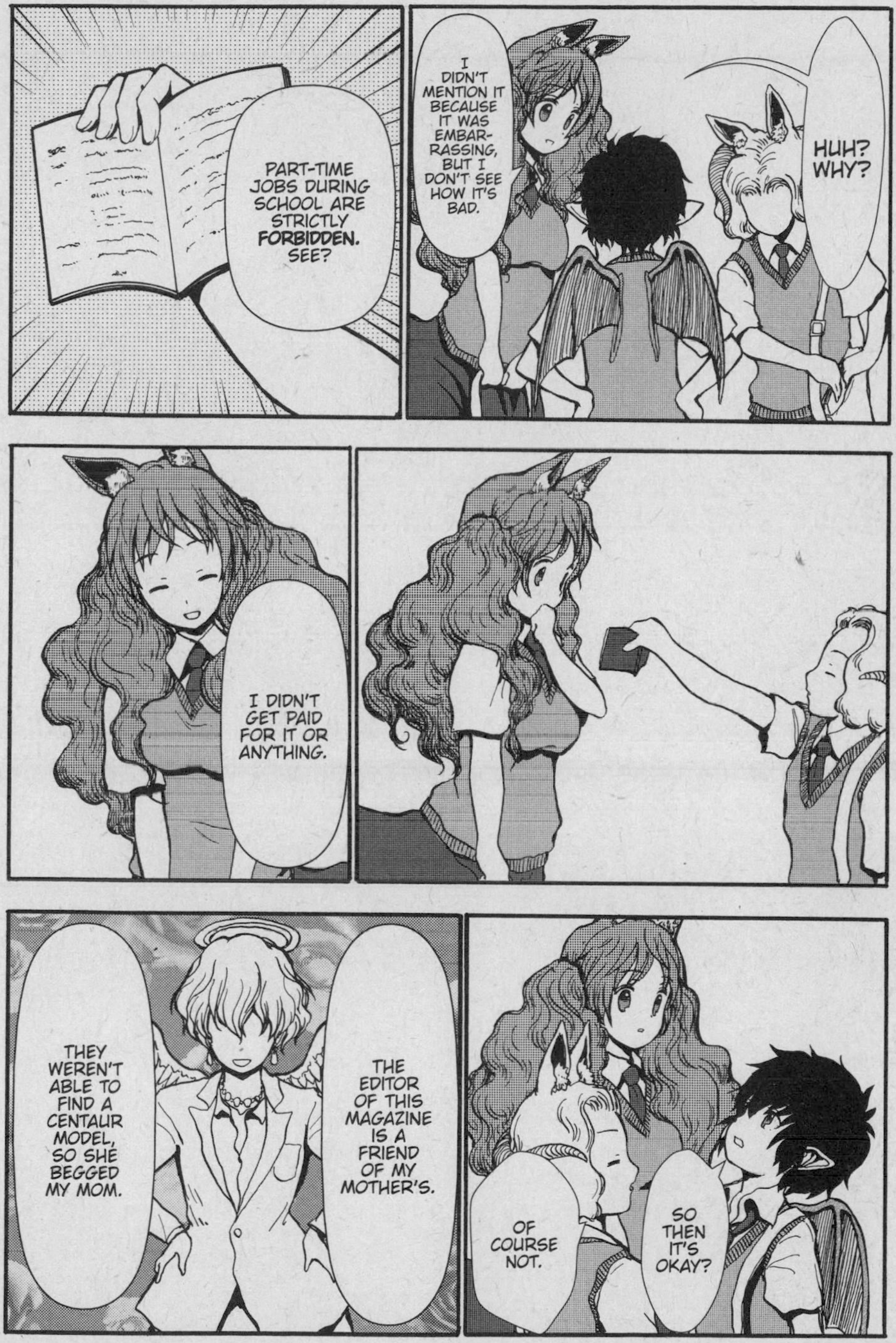
HUH? WHY?
I DIDN'T MENTION IT BECAUSE IT WAS EMBARRASSING, BUT I DON'T SEE HOW IT'S BAD.
PART-TIME JOBS DURING SCHOOL ARE STRICTLY FORBIDDEN. SEE?
I DIDN'T GET PAID FOR IT OR ANYTHING.
SO THEN IT'S OKAY?
OF COURSE NOT.
THE EDITOR OF THIS MAGAZINE IS A FRIEND OF MY MOTHER'S.
THEY WEREN'T ABLE TO FIND A CENTAUR MODEL, SO SHE BEGGED MY MOM.

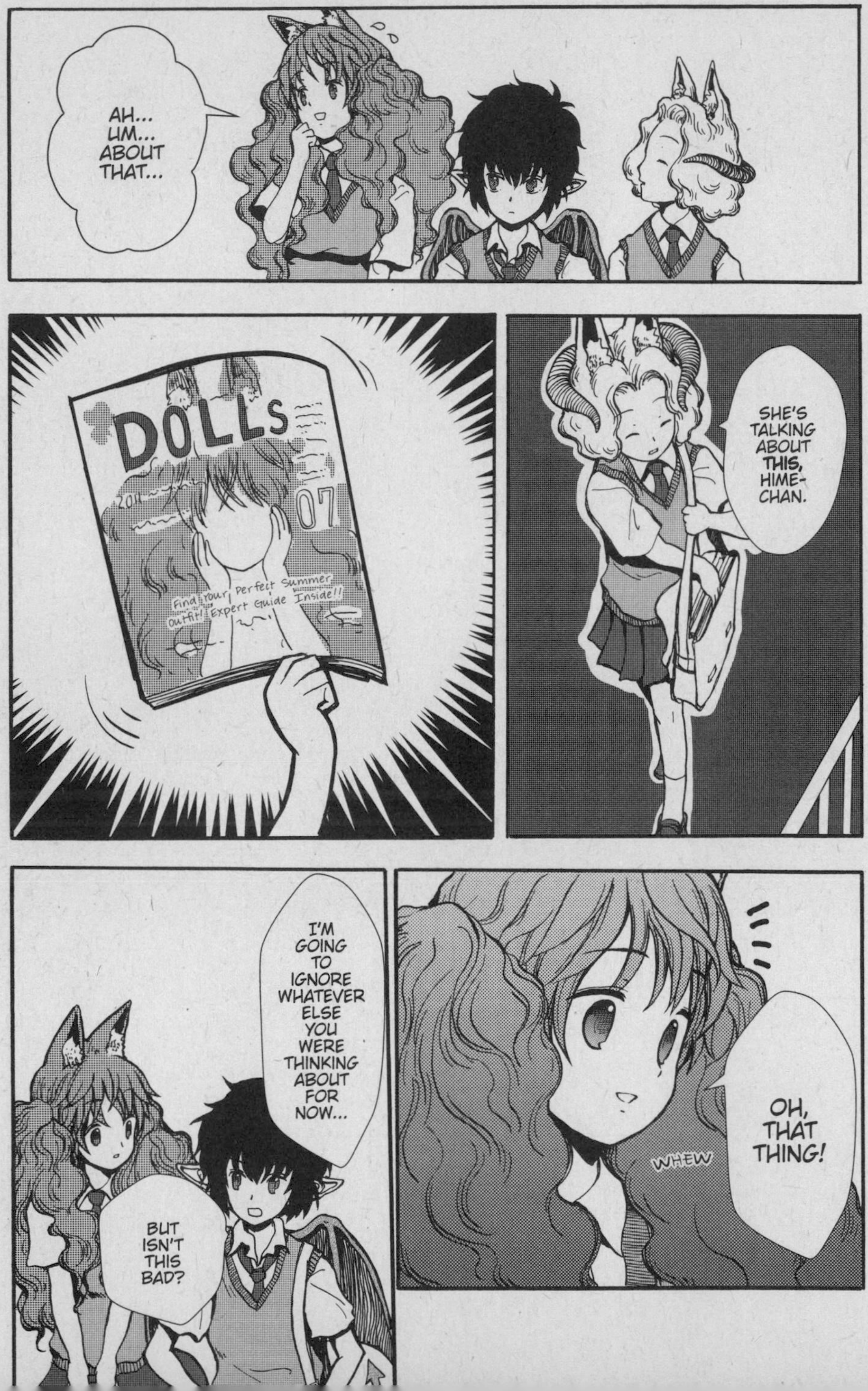
AH... UM... ABOUT THAT...
SHE'S TALKING ABOUT THIS, HIME-CHAN.
DOLLS
07
Find Your Perfect Summer Outfit! Expert Guide Inside!!
OH, THAT THING!
WHEW
I'M GOING TO IGNORE WHATEVER ELSE YOU WERE THINKING ABOUT FOR NOW...
BUT ISN'T THIS BAD?

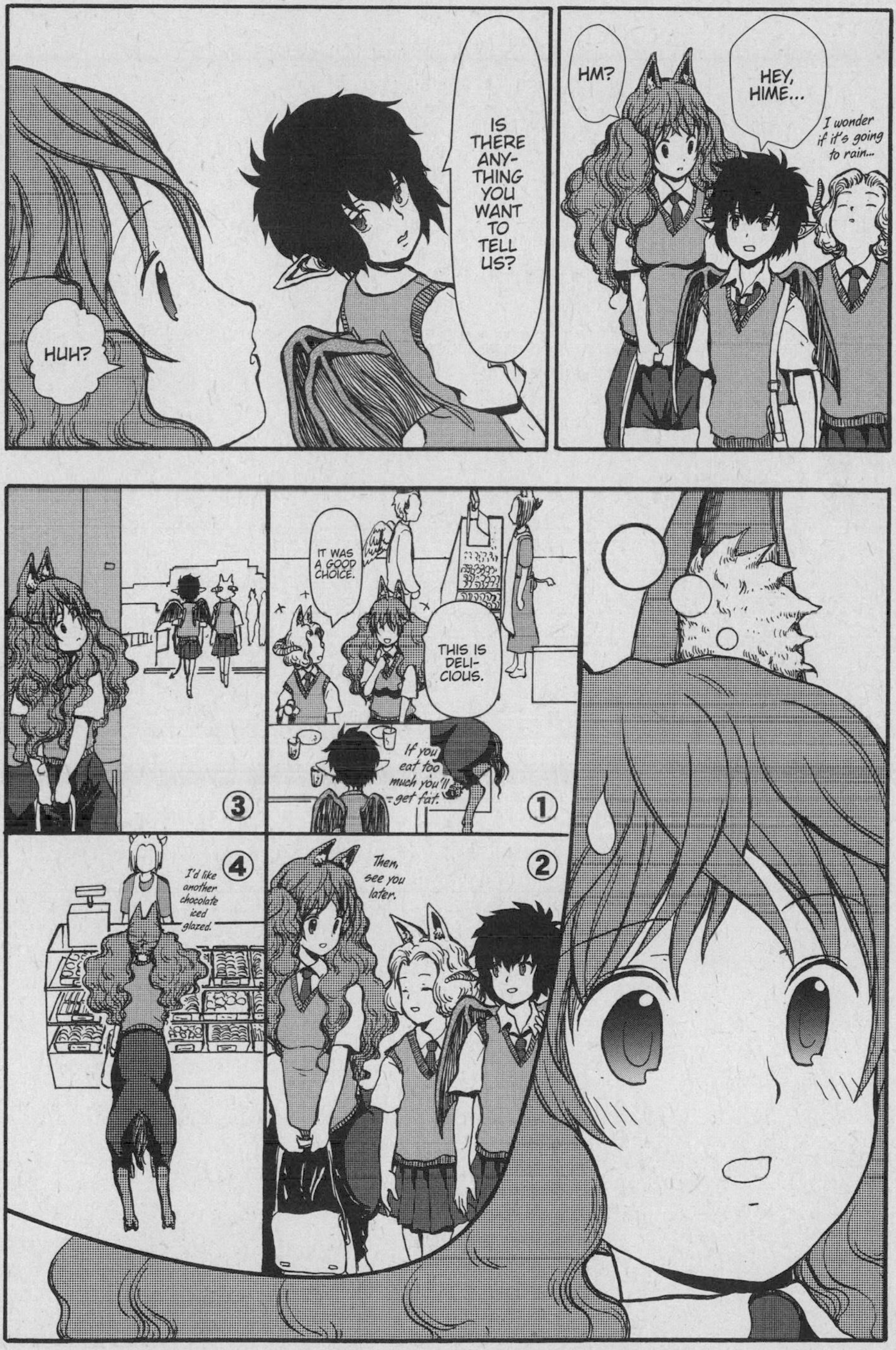
HEY, HIME...
HM?
I wonder if it's going to rain...
IS THERE ANYTHING YOU WANT TO TELL US?
HUH?
①
THIS IS DELICIOUS.
IT WAS A GOOD CHOICE.
If you eat too much you'll get fat.
②
Then, see you later.
③
④
I'd like another chocolate iced glazed.

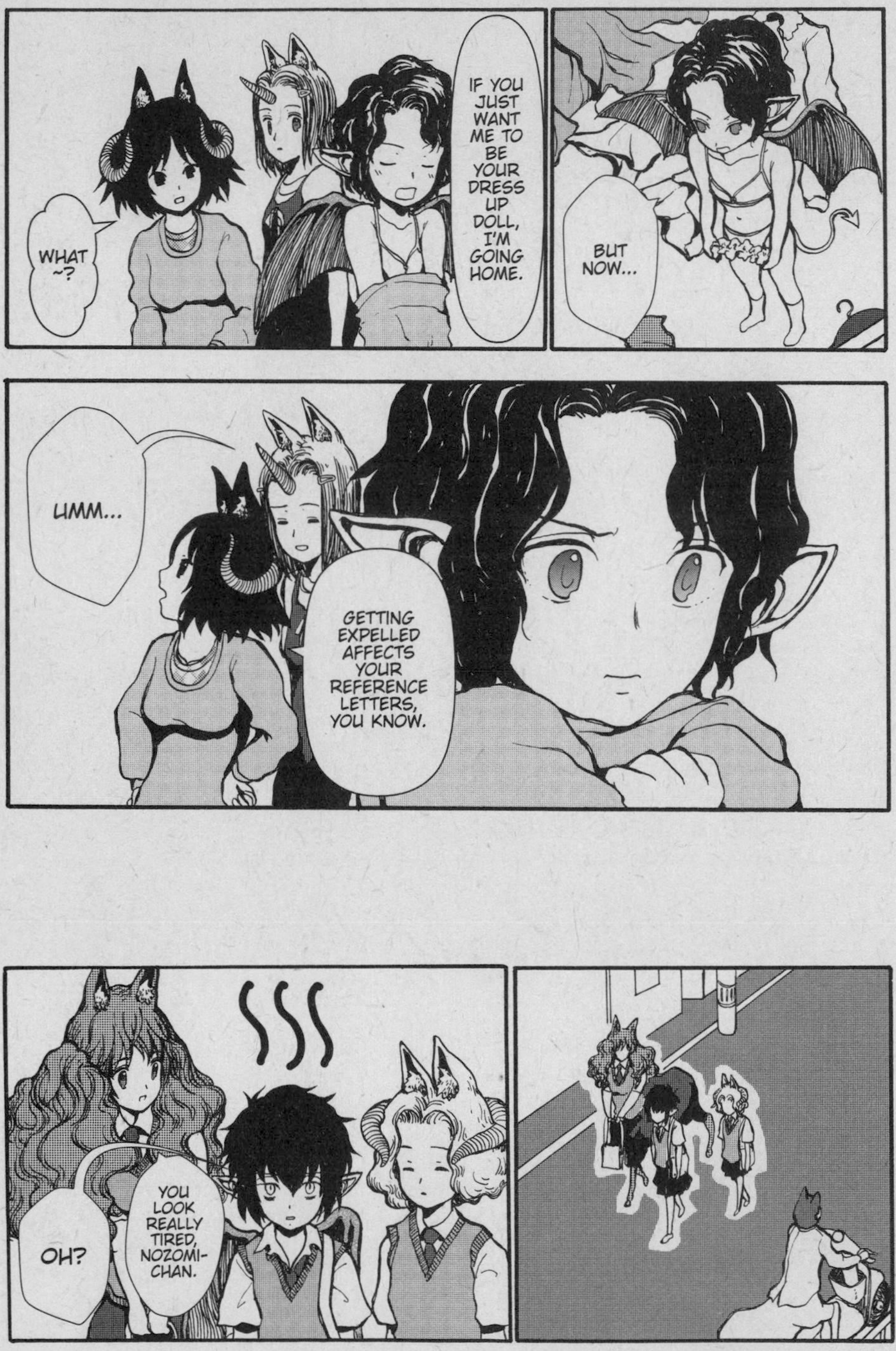
BUT NOW...
IF YOU JUST WANT ME TO BE YOUR DRESS UP DOLL, I'M GOING HOME.
WHAT ~?
UMM...
GETTING EXPELLED AFFECTS YOUR REFERENCE LETTERS, YOU KNOW.
YOU LOOK REALLY TIRED, NOZOMI-CHAN.
OH?

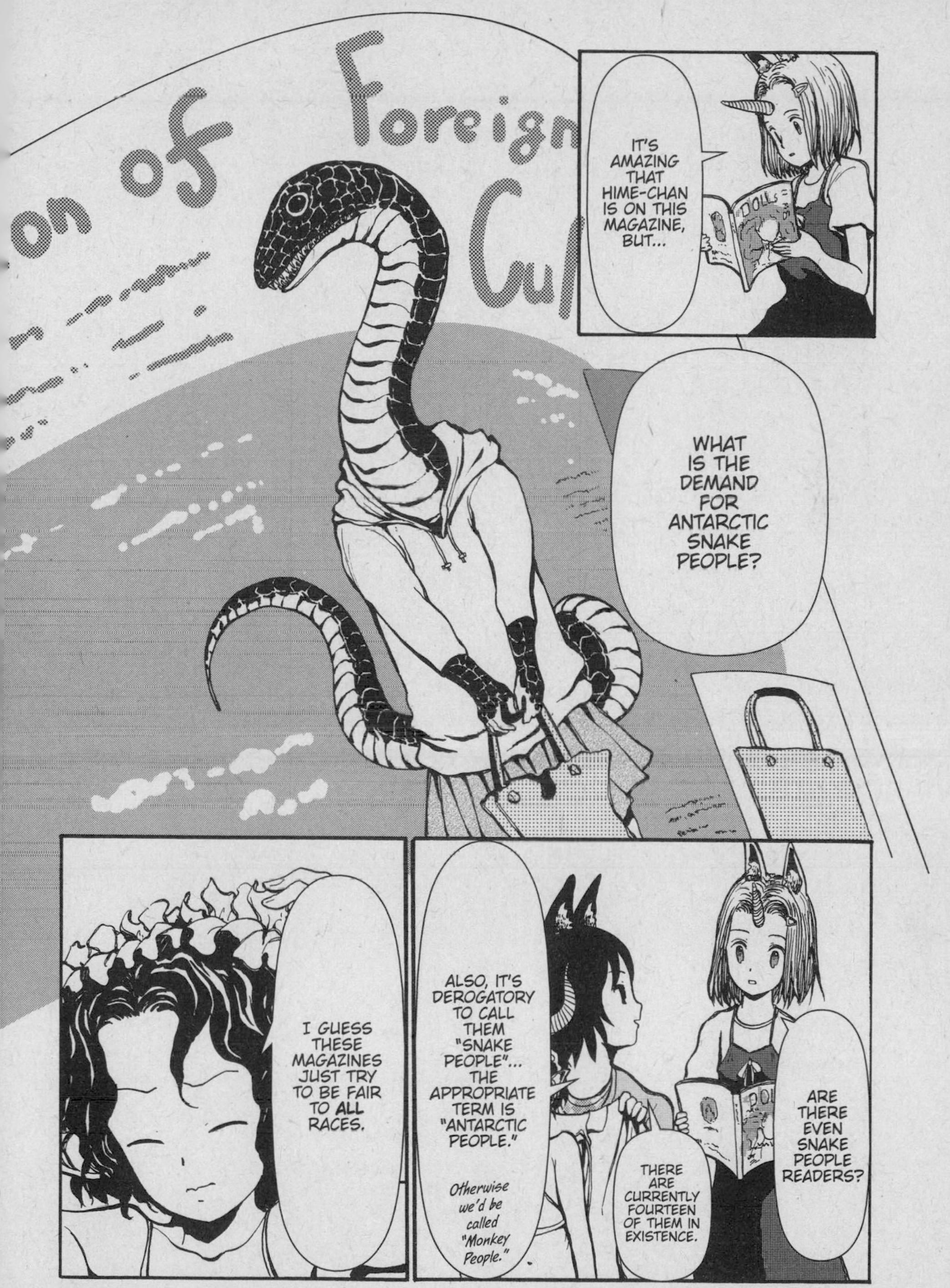
IT'S AMAZING THAT HIME-CHAN IS ON THIS MAGAZINE, BUT...
on of Foreign Cul
WHAT IS THE DEMAND FOR ANTARCTIC SNAKE PEOPLE?
ARE THERE EVEN SNAKE PEOPLE READERS?
THERE ARE CURRENTLY FOURTEEN OF THEM IN EXISTENCE.
ALSO, IT'S DEROGATORY TO CALL THEM "SNAKE PEOPLE"... THE APPROPRIATE TERM IS "ANTARCTIC PEOPLE."
Otherwise we'd be called "Monkey People."
I GUESS THESE MAGAZINES JUST TRY TO BE FAIR TO **ALL** RACES.

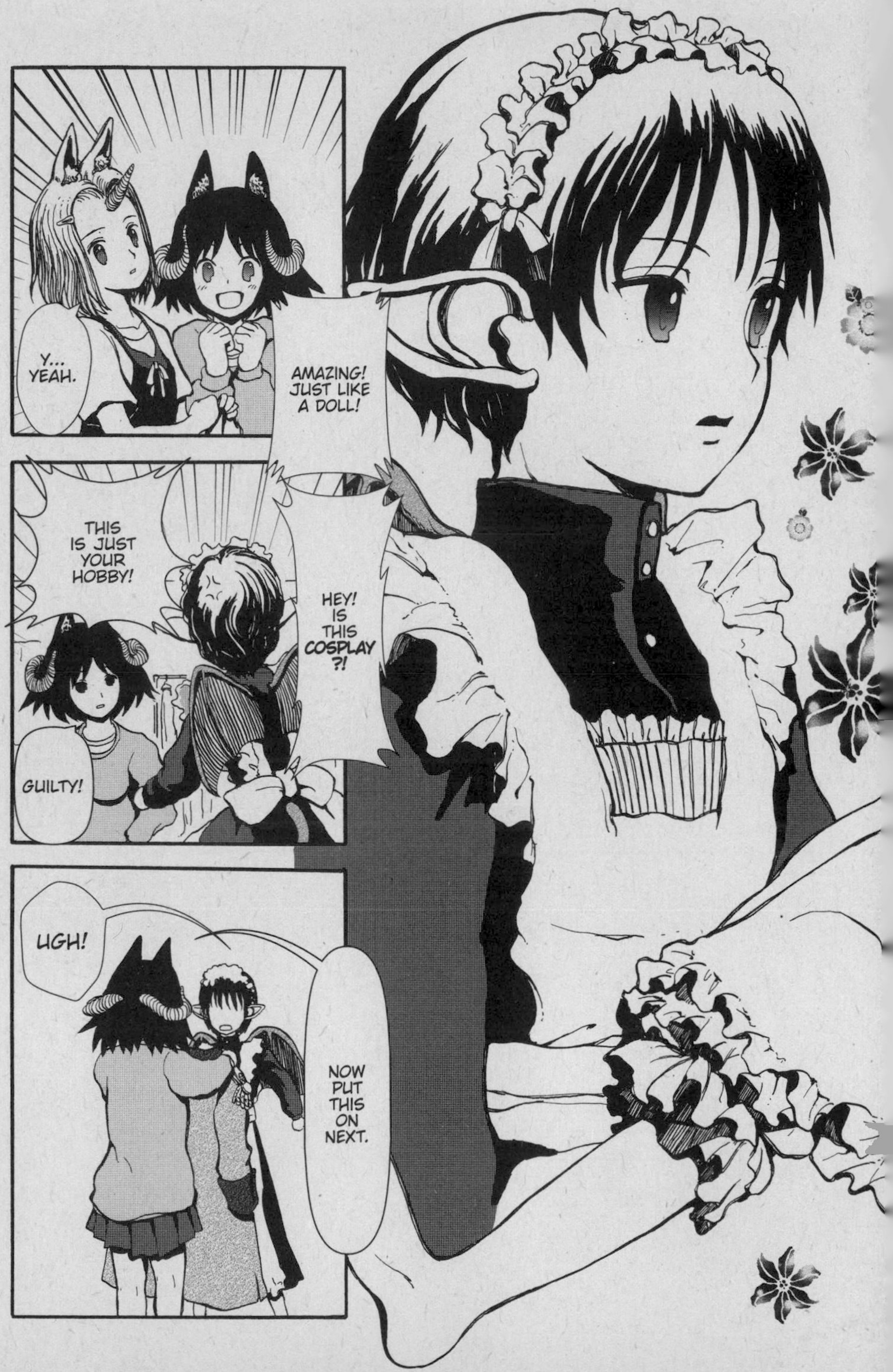
AMAZING! JUST LIKE A DOLL!
Y... YEAH.
HEY! IS THIS COSPLAY ?!
THIS IS JUST YOUR HOBBY!
GUILTY!
NOW PUT THIS ON NEXT.
UGH!

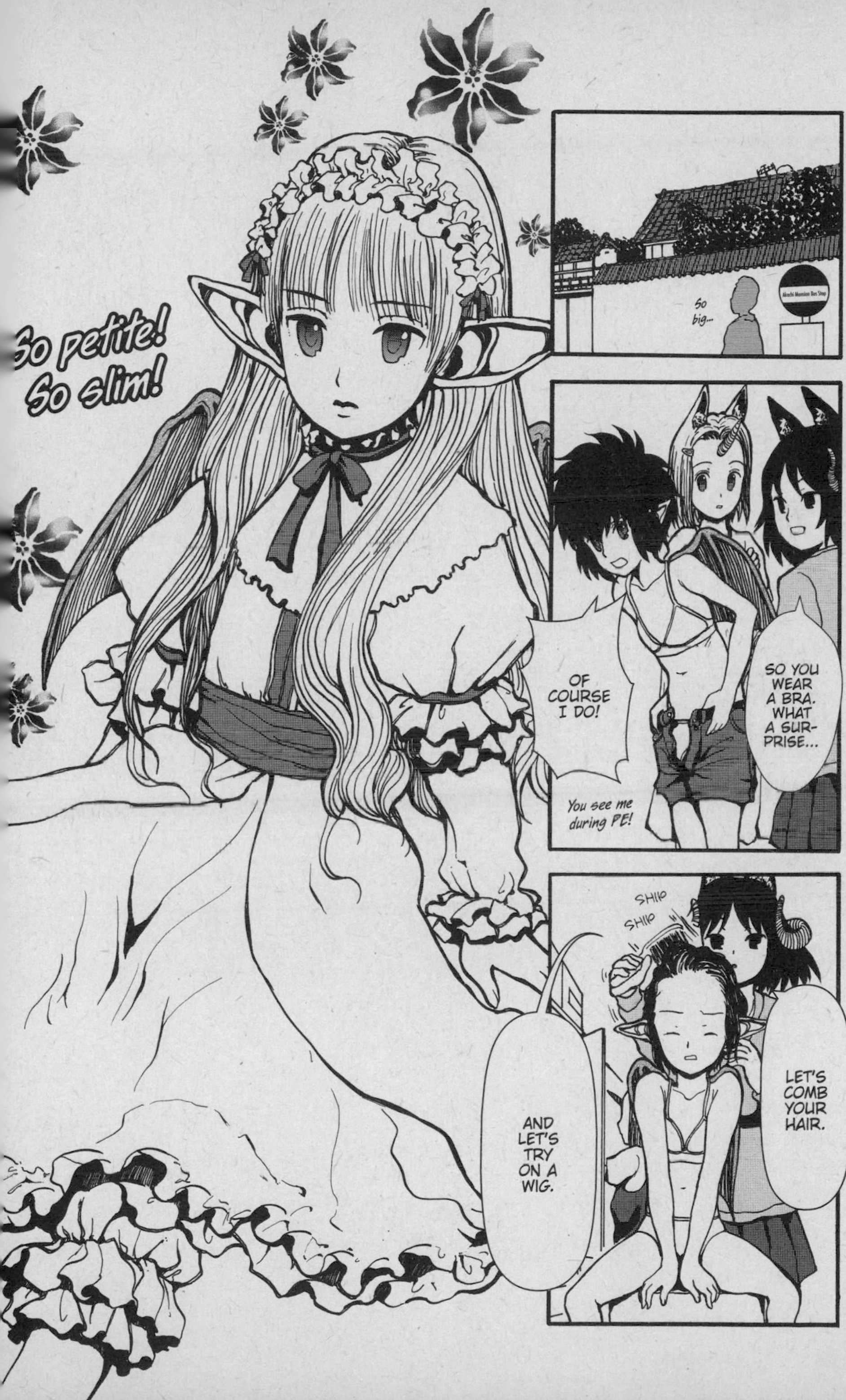
Akechi Mansion Bus Stop
So big...
SO YOU WEAR A BRA. WHAT A SUR-PRISE...
OF COURSE I DO!
You see me during PE!
SHIP
SHIP
LET'S COMB YOUR HAIR.
AND LET'S TRY ON A WIG.
So petite! So slim!

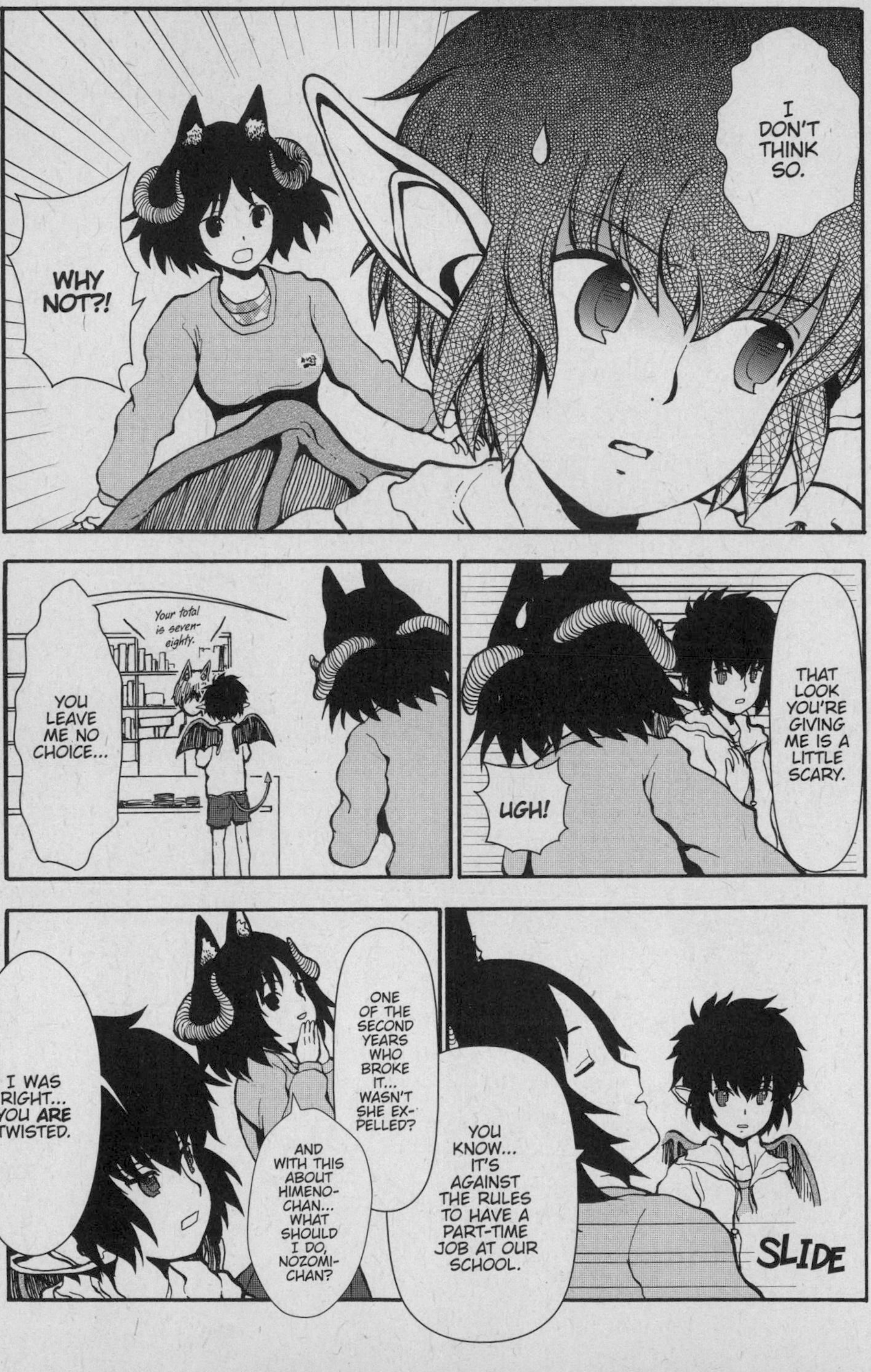
I DON'T THINK SO.
WHY NOT?!
THAT LOOK YOU'RE GIVING ME IS A LITTLE SCARY.
UGH!
Your total is seven-eighty.
YOU LEAVE ME NO CHOICE...
YOU KNOW... IT'S AGAINST THE RULES TO HAVE A PART-TIME JOB AT OUR SCHOOL.
SLIDE
ONE OF THE SECOND YEARS WHO BROKE IT... WASN'T SHE EXPELLED?
AND WITH THIS ABOUT HIMENO-CHAN... WHAT SHOULD I DO, NOZOMI-CHAN?
I WAS RIGHT... YOU ARE TWISTED.

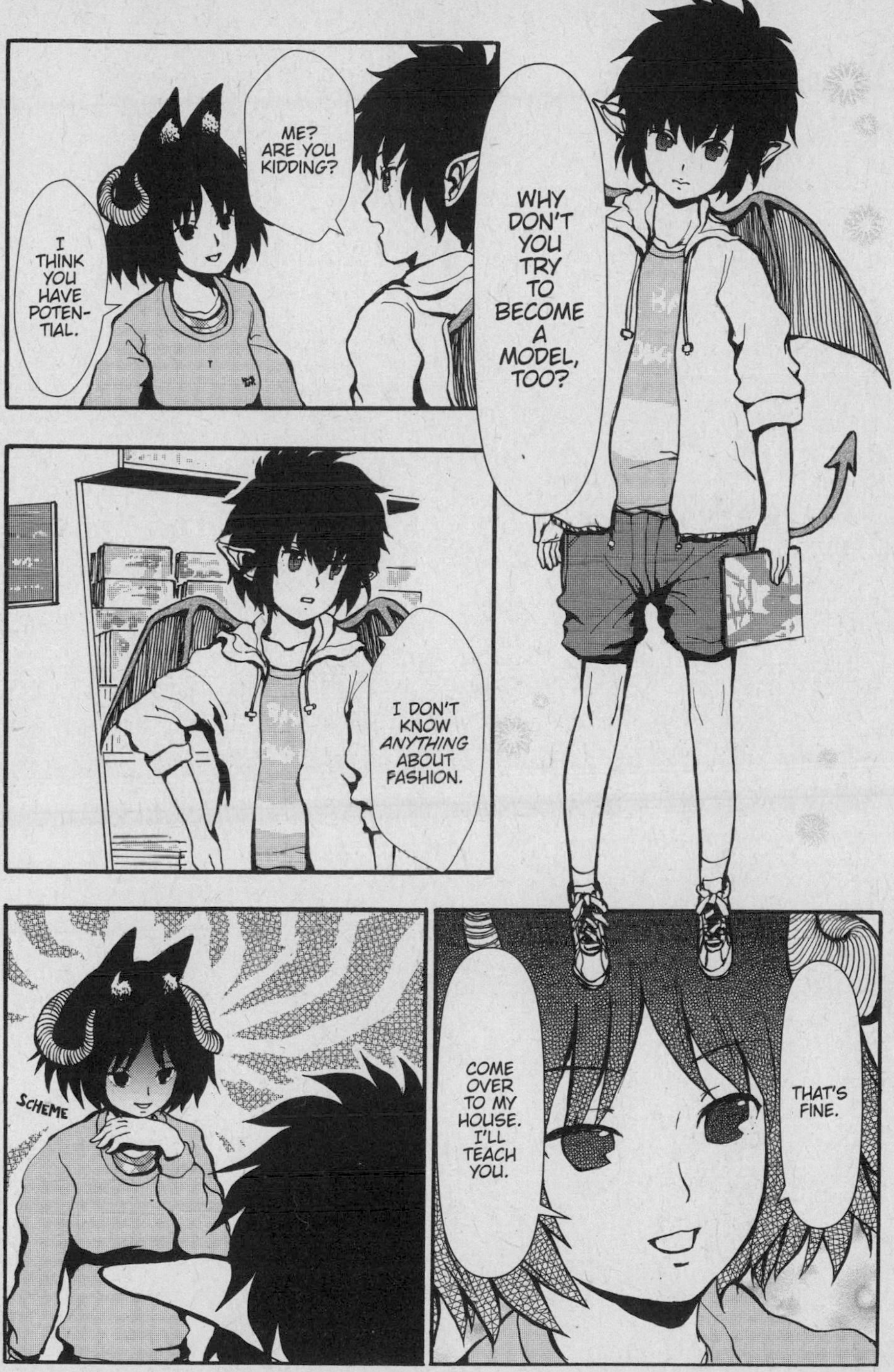
WHY DON'T YOU TRY TO BECOME A MODEL, TOO?
ME? ARE YOU KIDDING?
I THINK YOU HAVE POTEN-TIAL.
I DON'T KNOW *ANYTHING* ABOUT FASHION.
THAT'S FINE.
COME OVER TO MY HOUSE. I'LL TEACH YOU.
SCHEME

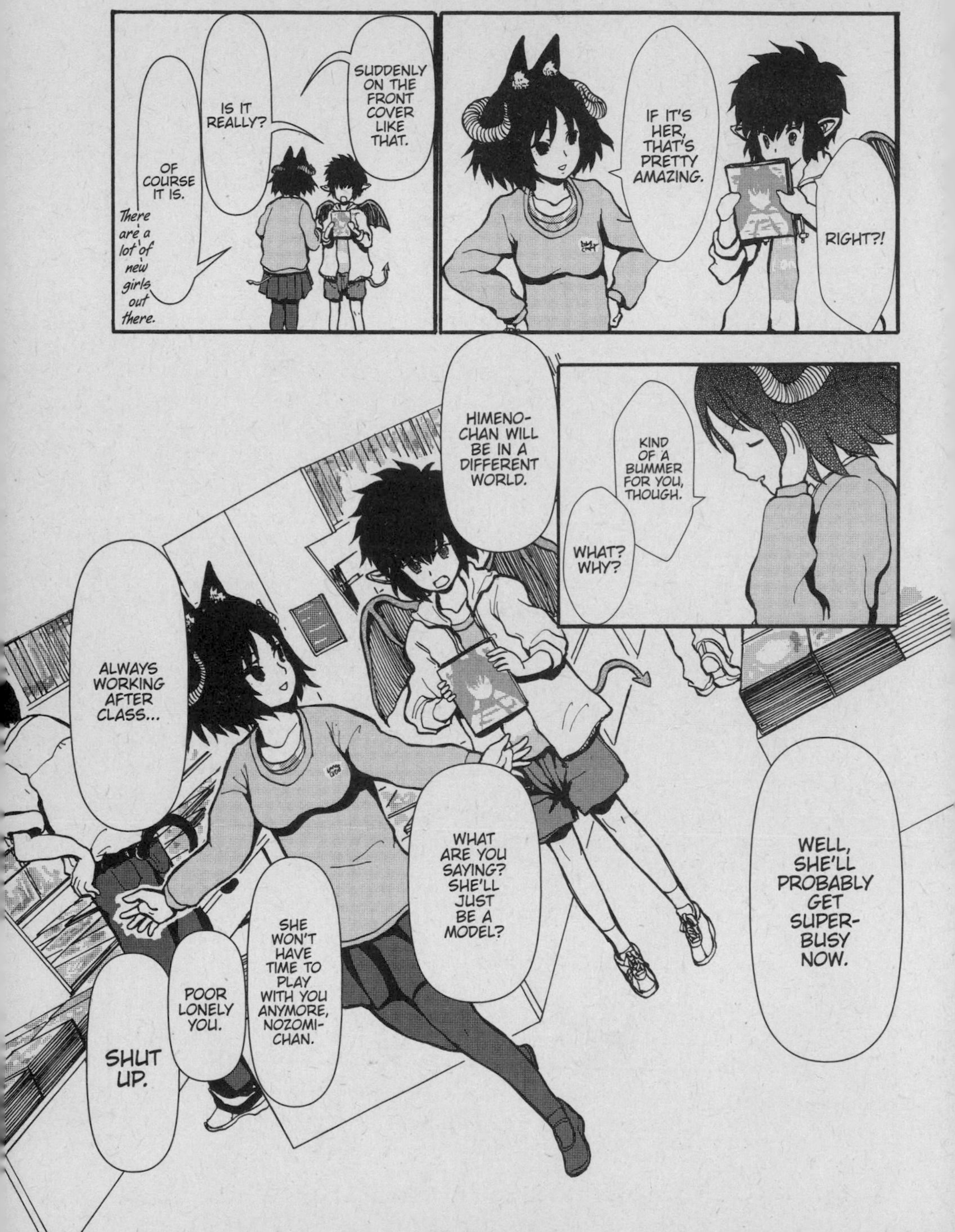
IF IT'S HER, THAT'S PRETTY AMAZING.
RIGHT?!
SUDDENLY ON THE FRONT COVER LIKE THAT.
IS IT REALLY?
OF COURSE IT IS.
There are a lot of new girls out there.
KIND OF A BUMMER FOR YOU, THOUGH.
WHAT? WHY?
HIMENO-CHAN WILL BE IN A DIFFERENT WORLD.
WELL, SHE'LL PROBABLY GET SUPER-BUSY NOW.
ALWAYS WORKING AFTER CLASS...
WHAT ARE YOU SAYING? SHE'LL JUST BE A MODEL?
SHE WON'T HAVE TIME TO PLAY WITH YOU ANYMORE, NOZOMI-CHAN.
POOR LONELY YOU.
SHUT UP.

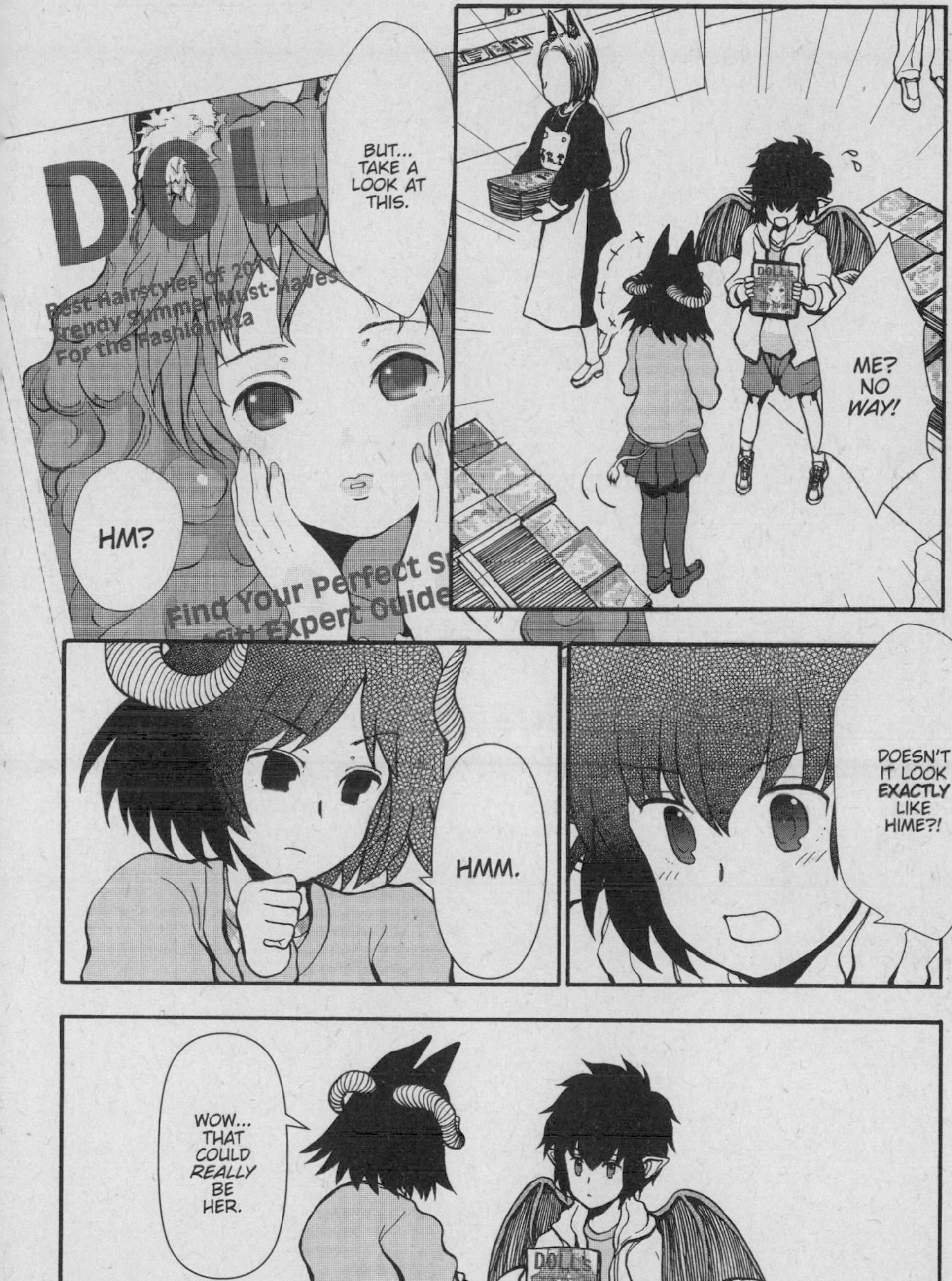
ME? NO WAY!
BUT... TAKE A LOOK AT THIS.
Trendy Summer Must-Haves
For the Fashionista
HM?
Expert Guide
DOESN'T IT LOOK **EXACTLY** LIKE HIME?!
HMM.
WOW... THAT COULD *REALLY* BE HER.
DOLLs

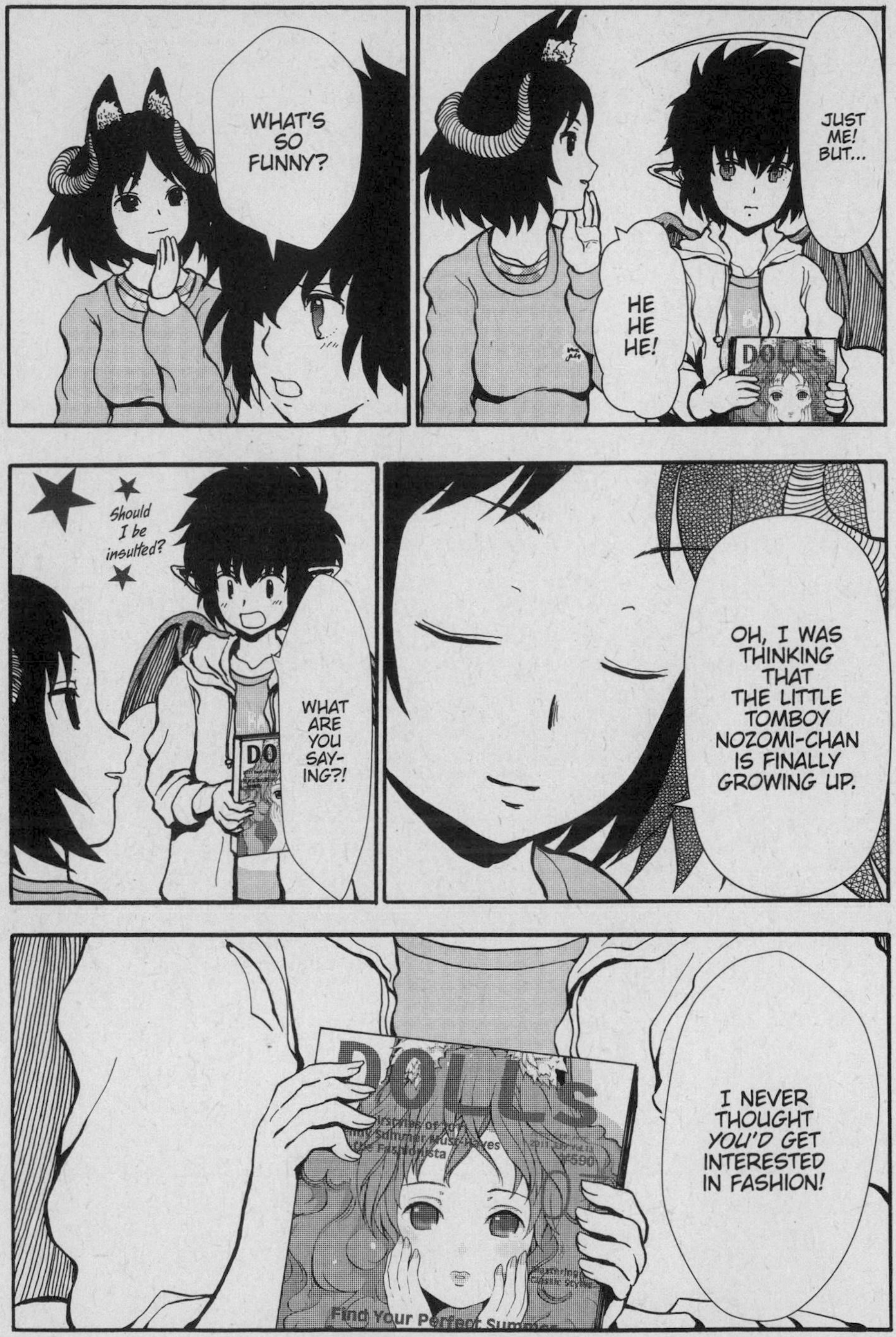
JUST ME! BUT...
HE HE HE!
DOLL's
WHAT'S SO FUNNY?
OH, I WAS THINKING THAT THE LITTLE TOMBOY NOZOMI-CHAN IS FINALLY GROWING UP.
WHAT ARE YOU SAY-ING?!
Should I be insulted?
I NEVER THOUGHT *YOU'D* GET INTERESTED IN FASHION!
DOLL's

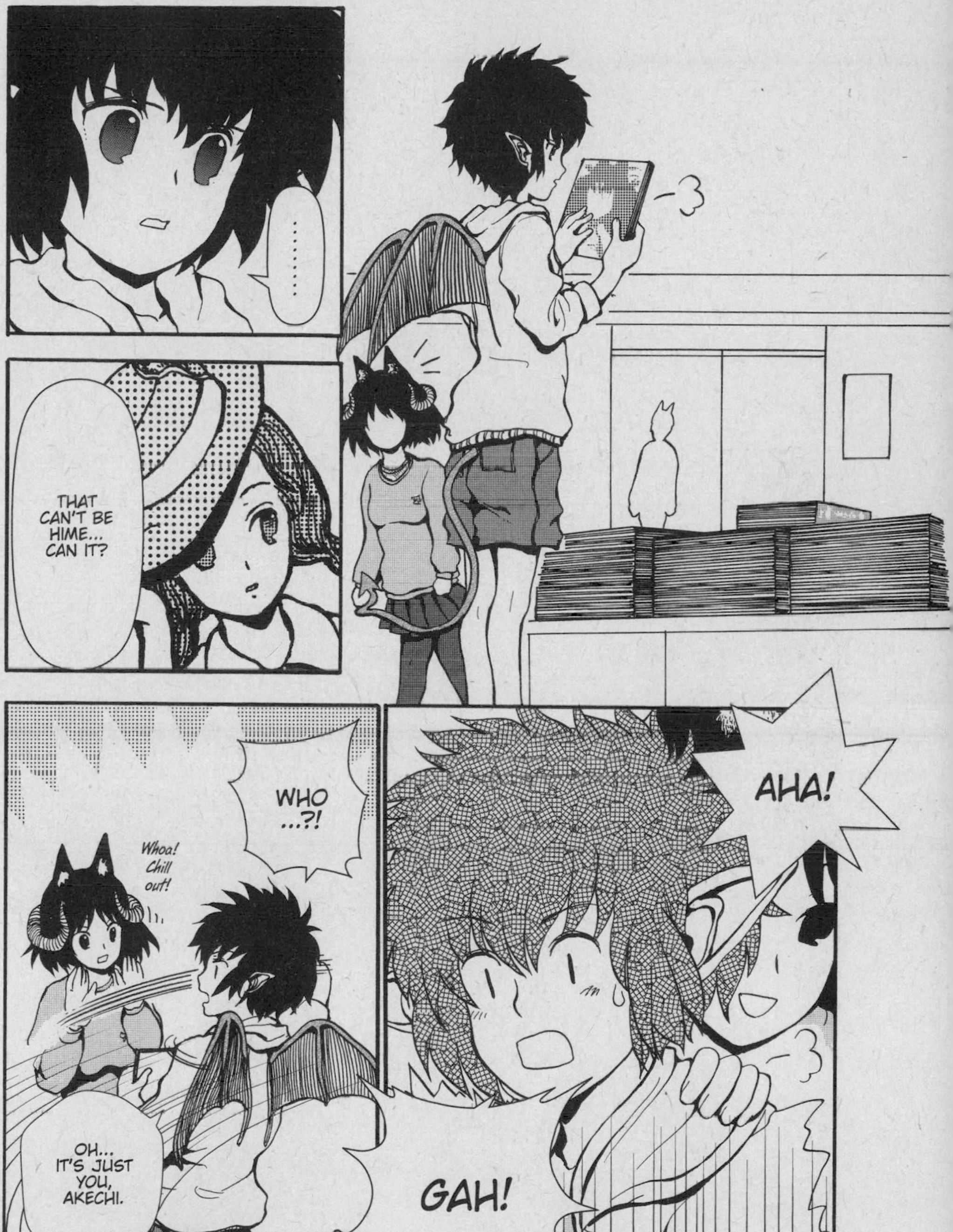
......
THAT CAN'T BE HIME... CAN IT?
AHA!
GAH!
WHO ...?!
Whoa! Chill out!
OH... IT'S JUST YOU, AKECHI.

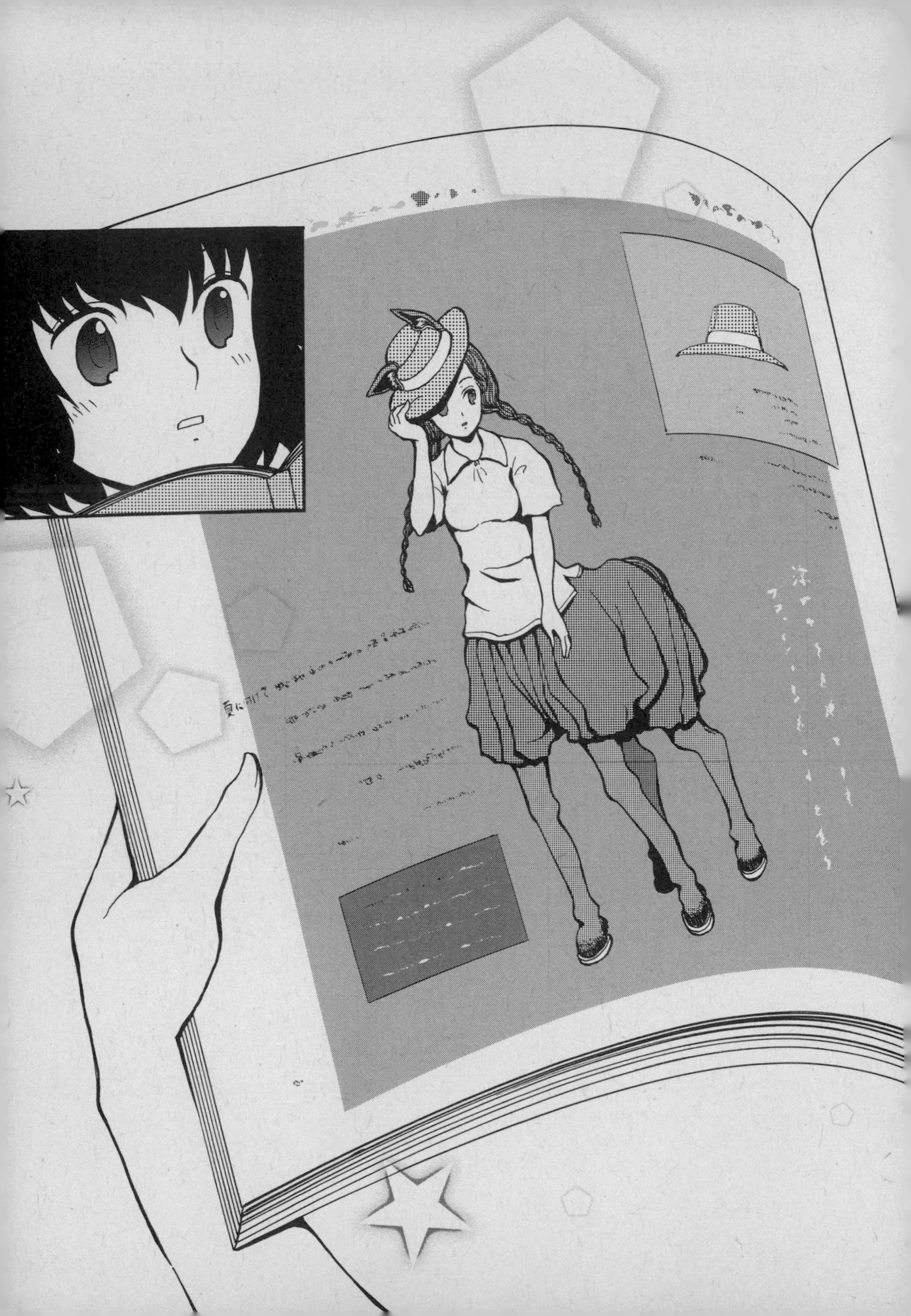
夏に向けて

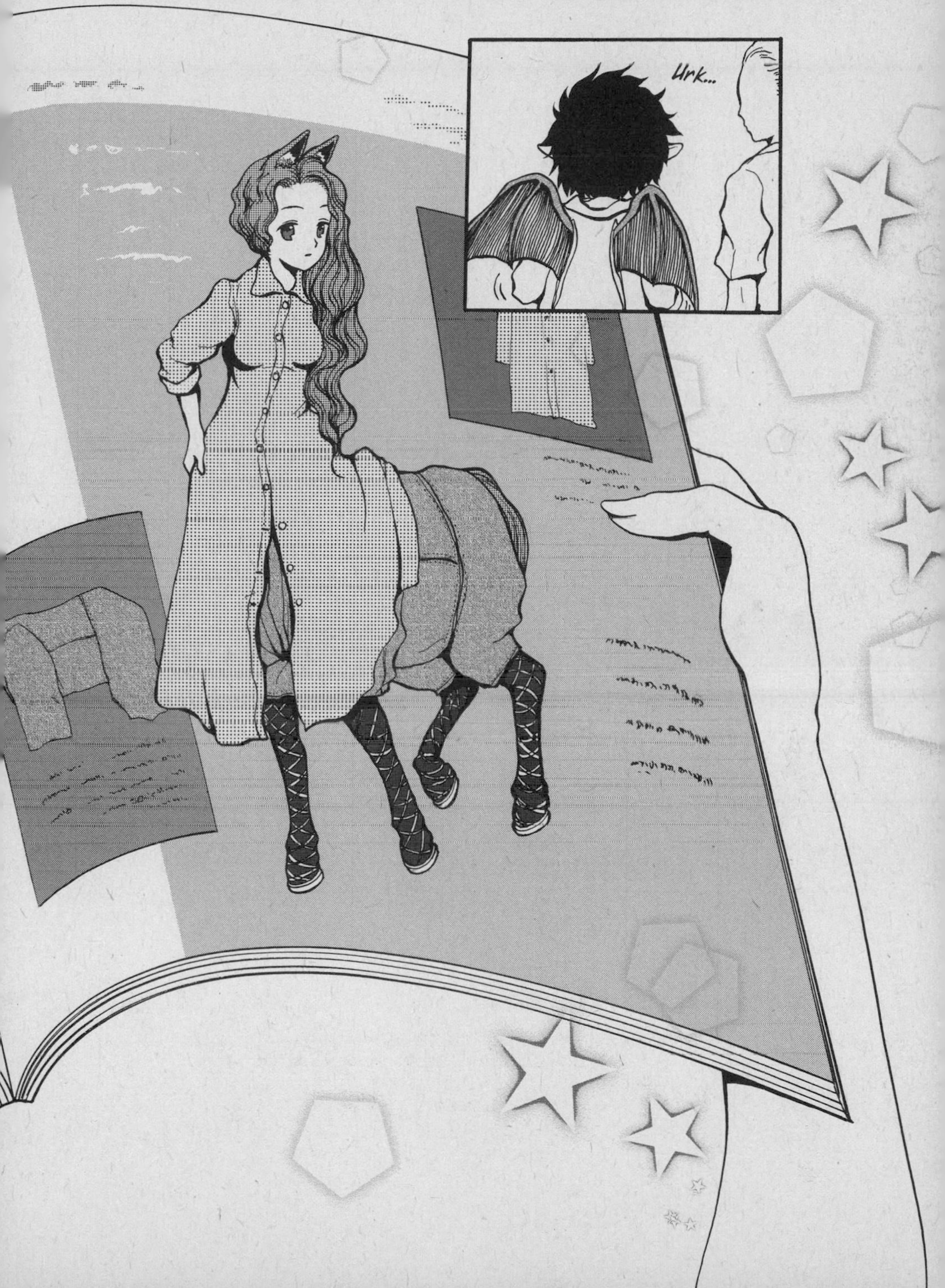
Urk...

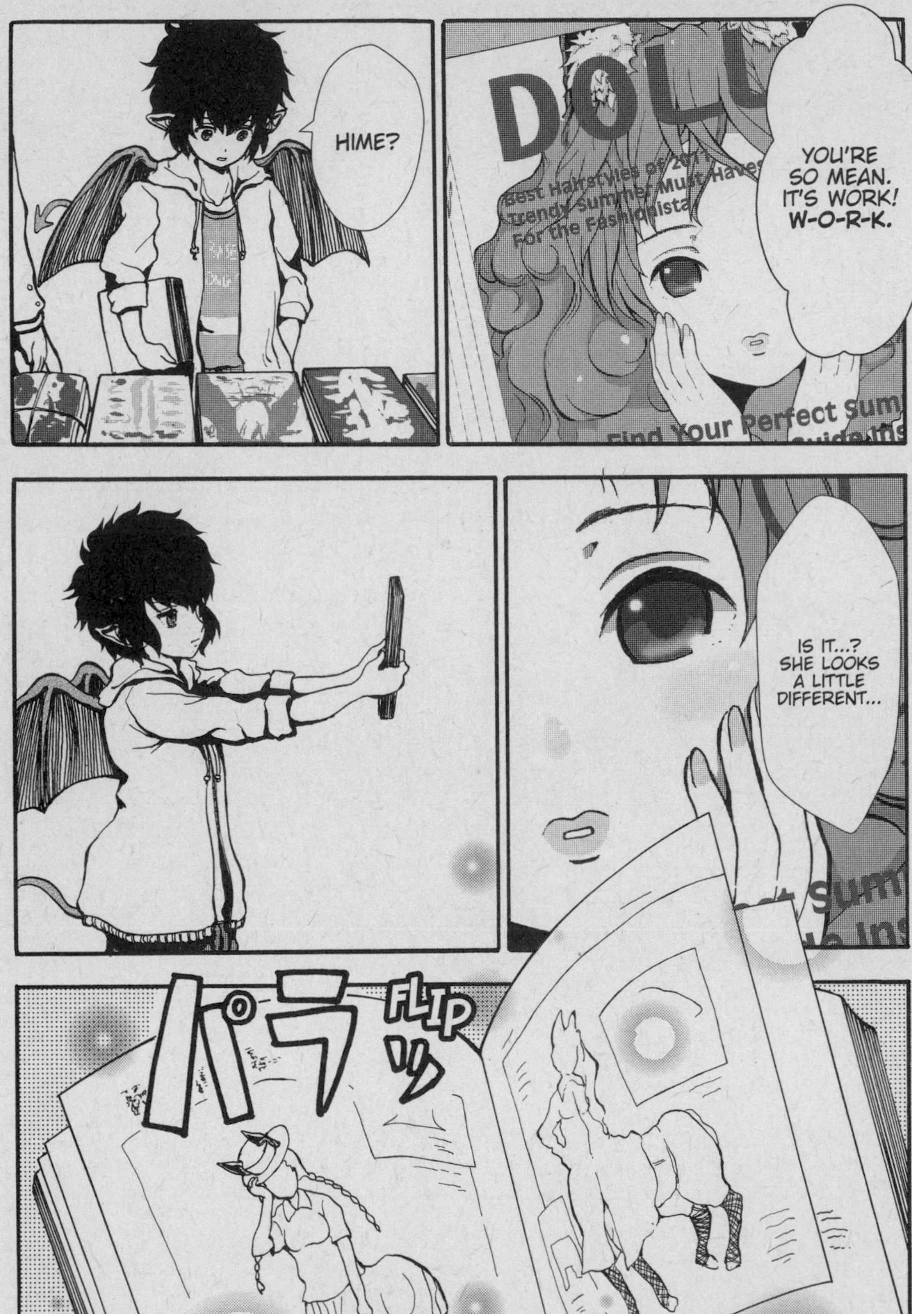
YOU'RE SO MEAN. IT'S WORK! W-O-R-K.
For the Fashionista
HIME?
IS IT...? SHE LOOKS A LITTLE DIFFERENT...
パラッ
FLIP

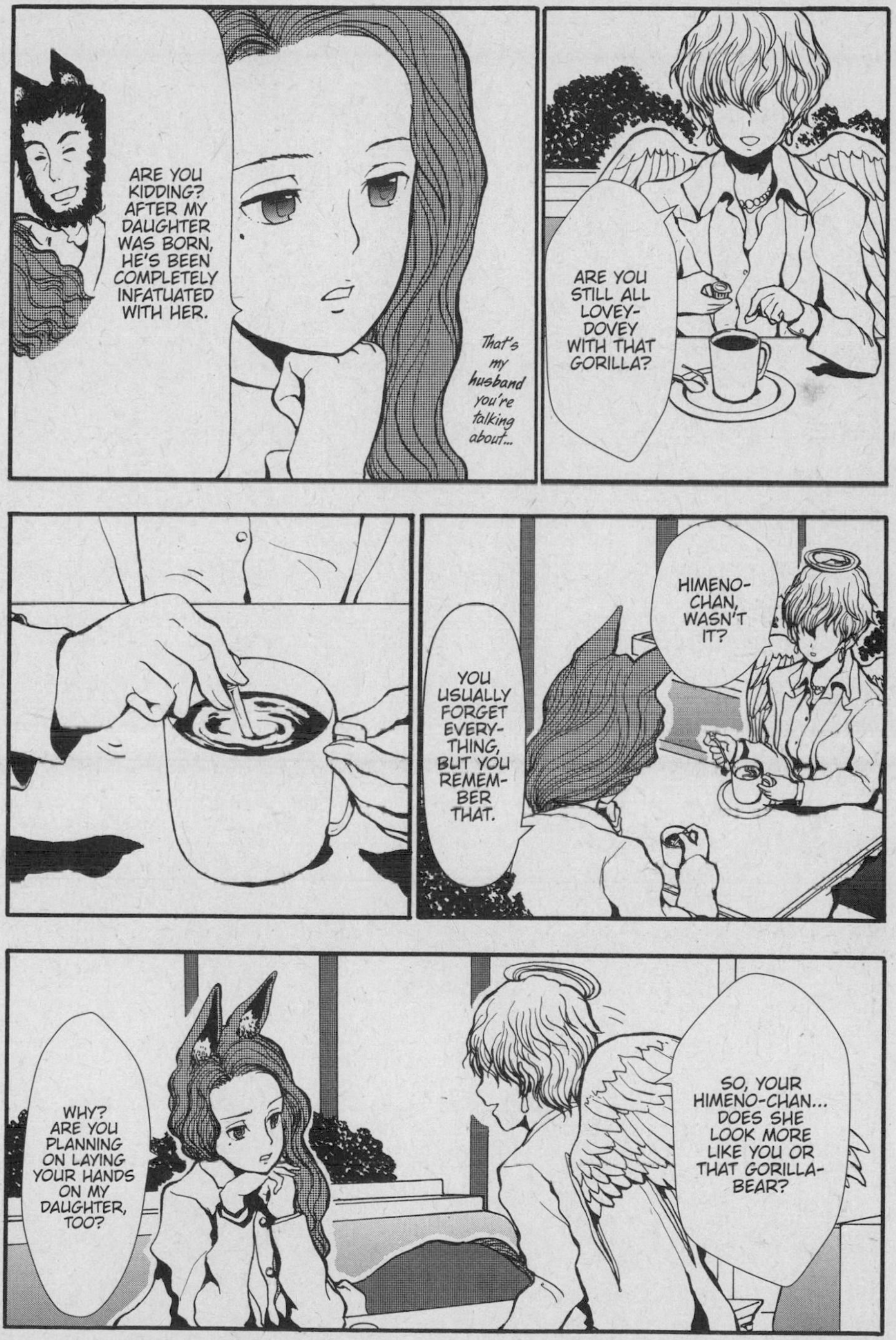
ARE YOU STILL ALL LOVEY-DOVEY WITH THAT GORILLA?
ARE YOU KIDDING? AFTER MY DAUGHTER WAS BORN, HE'S BEEN COMPLETELY INFATUATED WITH HER.
That's my husband you're talking about...
HIMENO-CHAN, WASN'T IT?
YOU USUALLY FORGET EVERYTHING, BUT YOU REMEMBER THAT.
SO, YOUR HIMENO-CHAN... DOES SHE LOOK MORE LIKE YOU OR THAT GORILLA-BEAR?
WHY? ARE YOU PLANNING ON LAYING YOUR HANDS ON MY DAUGHTER, TOO?

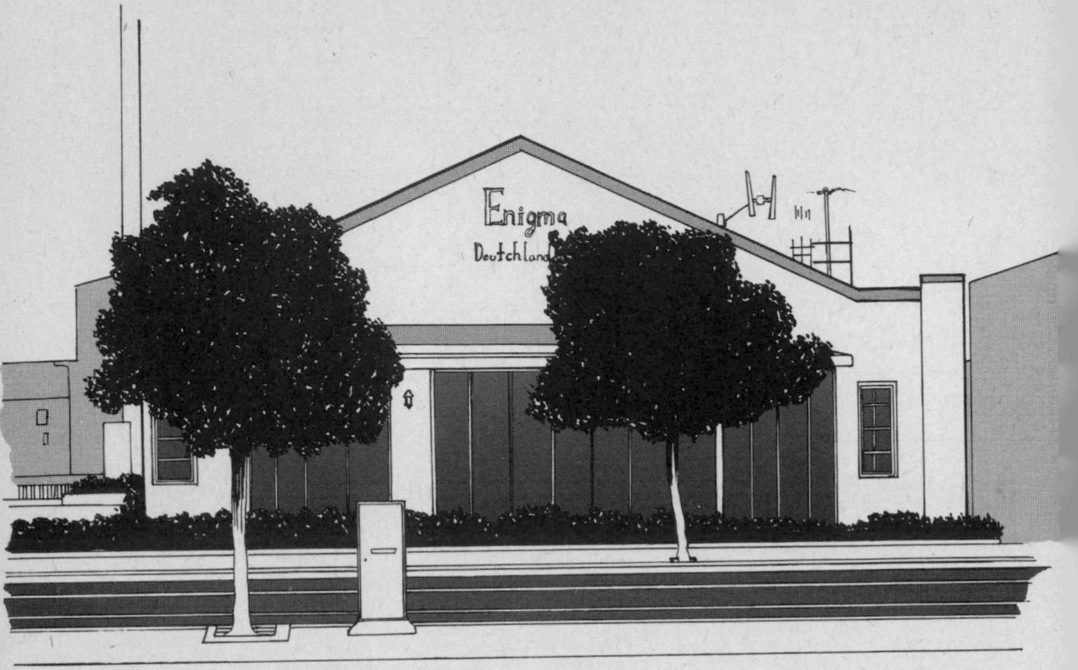
Enigma
Deutchland

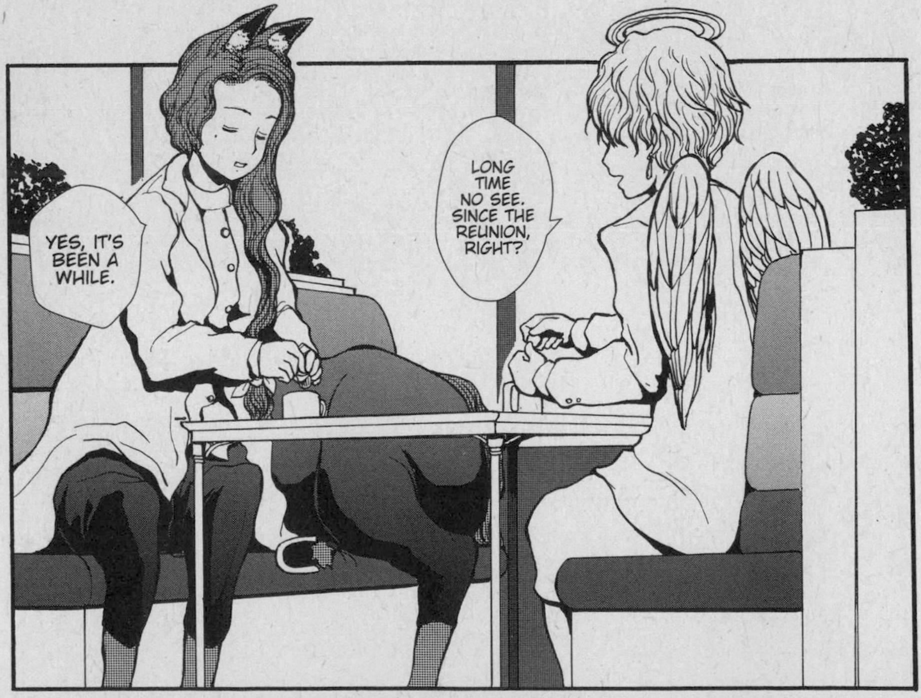
LONG TIME NO SEE. SINCE THE REUNION, RIGHT?
YES, IT'S BEEN A WHILE.

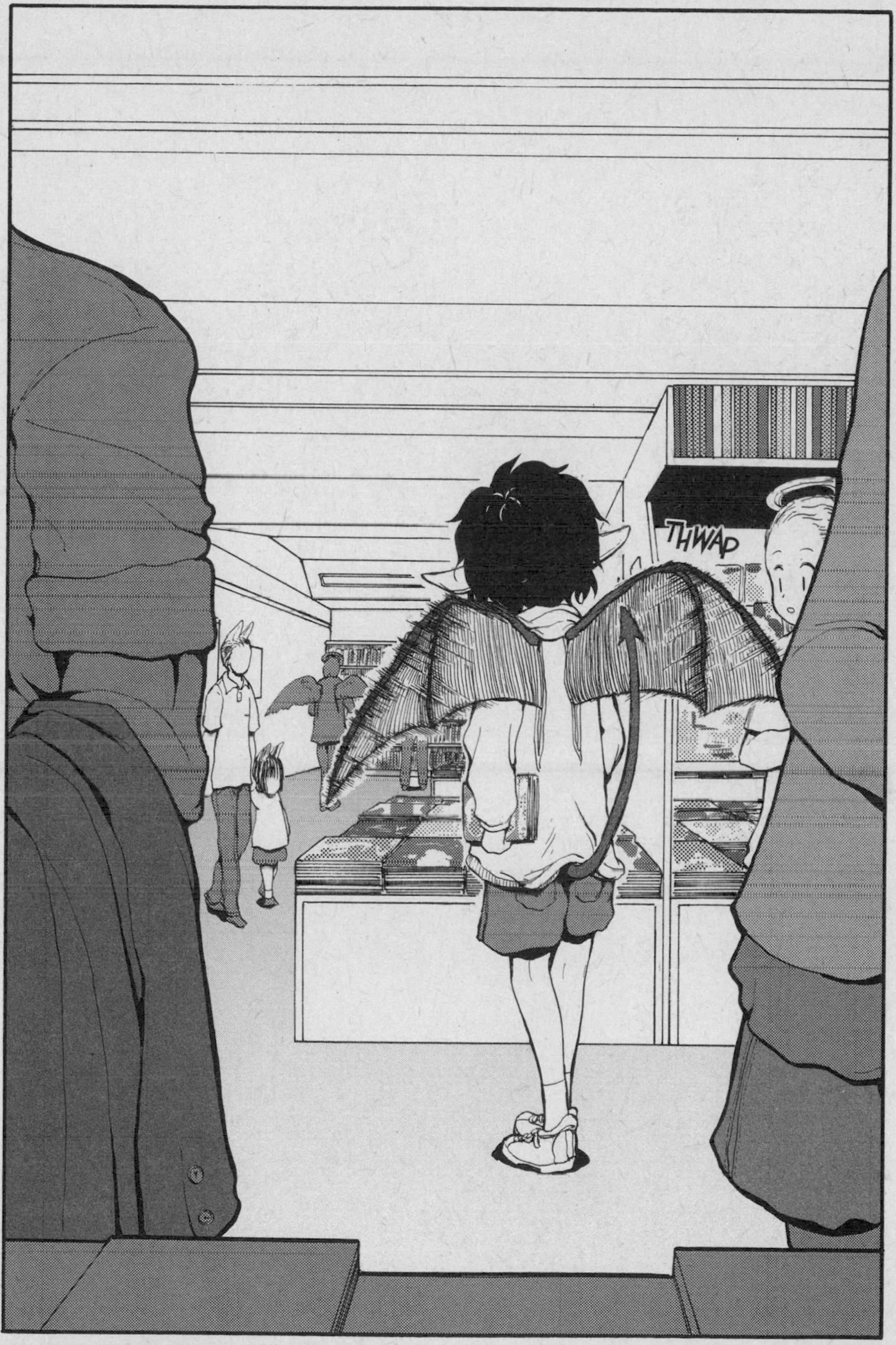
THWAP

CHAPTER 3

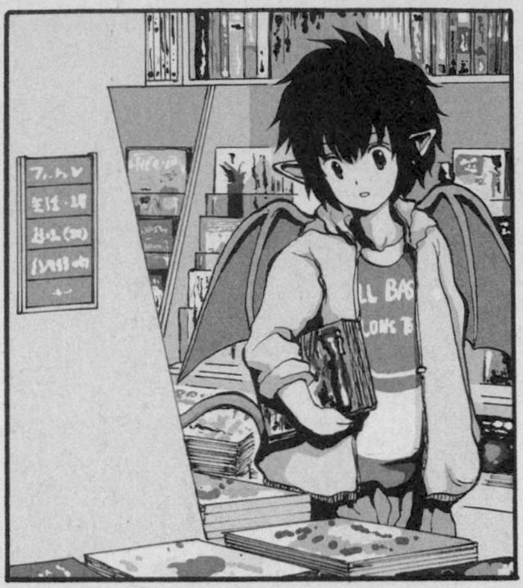

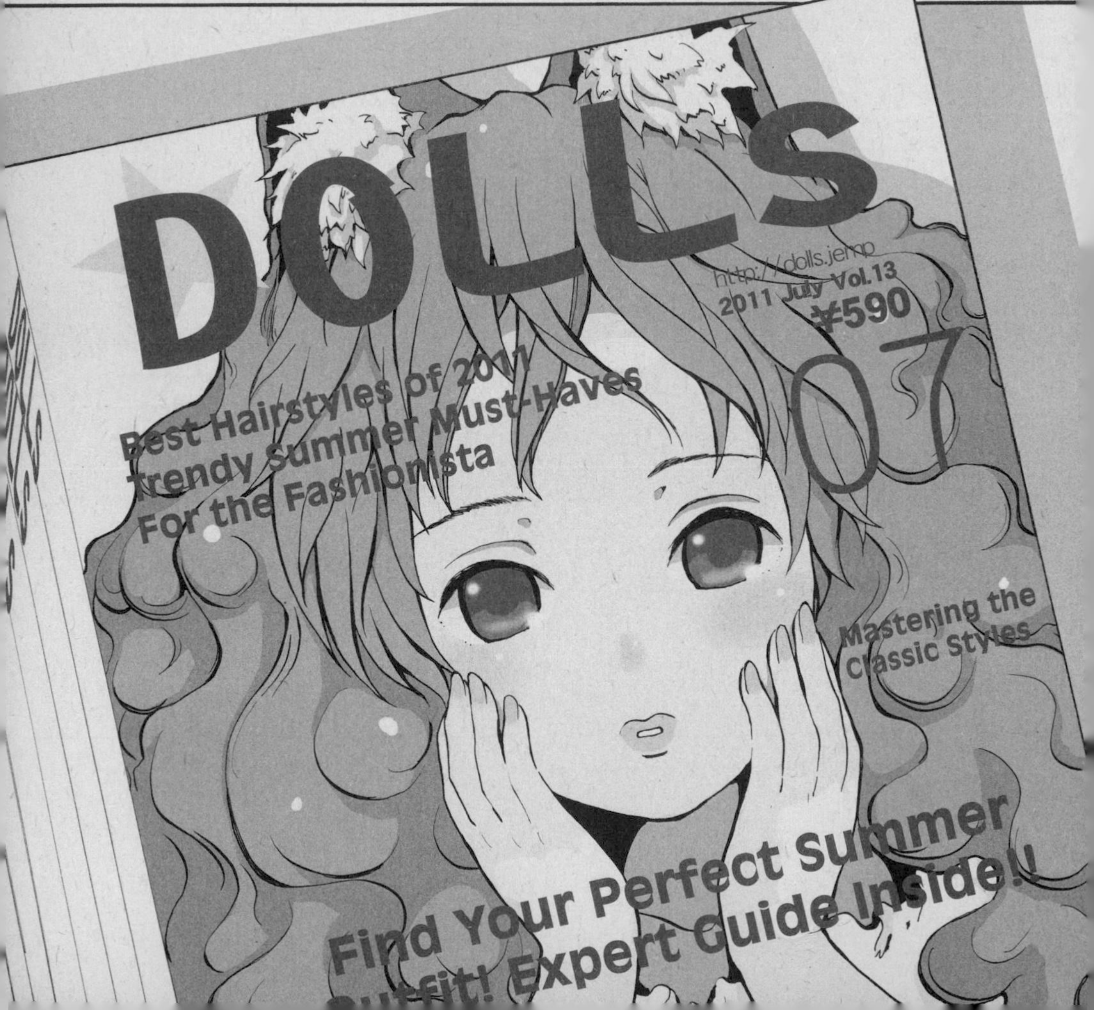
DOLLS
http://dolls.jemp
2011 July Vol.13
¥590
07
Best Hairstyles Of 2011
Trendy Summer Must-Haves
For the Fashionista
Mastering the Classic Styles
Find Your Perfect Summer
utfit! Expert Guide Inside!!
DOLLS

UNDERGARMENTS FOR PEOPLE WITH TAILS

THE TAILS ARE
THREADED THROUGH FIRST.

ALTERING GARMENTS FOR TAILS USED TO
BE A SPECIALIZED SKILL AMONG WOMEN,
BUT NOW MANY LESS EXPENSIVE GARMENTS
ARE MADE SPECIFICALLY TO ACCOMMODATE
TAILS. ADJUSTABLE STYLES THAT ALLOW
A CUSTOMIZED FIT FOR MULTIPLE TAIL
SIZES ARE ALSO AVAILABLE.

A Centaur's Life

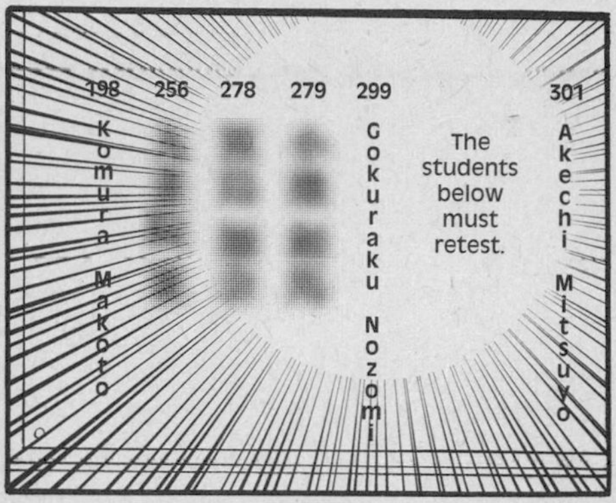
301
Akechi Mitsuyo
The students below must retest.
299
Gokuraku Nozomi
279
278
256
198
Komura Makoto
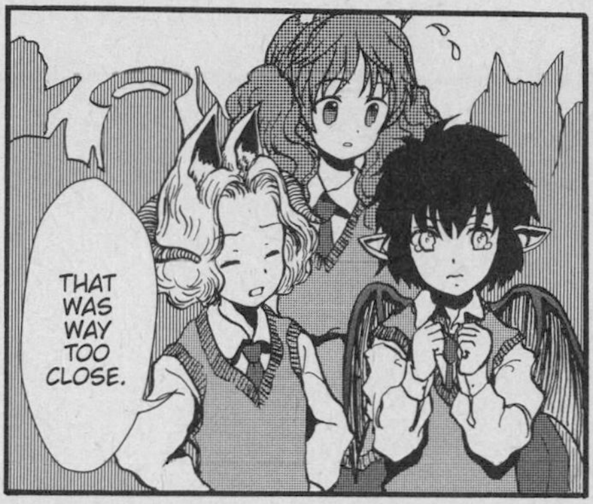
THAT WAS WAY TOO CLOSE.
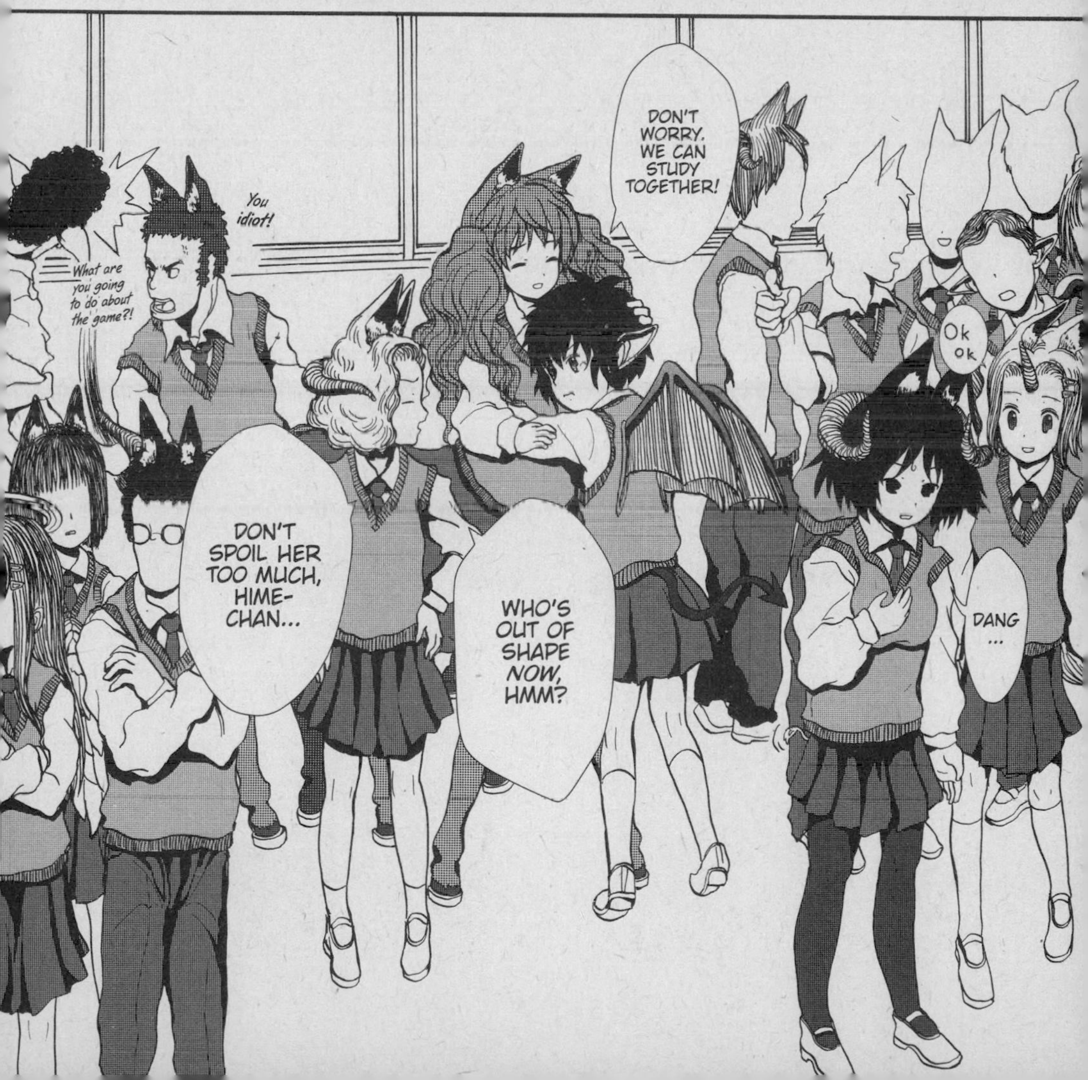
DON'T WORRY. WE CAN STUDY TOGETHER!
Ok ok
DANG ...
You idiot!
What are you going to do about the game?!
WHO'S OUT OF SHAPE NOW, HMM?
DON'T SPOIL HER TOO MUCH, HIME-CHAN...

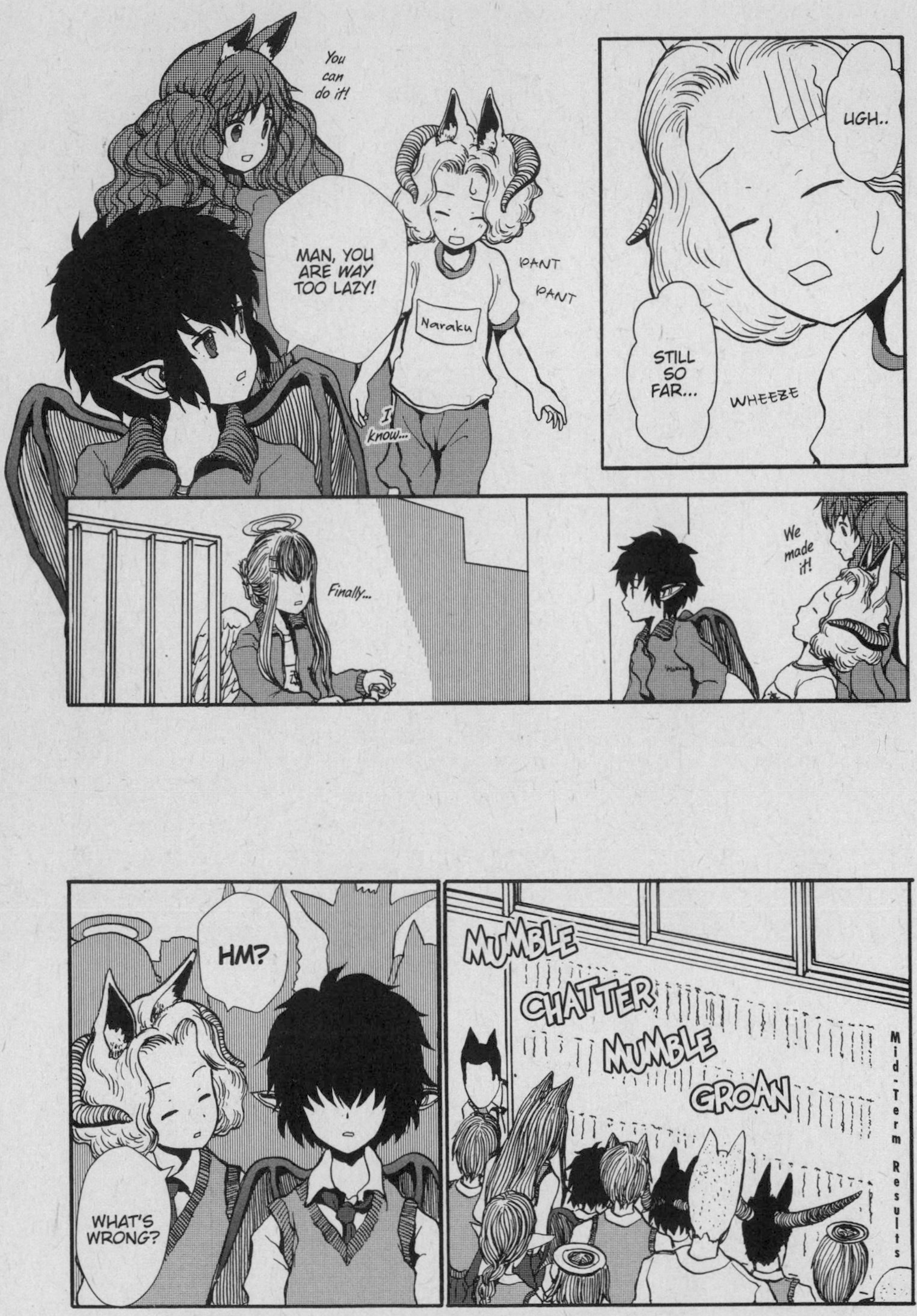
UGH..
STILL SO FAR...
WHEEZE
You can do it!
MAN, YOU ARE WAY TOO LAZY!
PANT
PANT
Naraku
I know...
We made it!
Finally...
Mid-Term Results
MUMBLE
CHATTER
MUMBLE
GROAN
HM?
WHAT'S WRONG?

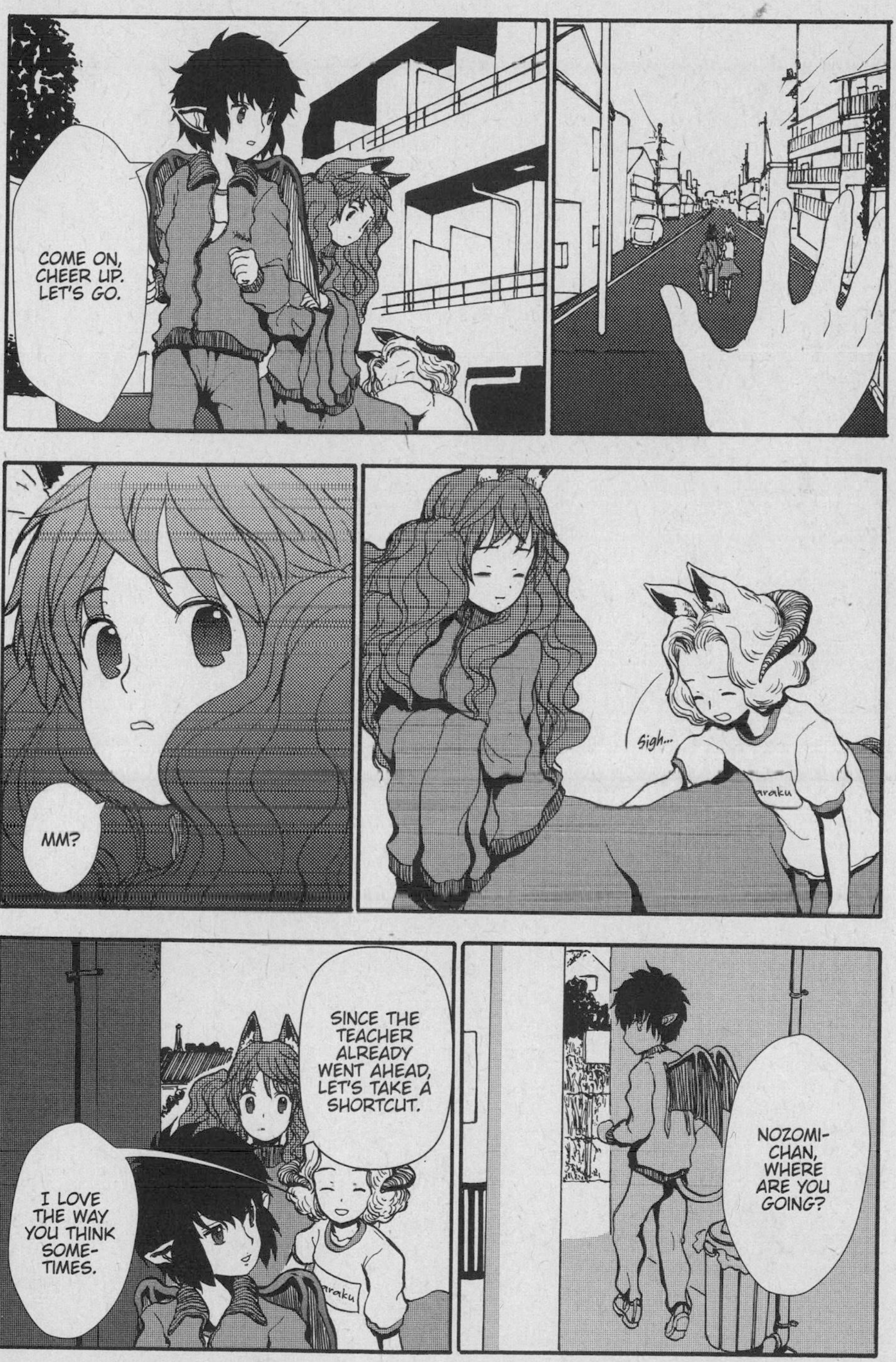
COME ON, CHEER UP. LET'S GO.
Sigh...
MM?
NOZOMI-CHAN, WHERE ARE YOU GOING?
SINCE THE TEACHER ALREADY WENT AHEAD, LET'S TAKE A SHORTCUT.
I LOVE THE WAY YOU THINK SOME-TIMES.

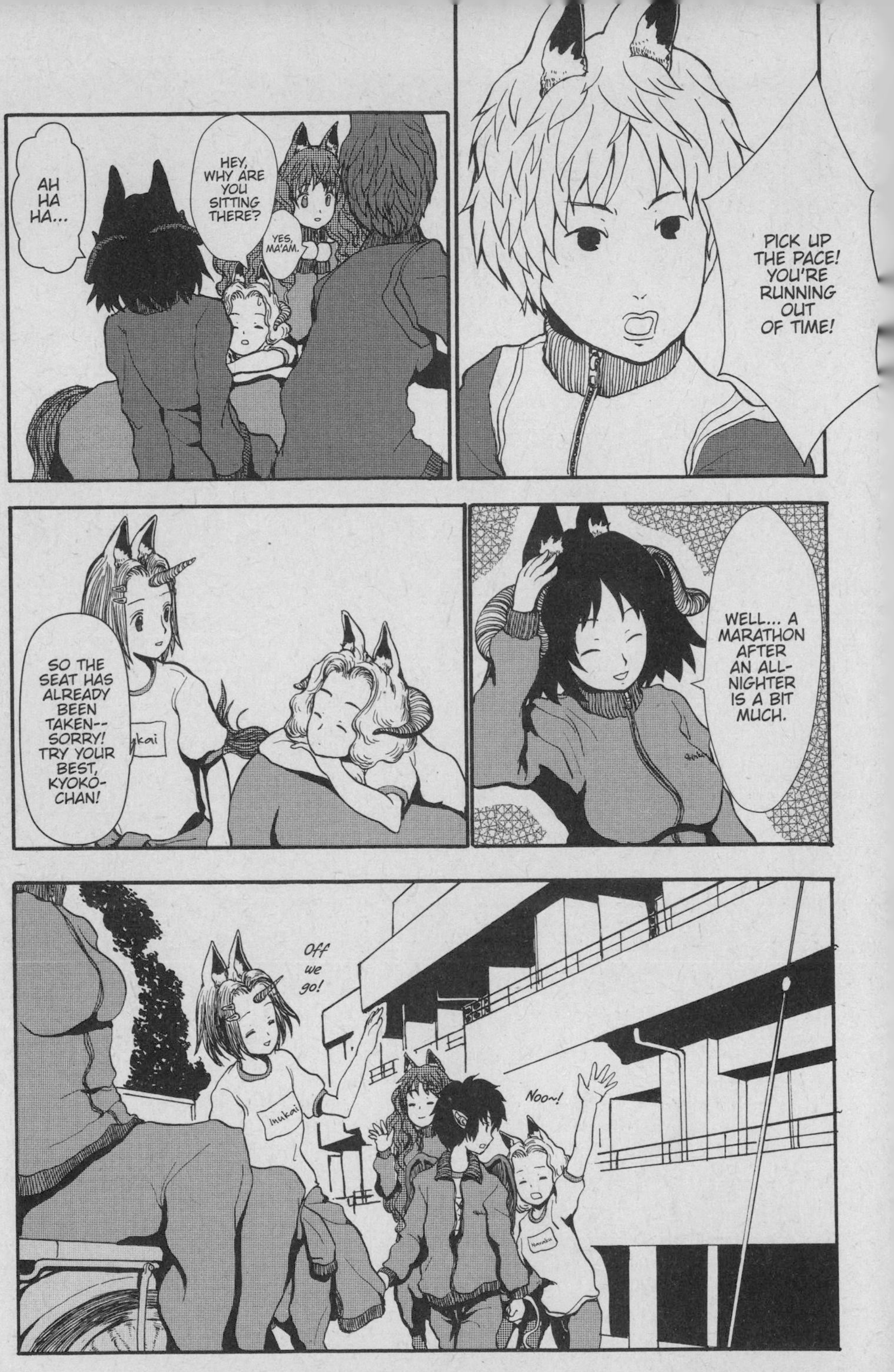
PICK UP THE PACE! YOU'RE RUNNING OUT OF TIME!
HEY, WHY ARE YOU SITTING THERE?
YES, MA'AM.
AH HA HA...
WELL... A MARATHON AFTER AN ALL-NIGHTER IS A BIT MUCH.
SO THE SEAT HAS ALREADY BEEN TAKEN-- SORRY! TRY YOUR BEST, KYOKO-CHAN!
Off we go!
Inukai
Noo~!

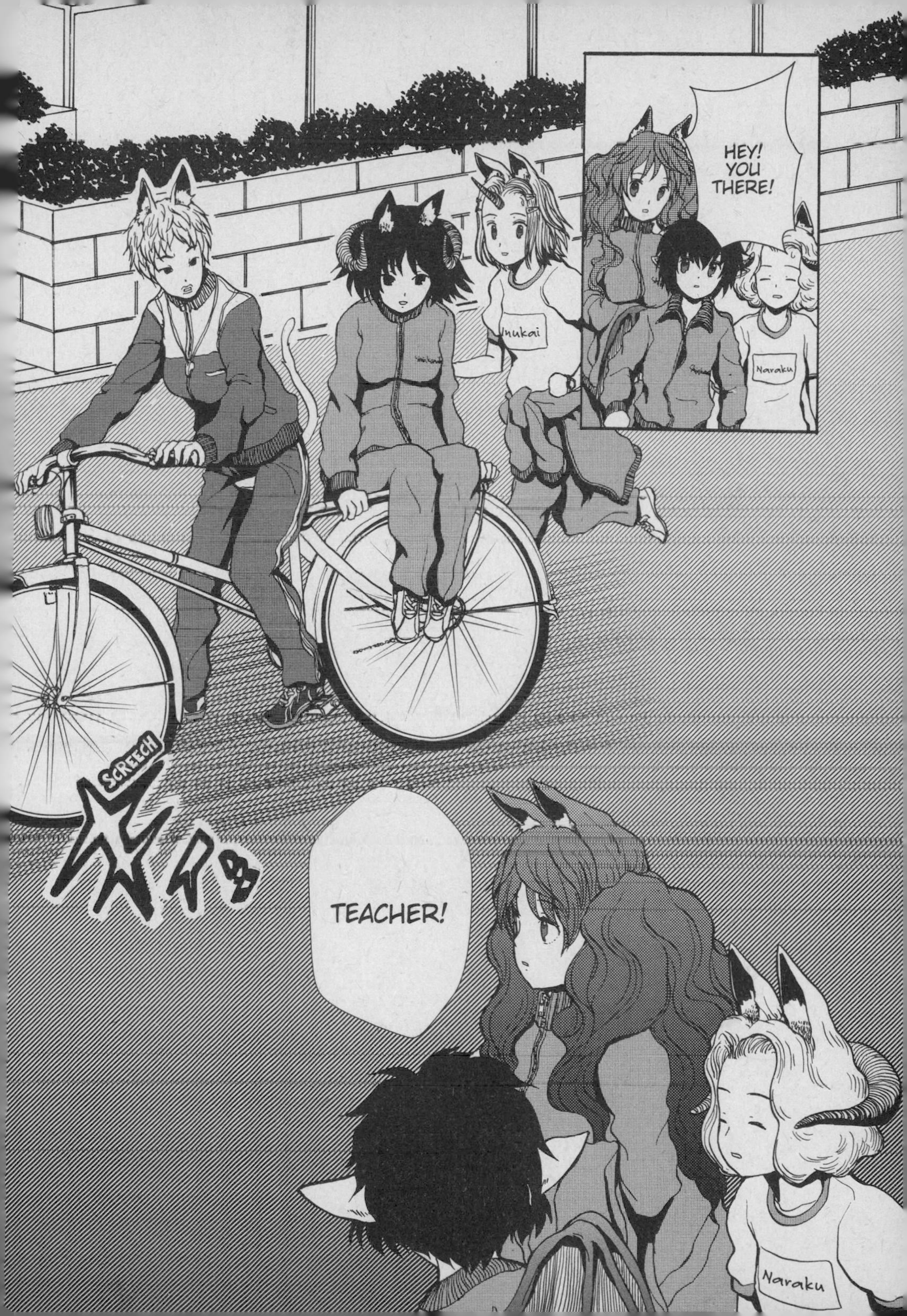
HEY! YOU THERE!
Inukai
Naraku
SCREECH
TEACHER!
Naraku

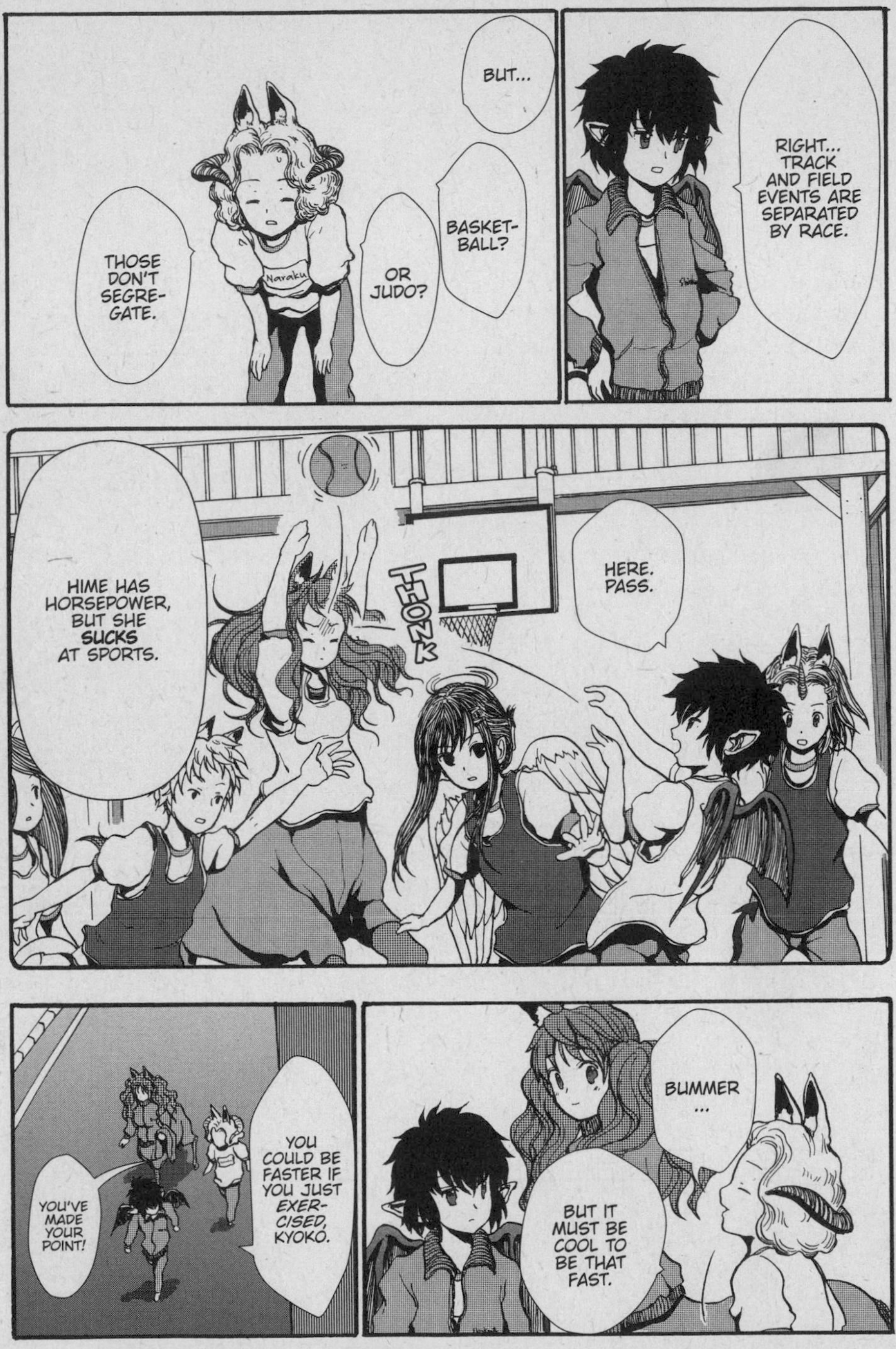
RIGHT... TRACK AND FIELD EVENTS ARE SEPARATED BY RACE.
BUT...
BASKET-BALL?
OR JUDO?
THOSE DON'T SEGRE-GATE.
HERE. PASS.
THONK
HIME HAS HORSEPOWER, BUT SHE **SUCKS** AT SPORTS.
BUMMER ...
BUT IT MUST BE COOL TO BE THAT FAST.
YOU COULD BE FASTER IF YOU JUST *EXER-CISED*, KYOKO.
YOU'VE MADE YOUR POINT!

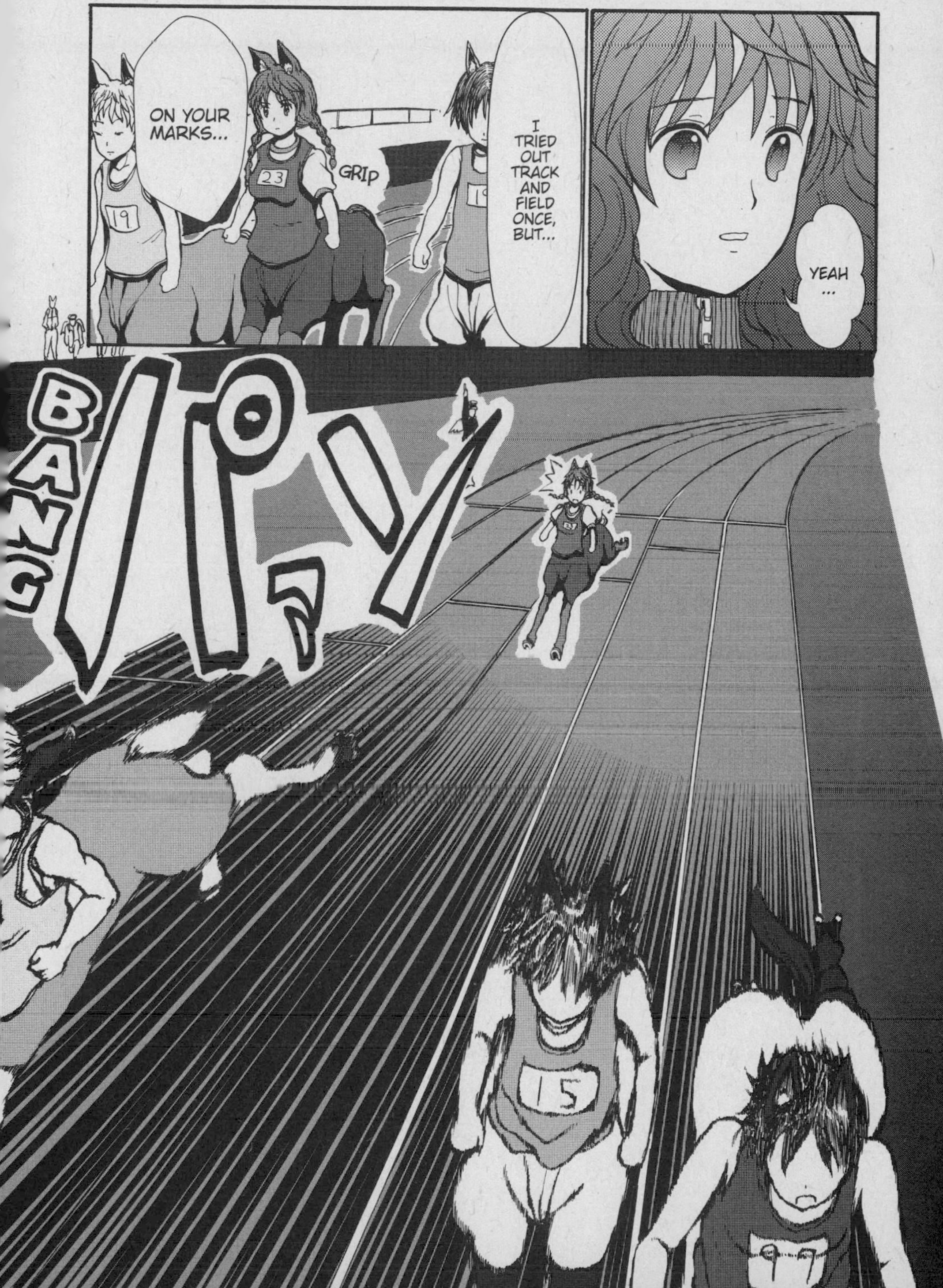
YEAH ...
I TRIED OUT TRACK AND FIELD ONCE, BUT...
ON YOUR MARKS...
GRIP
BANG

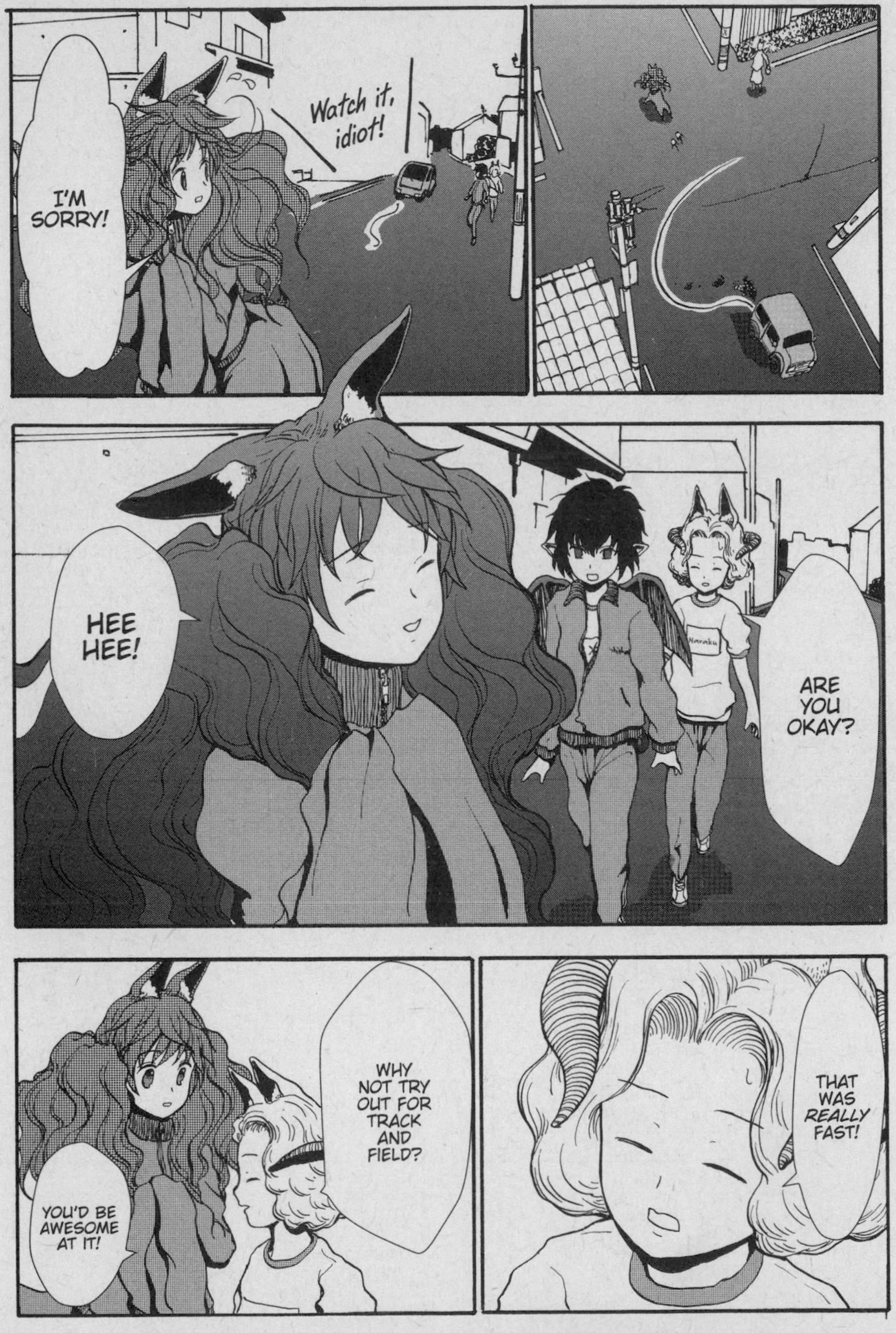
Watch it, idiot!
I'M SORRY!
ARE YOU OKAY?
HEE HEE!
THAT WAS *REALLY* FAST!
WHY NOT TRY OUT FOR TRACK AND FIELD?
YOU'D BE AWESOME AT IT!

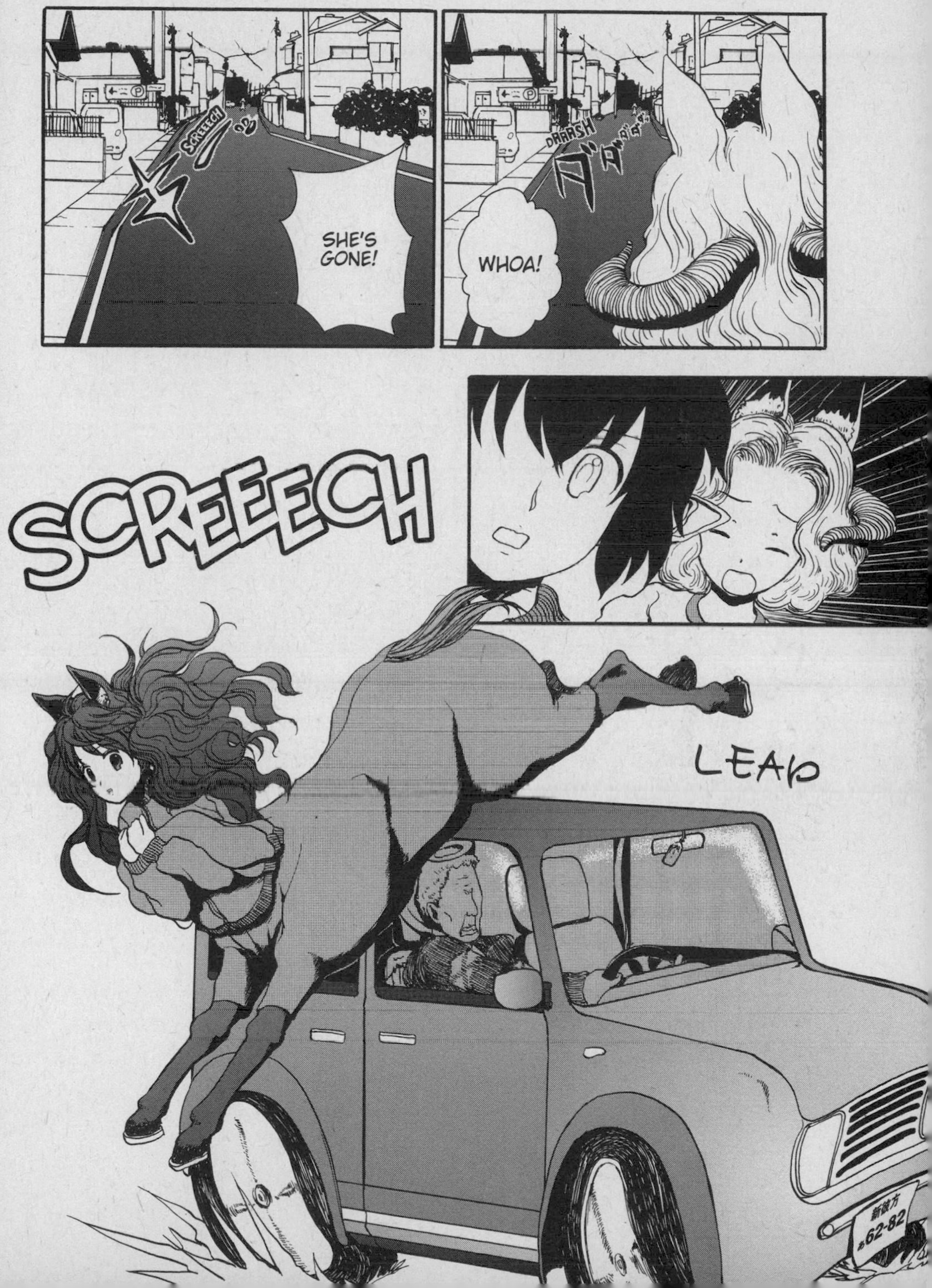
DRRRSH
WHOA!
SCREEECH
SHE'S GONE!
SCREEECH
LEAP

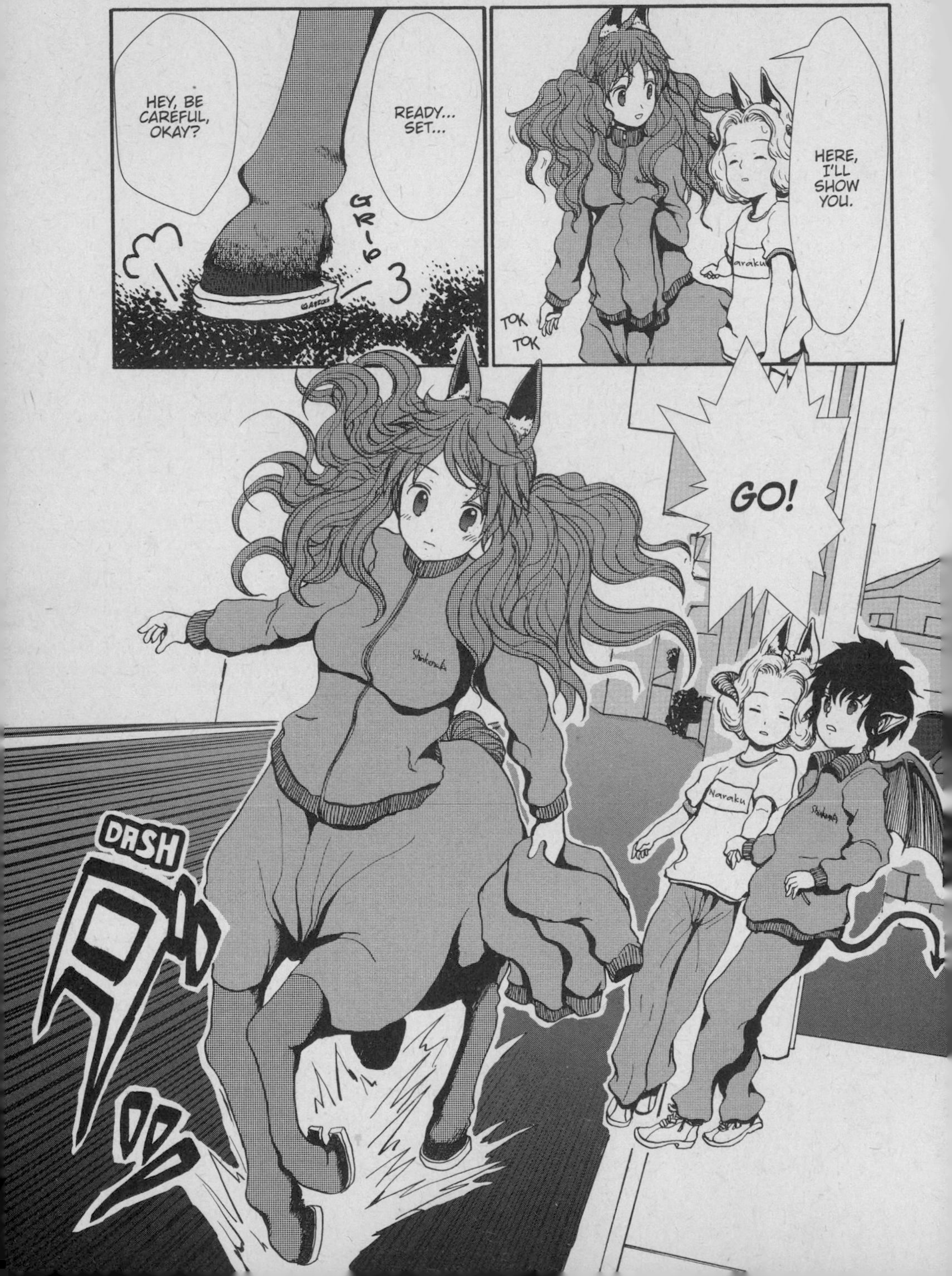
HERE, I'LL SHOW YOU.
TOK TOK
Naraku
READY... SET...
HEY, BE CAREFUL, OKAY?
GRIP
GO!
Naraku
DASH

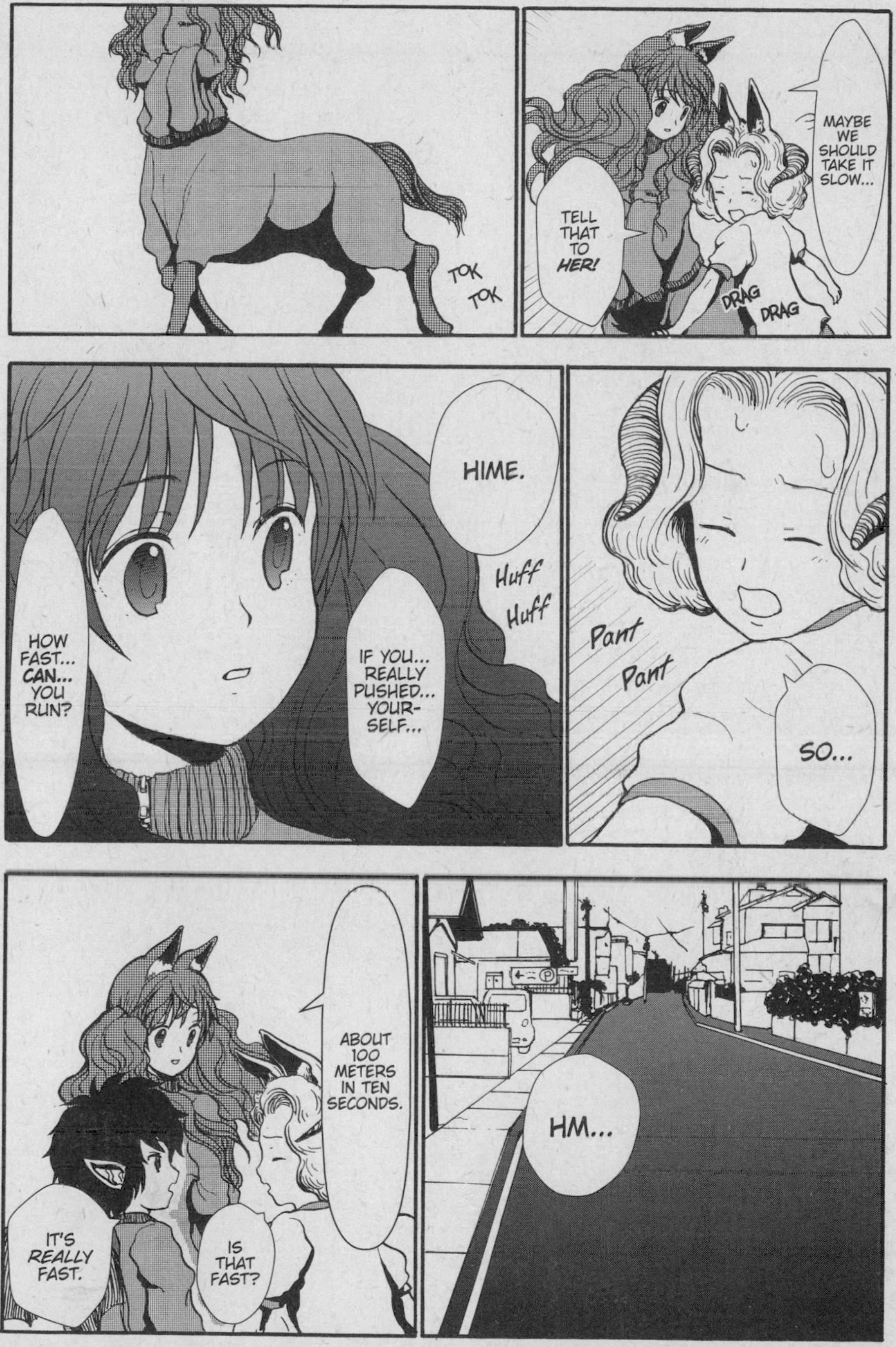
MAYBE WE SHOULD TAKE IT SLOW...
TELL THAT TO *HER!*
DRAG DRAG
TOK TOK
Pant Pant
SO...
HIME.
Huff Huff
IF YOU... REALLY PUSHED... YOUR-SELF...
HOW FAST... **CAN...** YOU RUN?
HM...
ABOUT 100 METERS IN TEN SECONDS.
IS THAT FAST?
IT'S *REALLY* FAST.

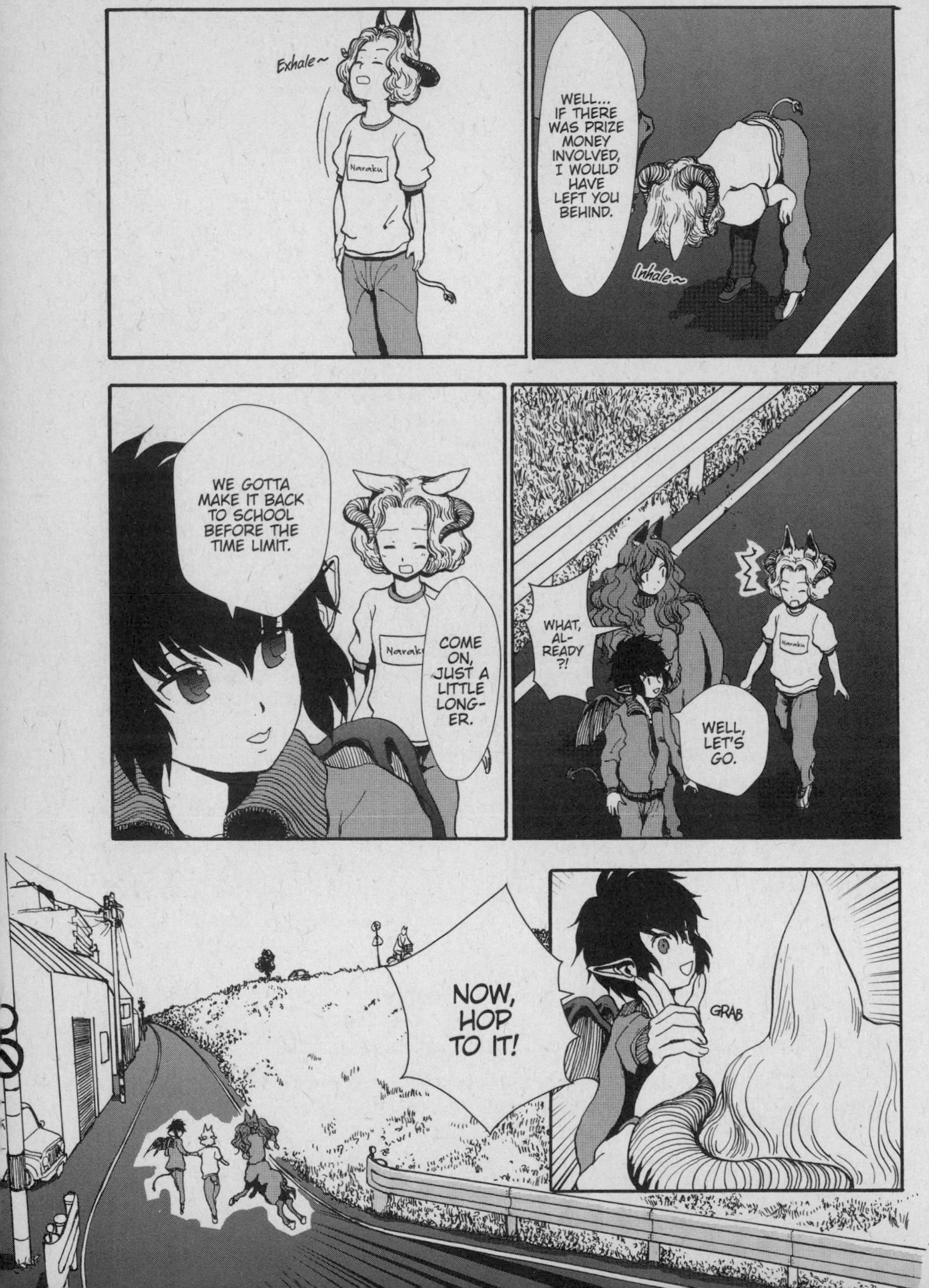
WELL... IF THERE WAS PRIZE MONEY INVOLVED, I WOULD HAVE LEFT YOU BEHIND.
Inhale~
Exhale~
WHAT, AL-READY ?!
WELL, LET'S GO.
WE GOTTA MAKE IT BACK TO SCHOOL BEFORE THE TIME LIMIT.
COME ON, JUST A LITTLE LONGER.
NOW, HOP TO IT!
GRAB

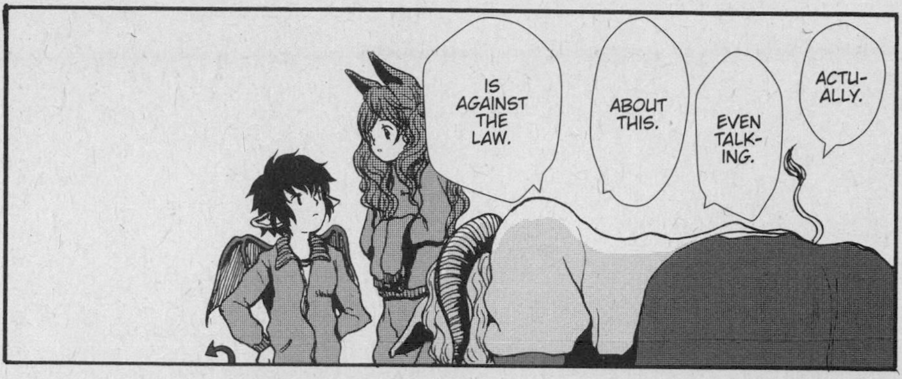
ACTU-ALLY.
EVEN TALK-ING.
ABOUT THIS.
IS AGAINST THE LAW.
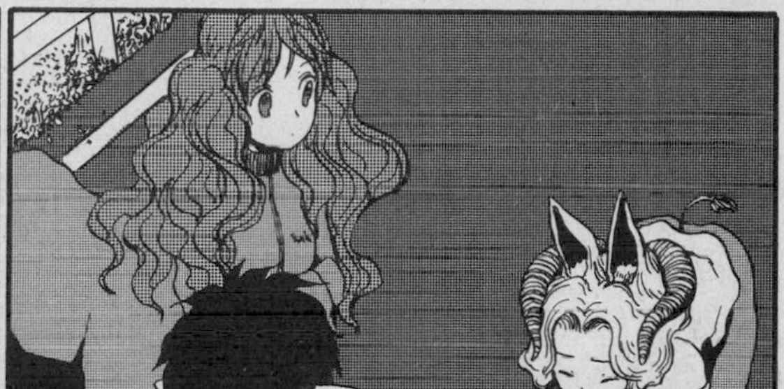
WELL... WE'LL CATCH UP AFTER YOU CATCH YOUR BREATH.
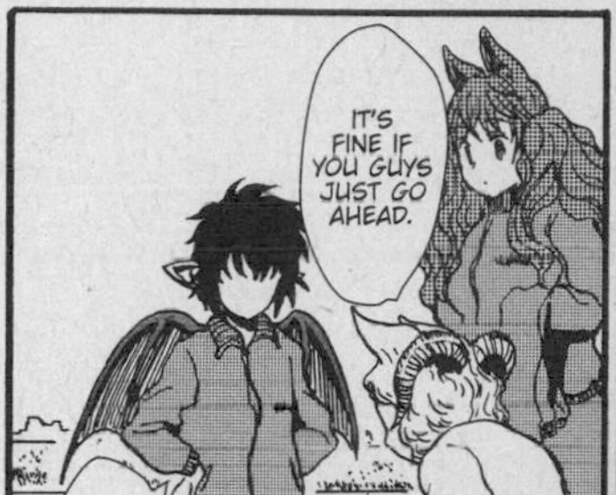
IT'S FINE IF YOU GUYS JUST GO AHEAD.
NEITHER OF US ARE AIM-ING TO BE FIRST ANYWAYS.
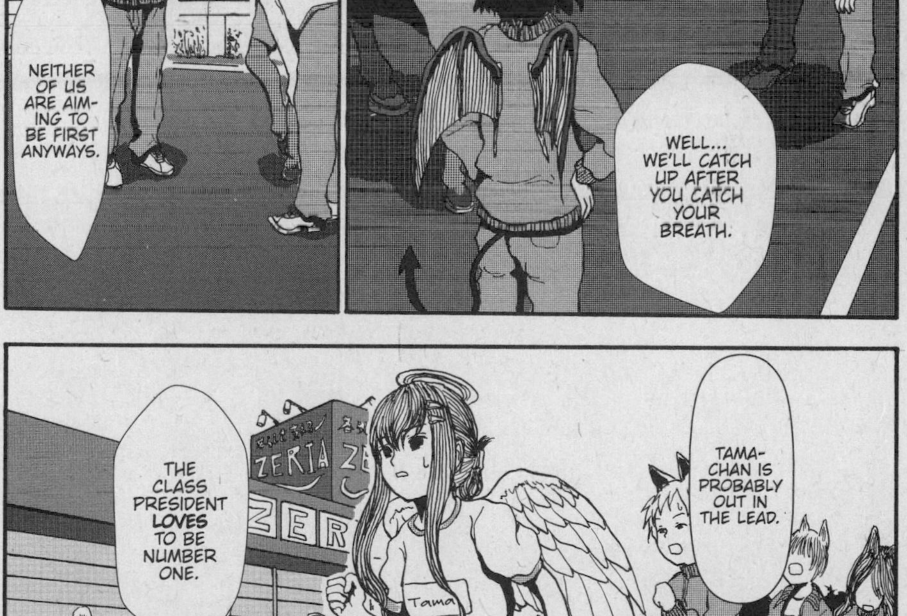
TAMA-CHAN IS PROBABLY OUT IN THE LEAD.
THE CLASS PRESIDENT **LOVES** TO BE NUMBER ONE.
ZERIA
Tama

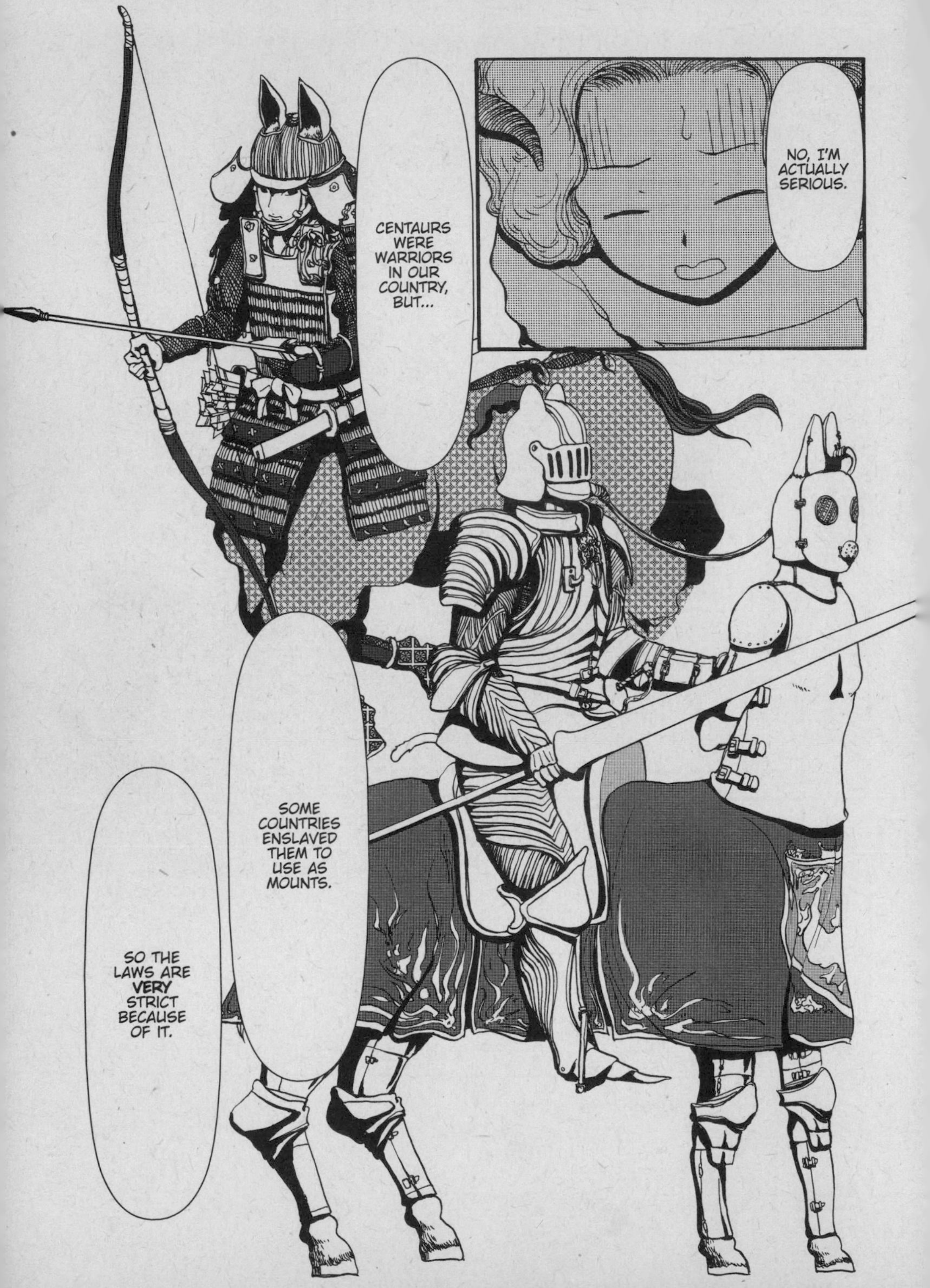
NO, I'M ACTUALLY SERIOUS.
CENTAURS WERE WARRIORS IN OUR COUNTRY, BUT...
SOME COUNTRIES ENSLAVED THEM TO USE AS MOUNTS.
SO THE LAWS ARE **VERY** STRICT BECAUSE OF IT.

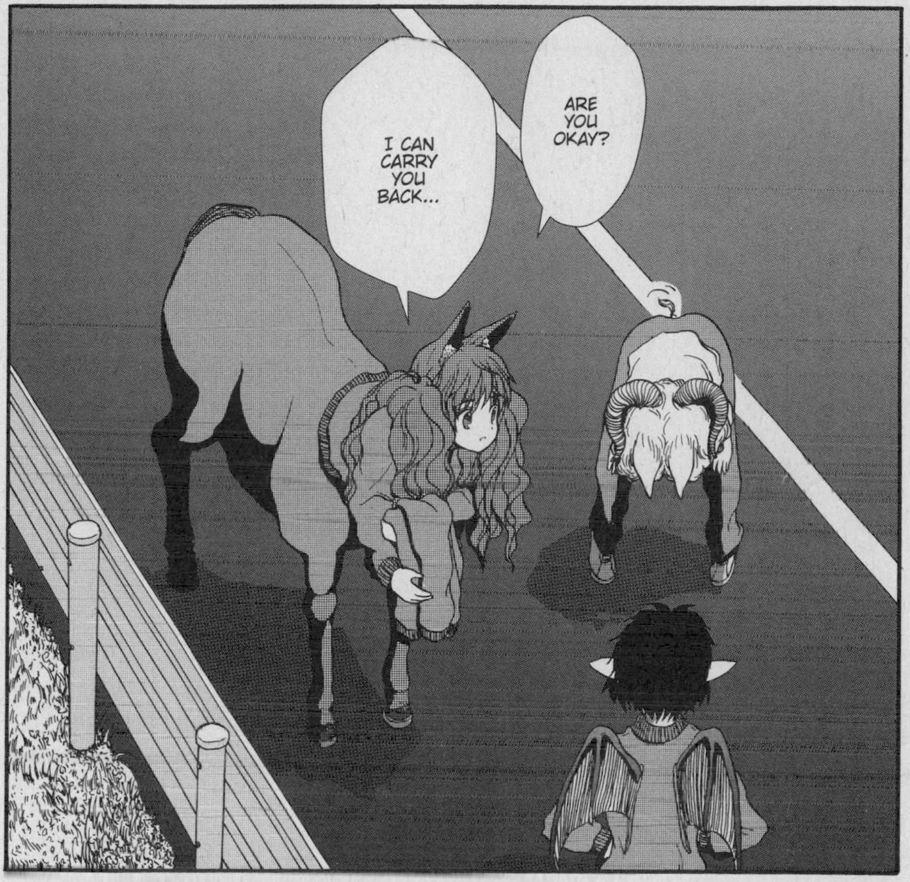
ARE YOU OKAY?
I CAN CARRY YOU BACK...
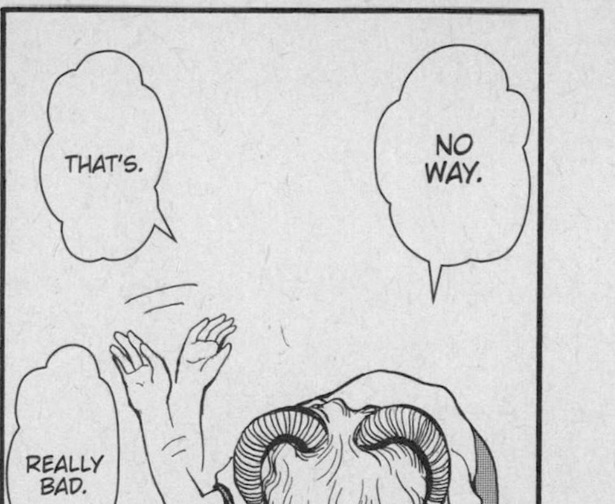
NO WAY.
THAT'S.
REALLY BAD.
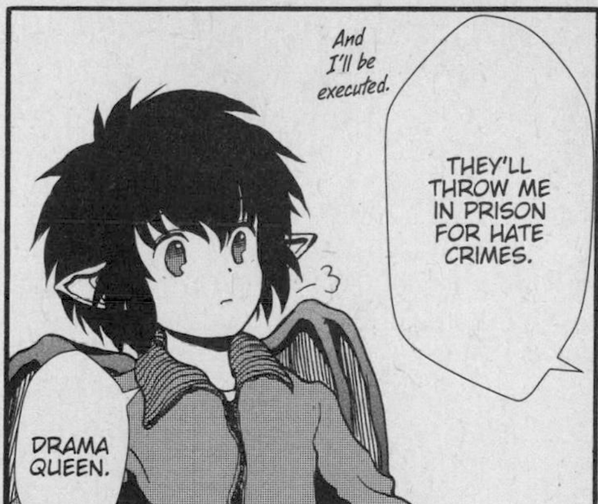
THEY'LL THROW ME IN PRISON FOR HATE CRIMES.
And I'll be executed.
DRAMA QUEEN.

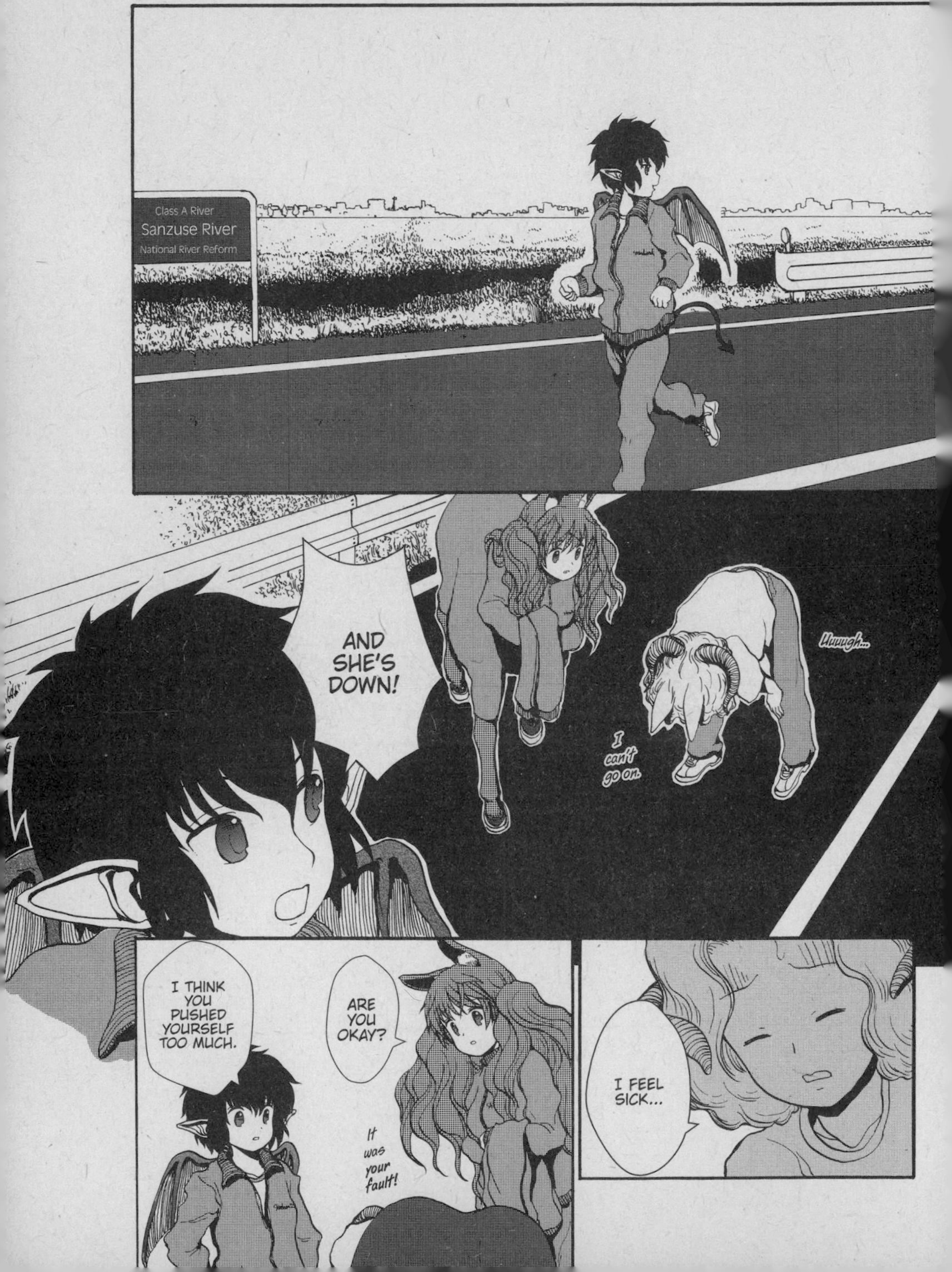
Class A River
Sanzuse River
National River Reform
Uuuugh...
I can't go on.
AND SHE'S DOWN!
I FEEL SICK...
ARE YOU OKAY?
I THINK YOU PUSHED YOURSELF TOO MUCH.
It was your fault!

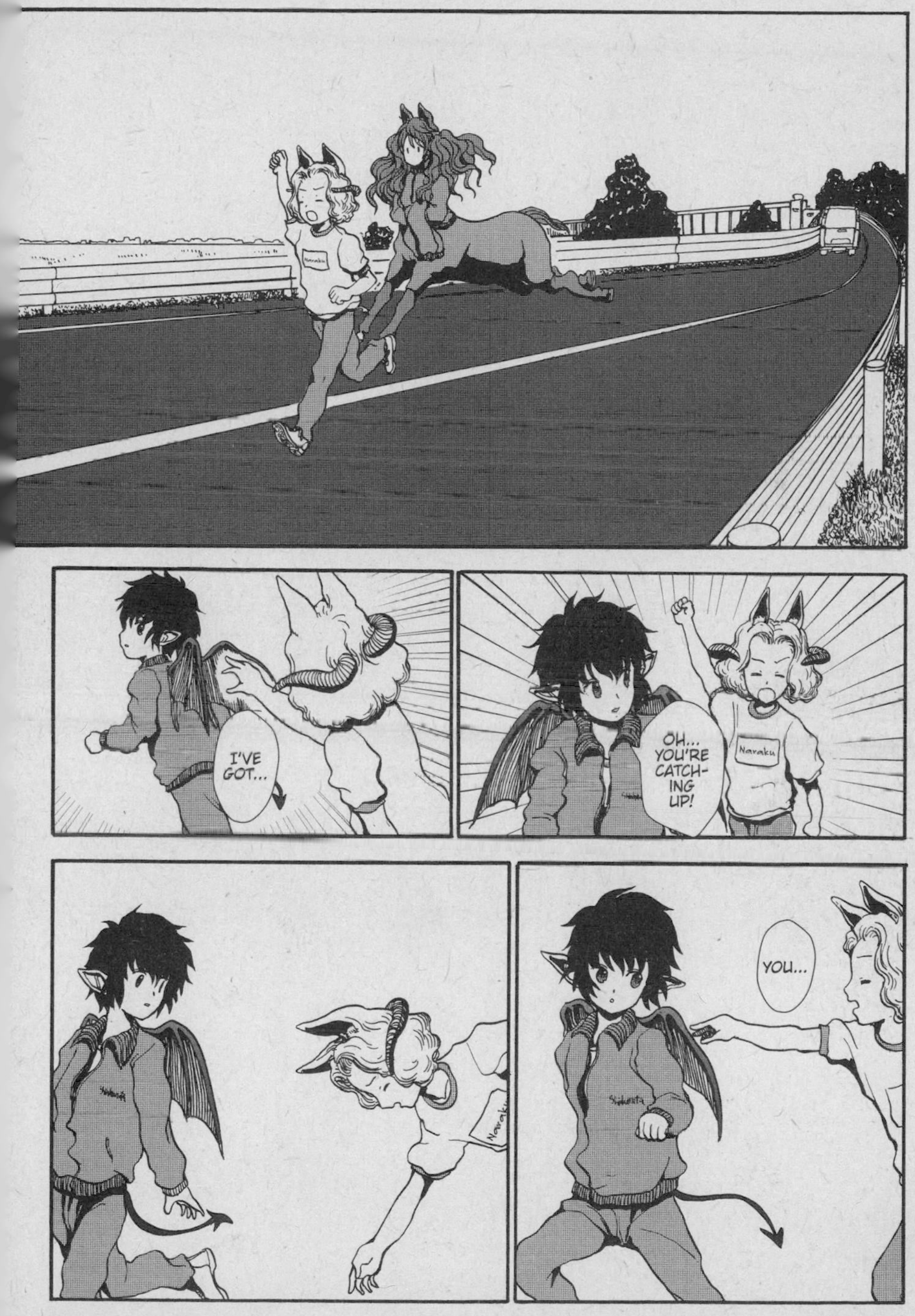
OH... YOU'RE CATCH-ING UP!
I'VE GOT...
YOU...

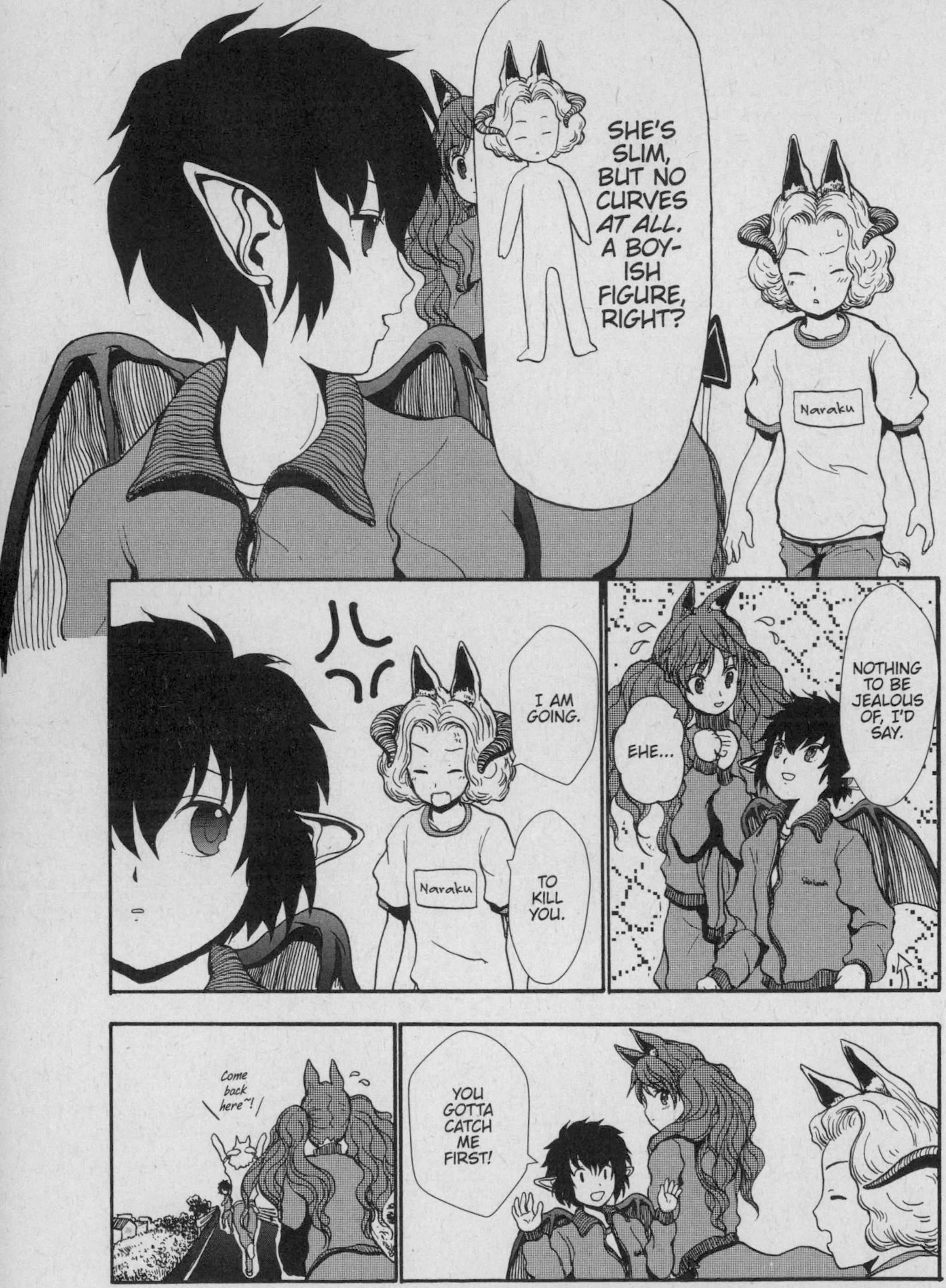
SHE'S SLIM, BUT NO CURVES AT ALL. A BOY-ISH FIGURE, RIGHT?
Naraku
NOTHING TO BE JEALOUS OF, I'D SAY.
EHE...
I AM GOING.
TO KILL YOU.
Naraku
YOU GOTTA CATCH ME FIRST!
Come back here~!

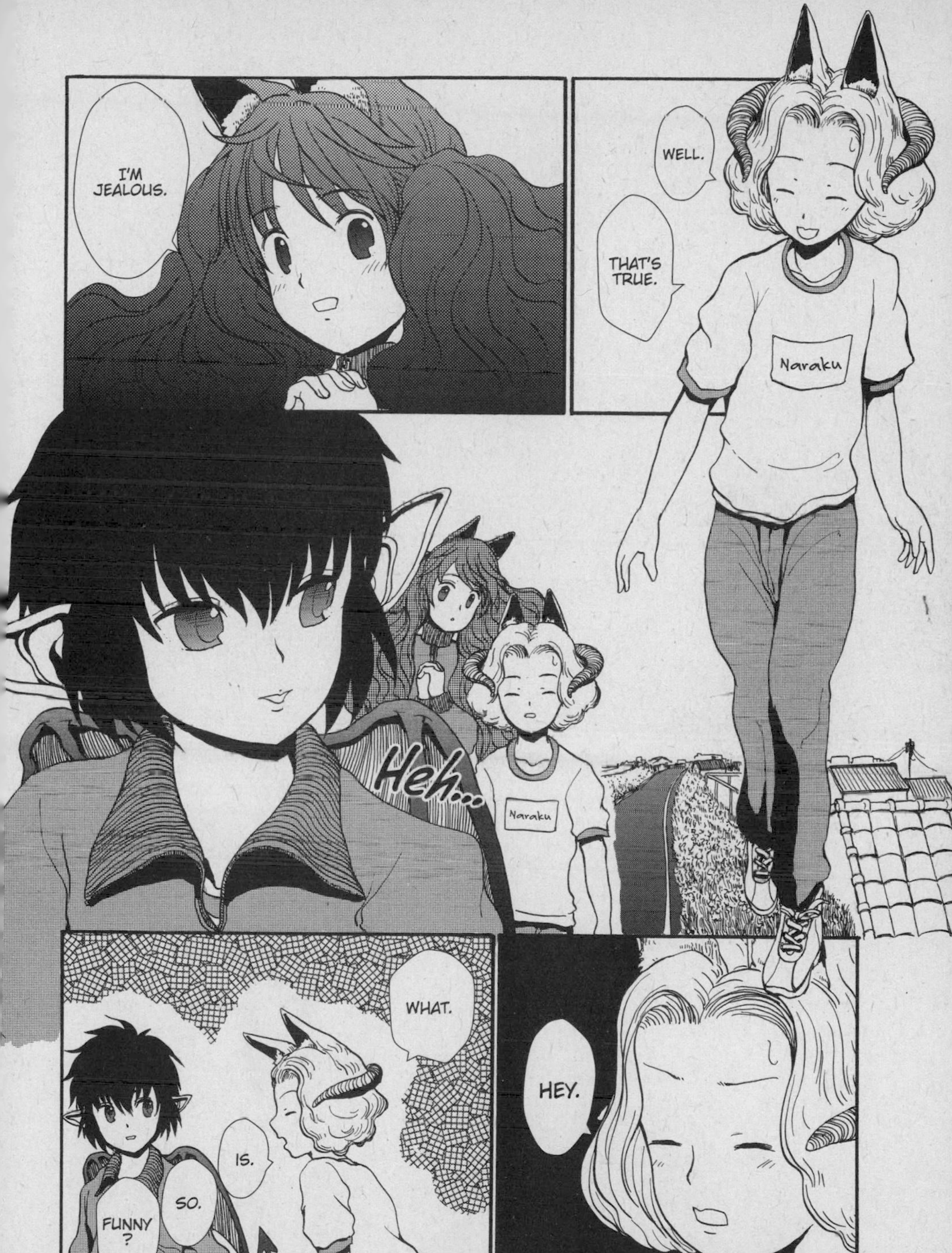
WELL.
THAT'S TRUE.
Naraku
I'M JEALOUS.
Heh...
Naraku
HEY.
WHAT.
IS.
SO.
FUNNY?

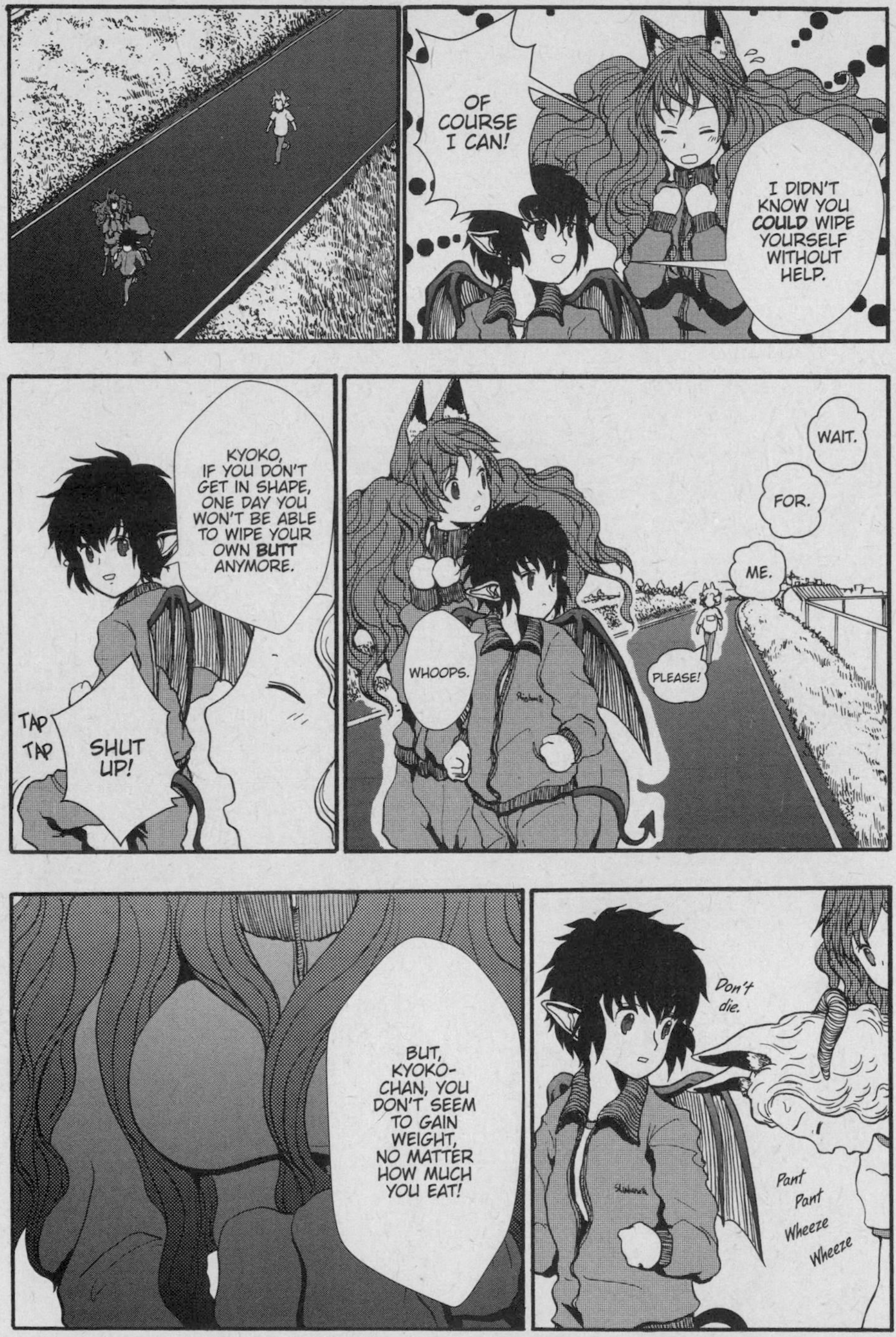
I DIDN'T KNOW YOU **COULD** WIPE YOURSELF WITHOUT HELP.
OF COURSE I CAN!
WAIT.
FOR.
ME.
PLEASE!
WHOOPS.
KYOKO, IF YOU DON'T GET IN SHAPE, ONE DAY YOU WON'T BE ABLE TO WIPE YOUR OWN **BUTT** ANYMORE.
SHUT UP!
TAP TAP
Don't die.
Pant Pant
Wheeze Wheeze
BUT, KYOKO-CHAN, YOU DON'T SEEM TO GAIN WEIGHT, NO MATTER HOW MUCH YOU EAT!

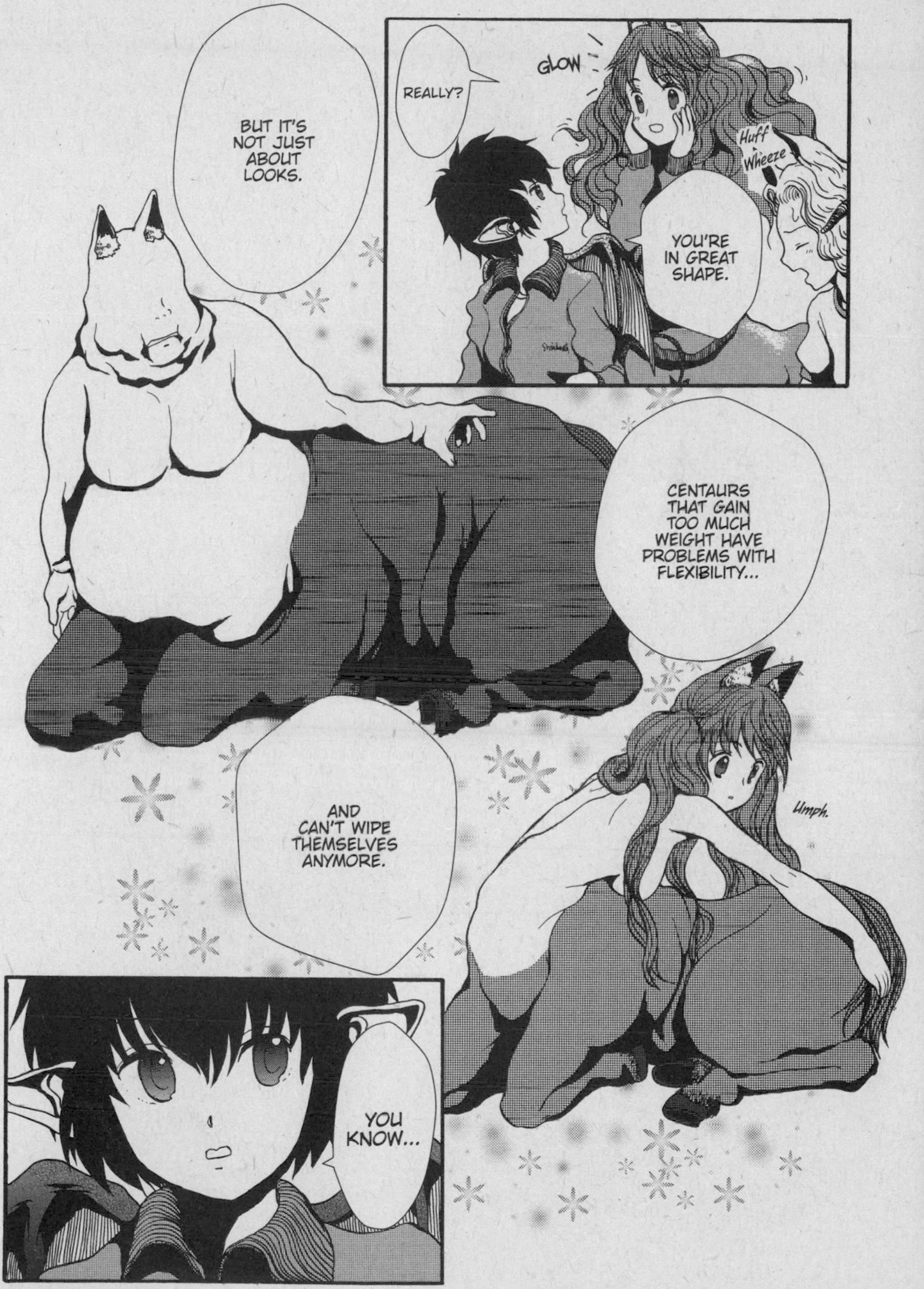
Huff
Wheeze
YOU'RE IN GREAT SHAPE.
GLOW
REALLY?
BUT IT'S NOT JUST ABOUT LOOKS.
CENTAURS THAT GAIN TOO MUCH WEIGHT HAVE PROBLEMS WITH FLEXIBILITY...
Umph.
AND CAN'T WIPE THEMSELVES ANYMORE.
YOU KNOW...

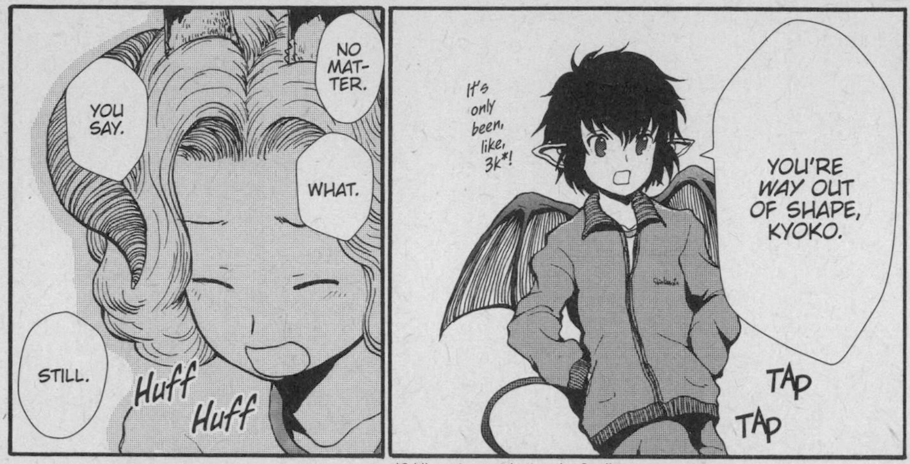
YOU'RE WAY OUT OF SHAPE, KYOKO.
TAP
TAP
It's only been, like, 3k*!
NO MATTER.
WHAT.
YOU SAY.
STILL.
Huff
Huff

*3 kilometers, or just under 2 miles.

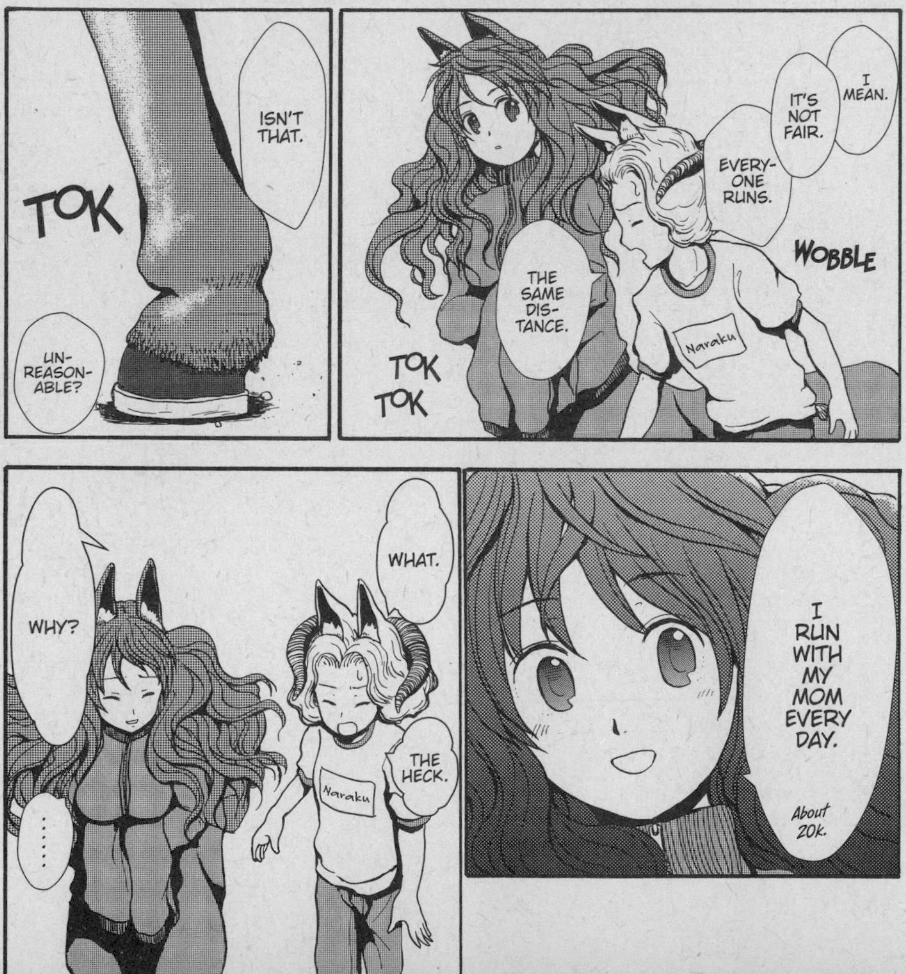
I MEAN.
IT'S NOT FAIR.
EVERYONE RUNS.
WOBBLE
THE SAME DISTANCE.
Naraku
TOK
TOK
ISN'T THAT.
TOK
UNREASONABLE?
I RUN WITH MY MOM EVERY DAY.
About 20k.
WHAT.
THE HECK.
Naraku
WHY?
......

CHAPTER 2

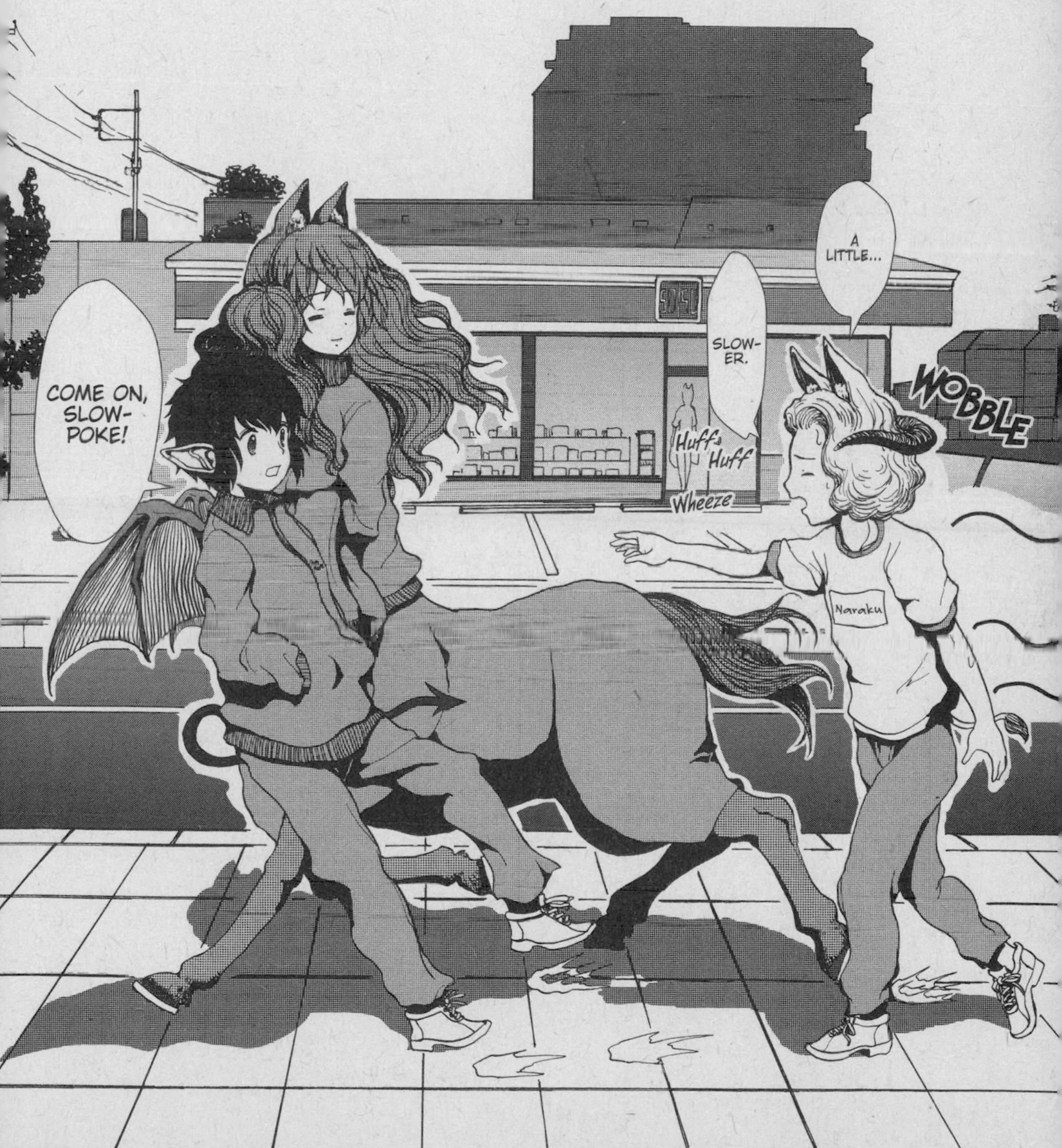
A LITTLE...
WOBBLE
SLOW-ER.
Huff Huff
Wheeze
Naraku
COME ON, SLOW-POKE!

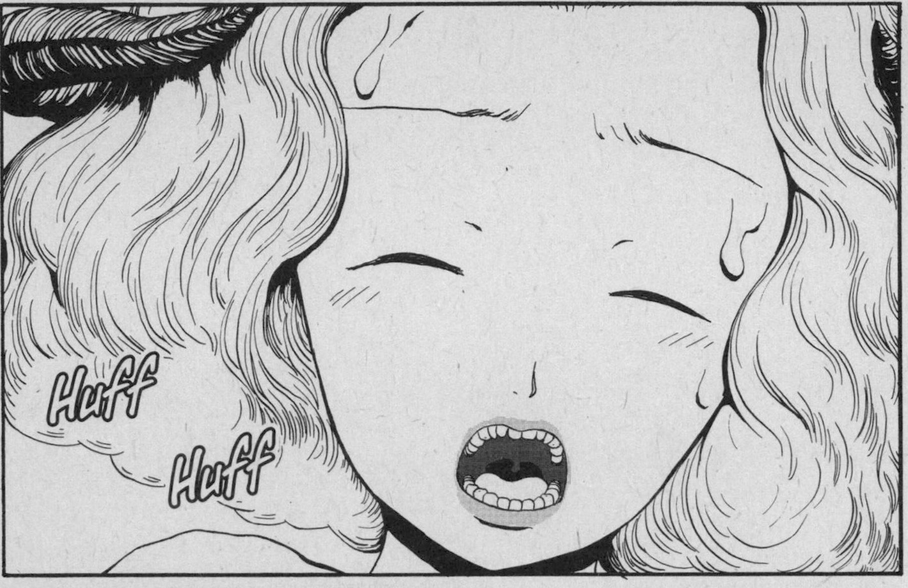
Huff
Huff
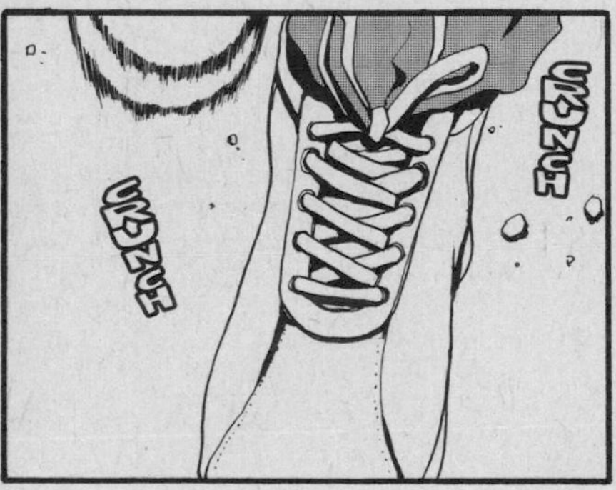
CRUNCH
CRUNCH
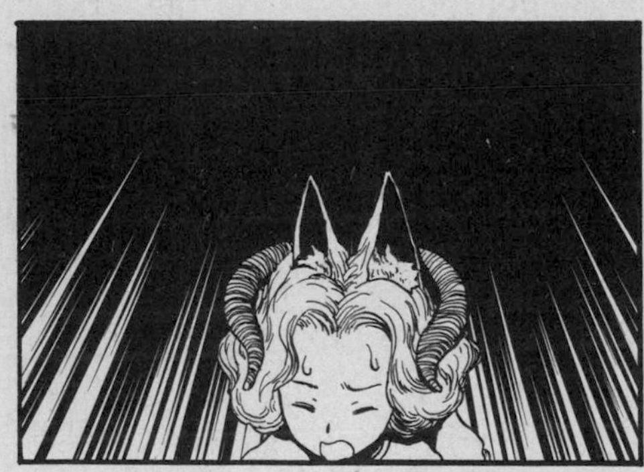
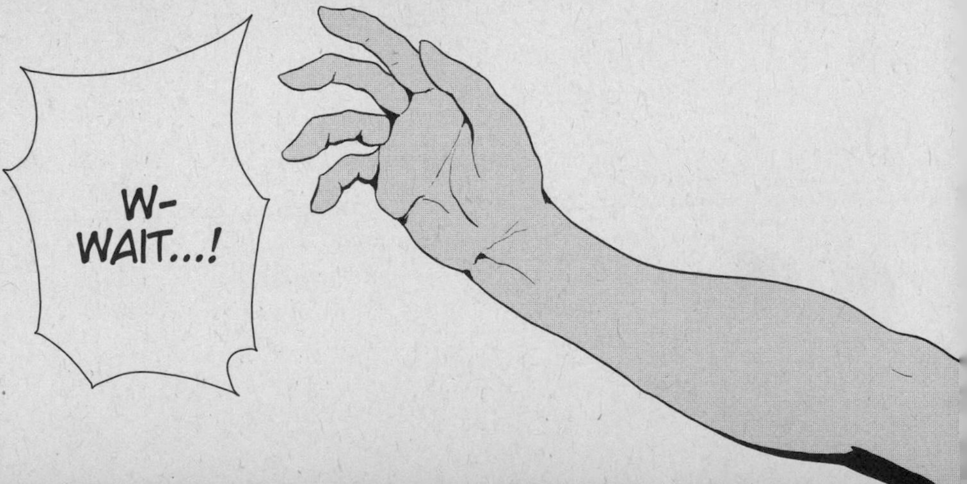
W-
WAIT...!

CENTAUR FOOTWEAR

RUBBER HORSESHOES

THIS IS WHAT PEOPLE TYPICALLY
MEAN WHEN REFERRING TO HORSESHOES.
TRADITIONAL METAL HORSESHOES ARE
GENERALLY ONLY WORN BY THE ELDERLY
FROM BEFORE THE WAR. CENTAURS CAN ALSO
BUY BOOTS THAT COMPLETELY COVER THE HOOF
OR SPECIALIZED SHOES FOR RUNNING, HIKING,
AND TEA CEREMONIES, BUT OTHER RACES
USUALLY CAN'T TELL THE DIFFERENCE.
THERE ARE MANY STYLES AND BRANDS.

A CentaUr's Life

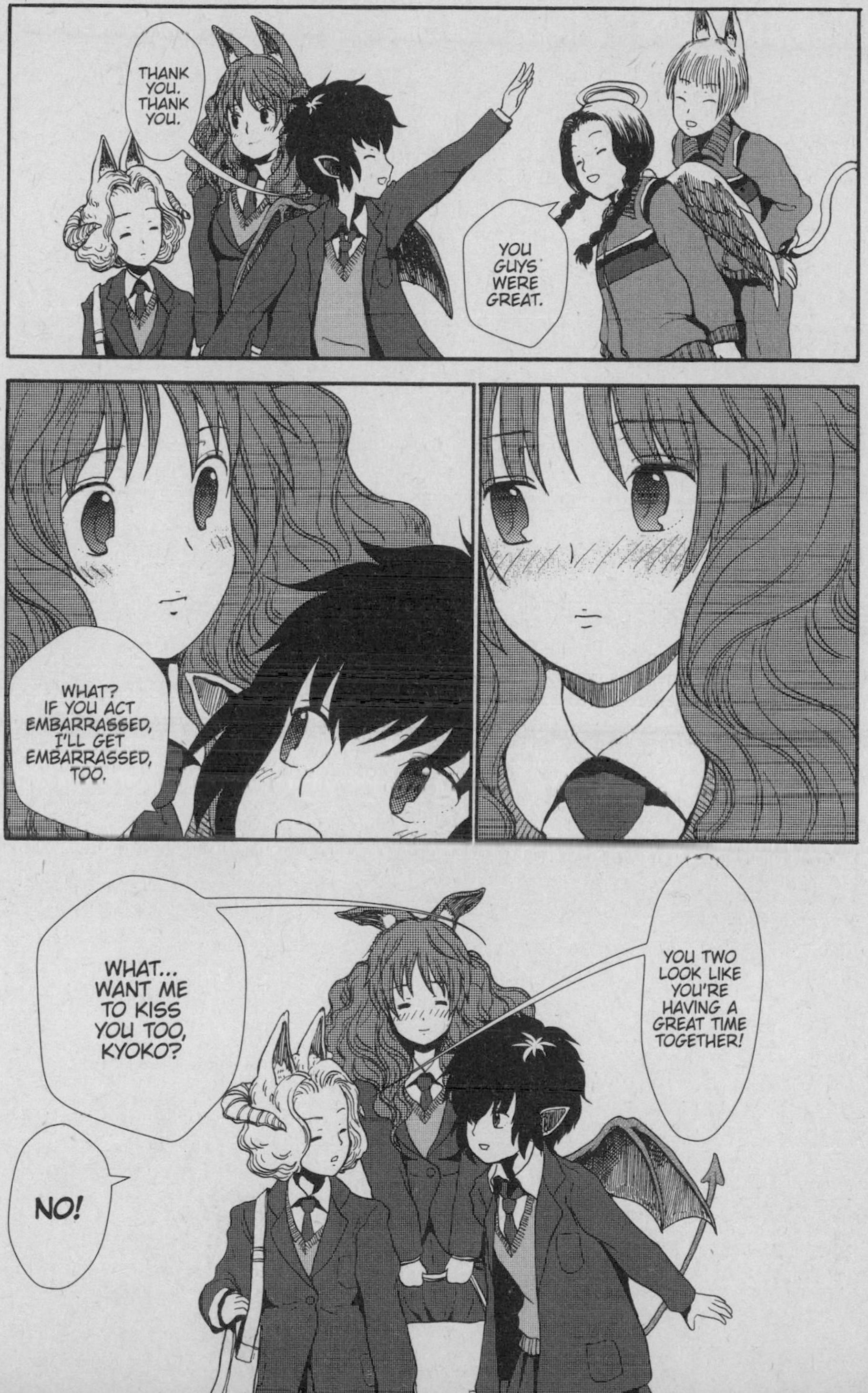
YOU GUYS WERE GREAT.
THANK YOU. THANK YOU.
WHAT? IF YOU ACT EMBARRASSED, I'LL GET EMBARRASSED, TOO.
YOU TWO LOOK LIKE YOU'RE HAVING A GREAT TIME TOGETHER!
WHAT... WANT ME TO KISS YOU TOO, KYOKO?
NO!

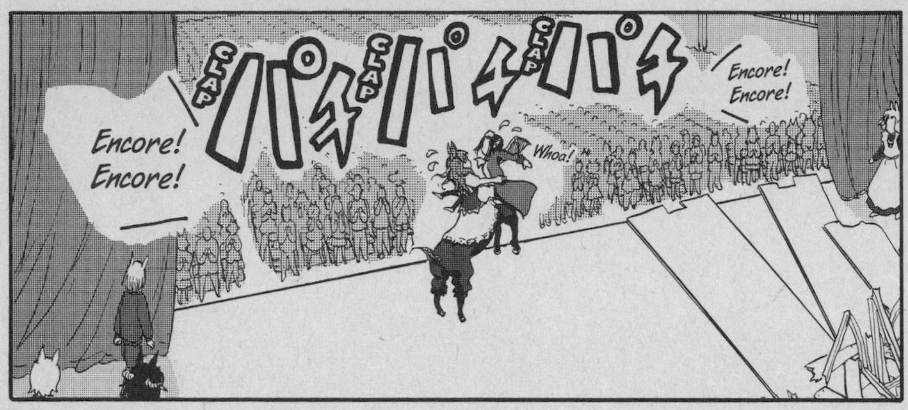
Encore! Encore!
CLAP パチ CLAP パチ CLAP パチ
Whoa!
Encore! Encore!

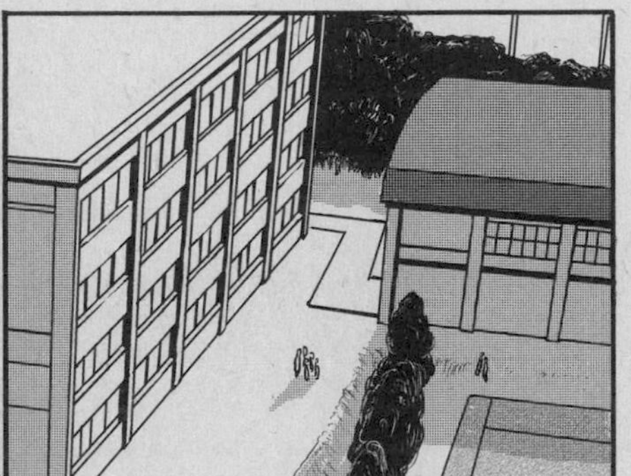

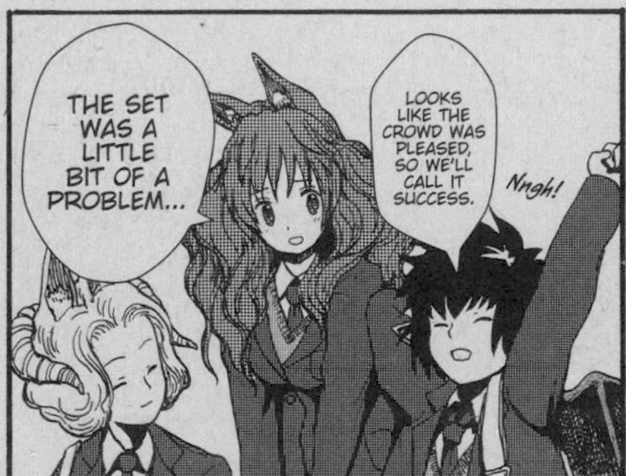
THE SET WAS A LITTLE BIT OF A PROBLEM...
LOOKS LIKE THE CROWD WAS PLEASED, SO WE'LL CALL IT SUCCESS.
Nngh!

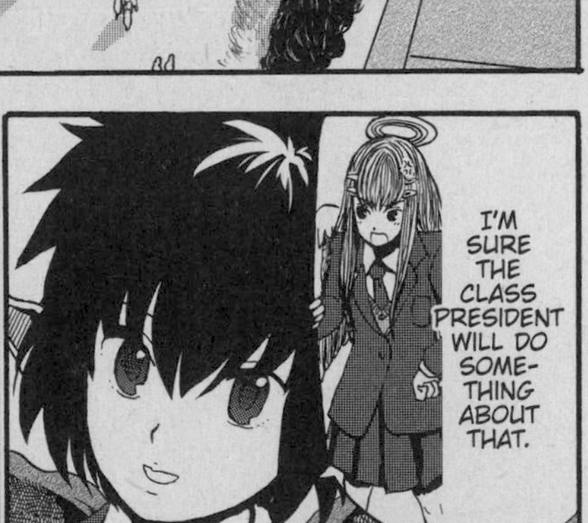
I'M SURE THE CLASS PRESIDENT WILL DO SOME-THING ABOUT THAT.

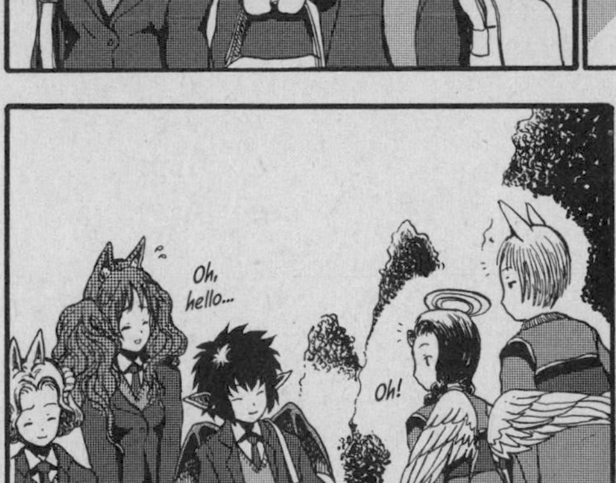
Oh!
Oh, hello...

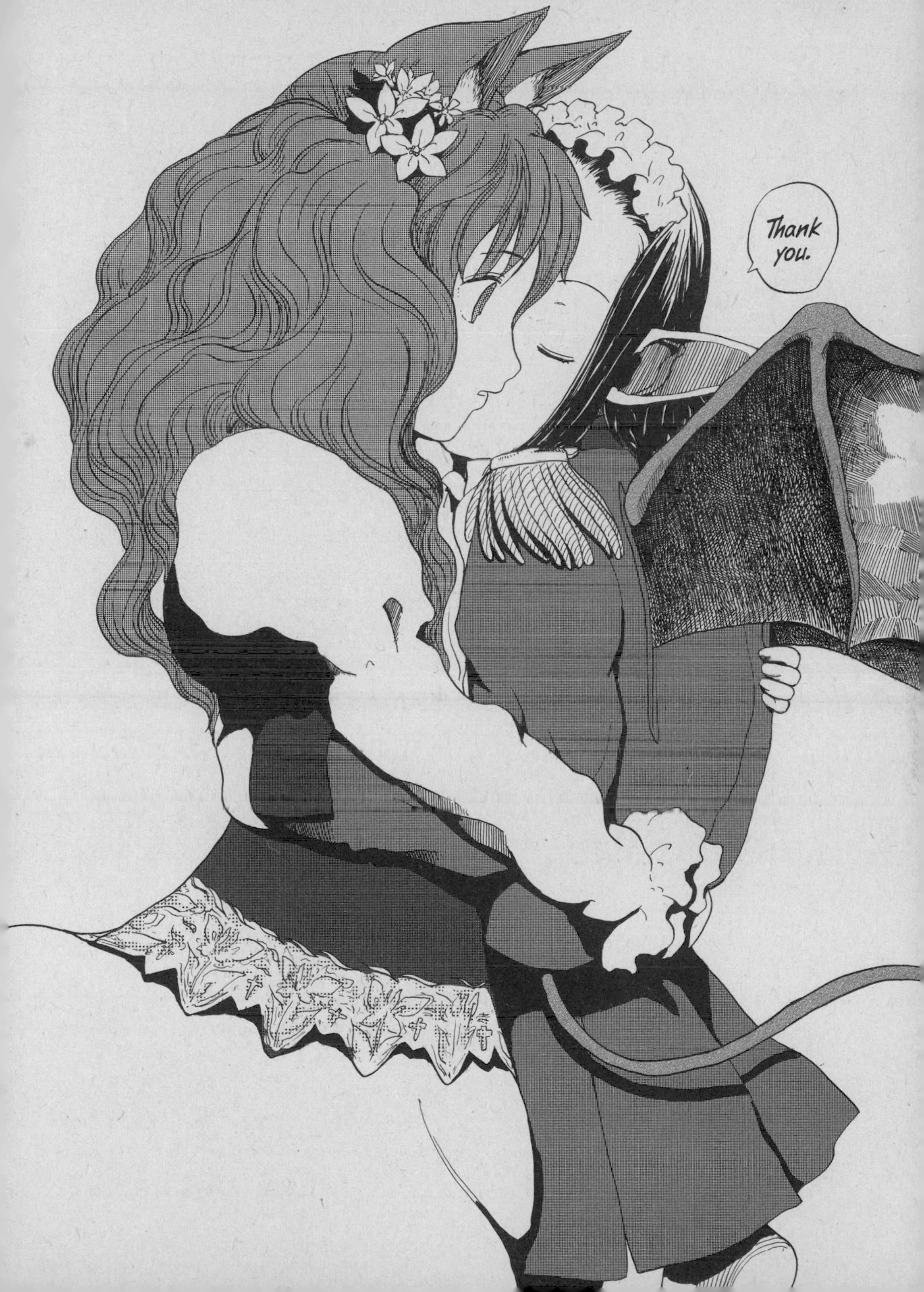
Thank you.

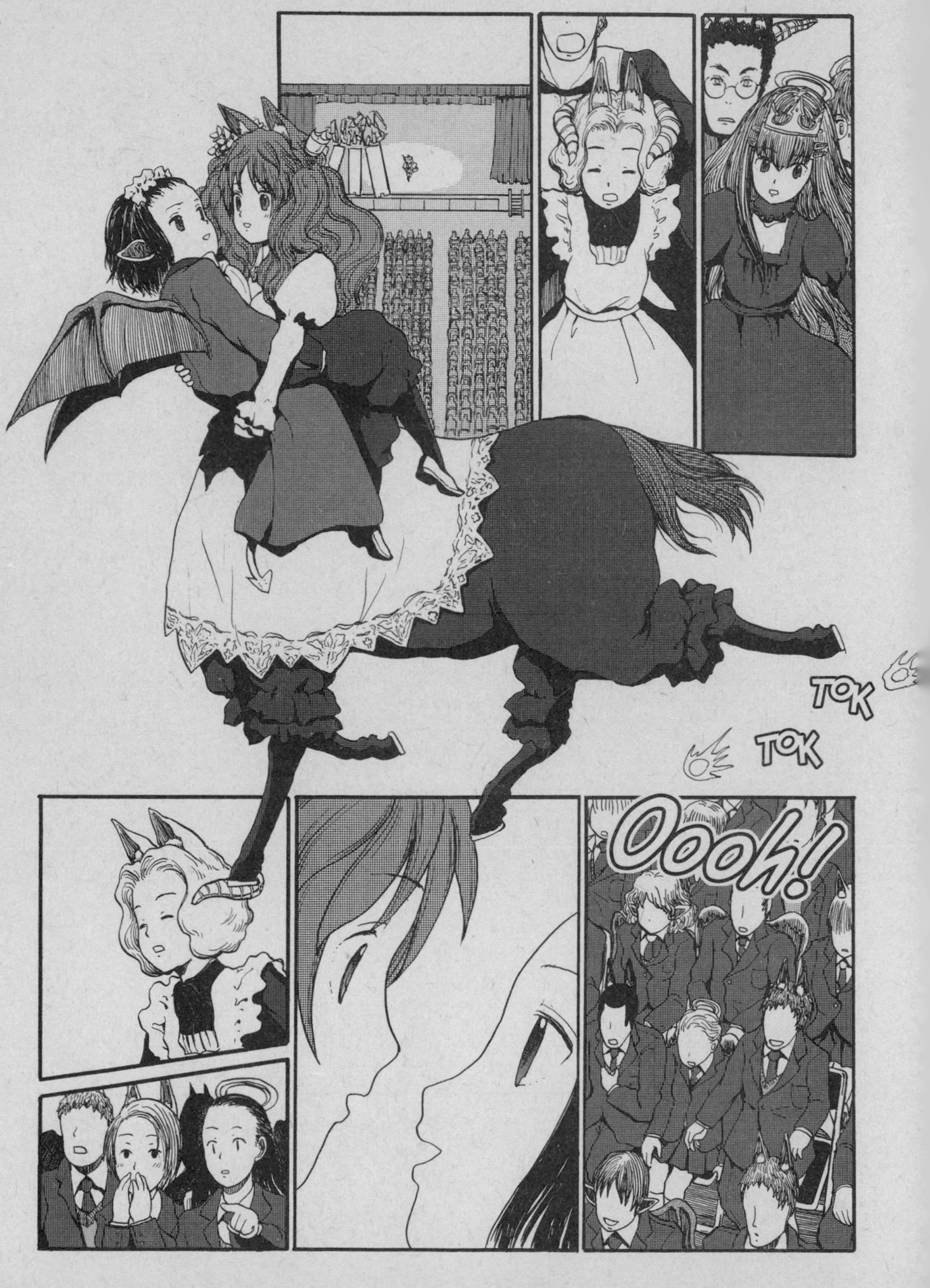
TOK
TOK
Oooh!

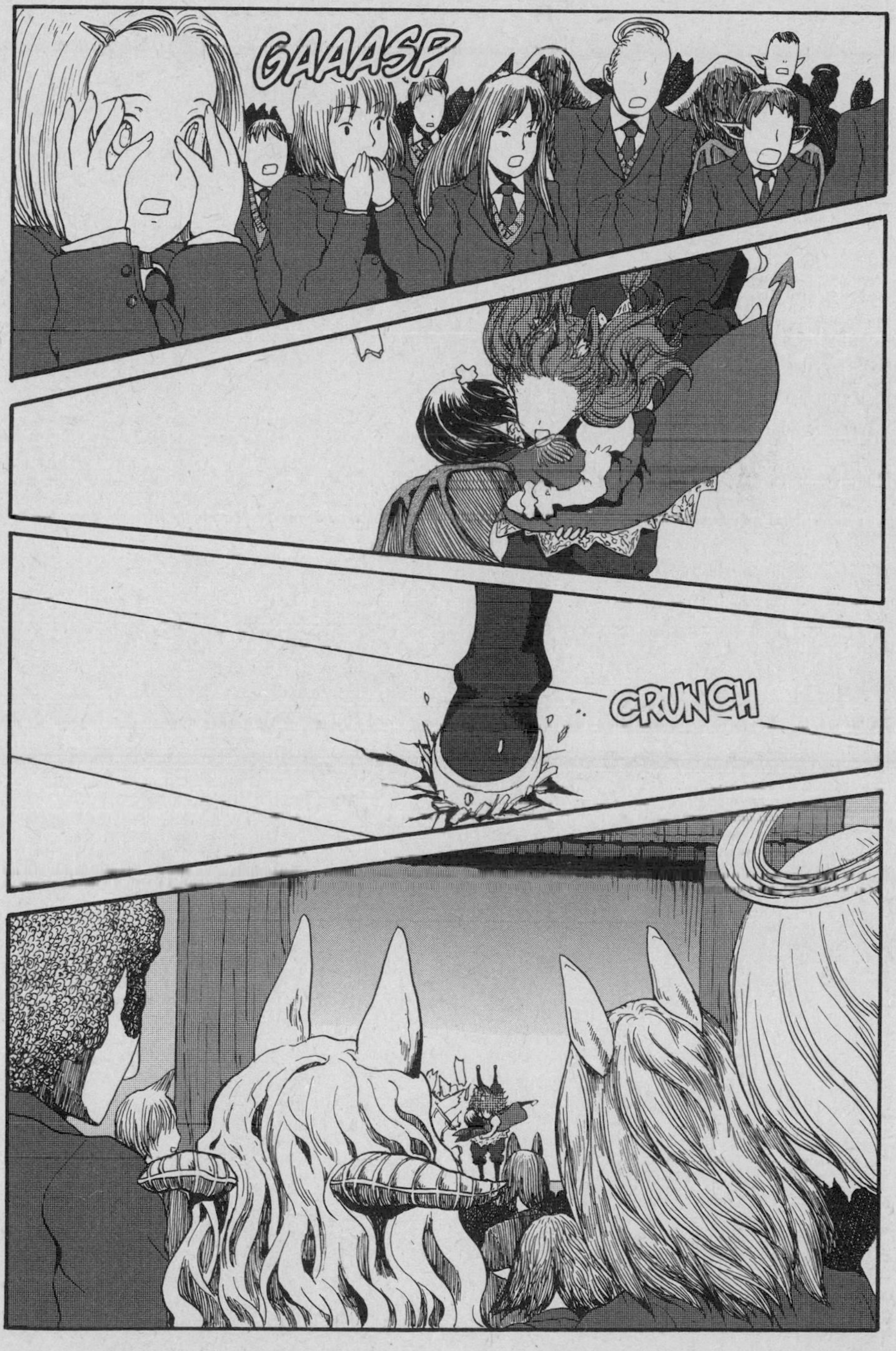
GAAASP
CRUNCH

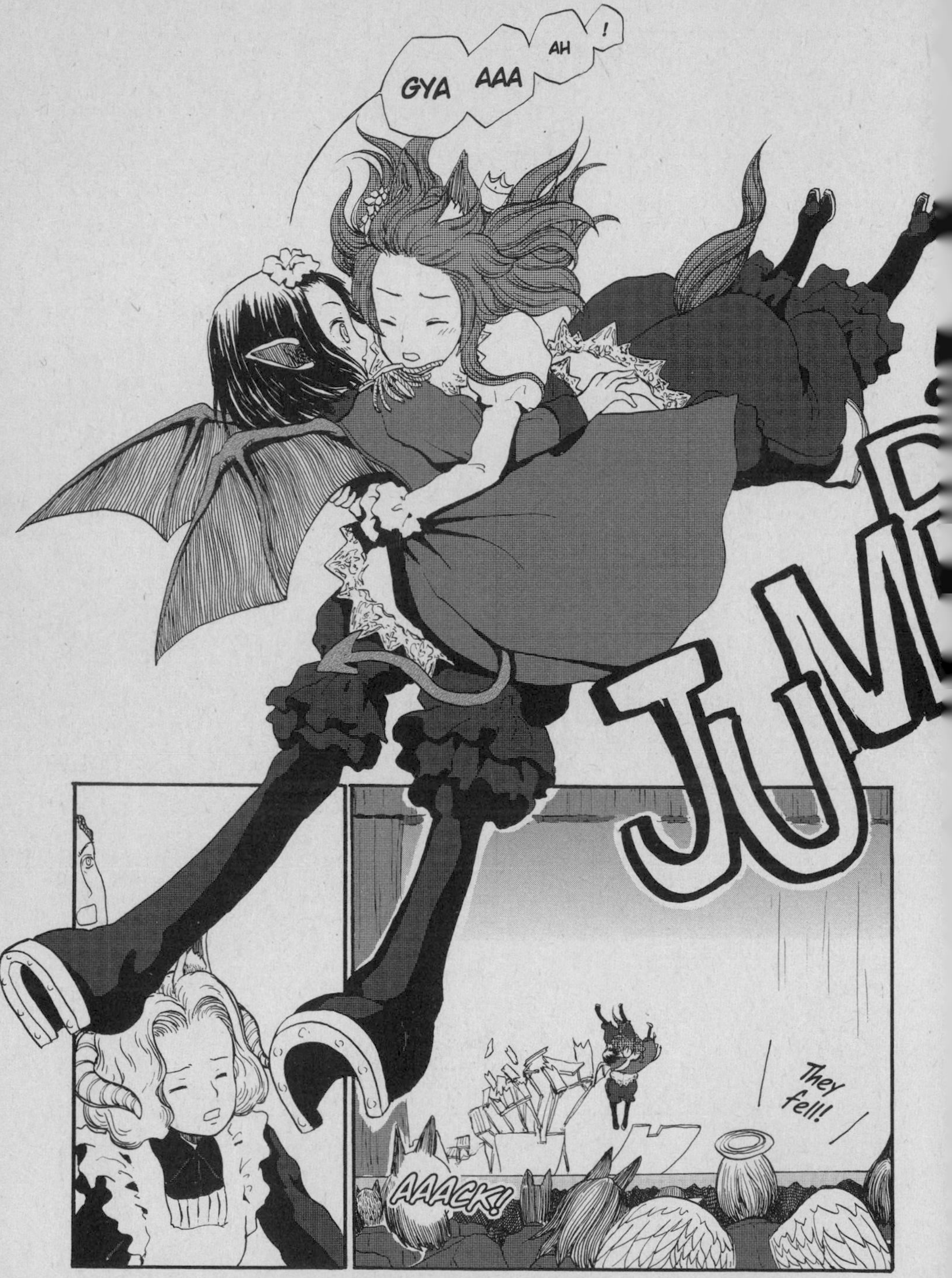
GYA AAA AH !
JUMP
They fell!
AAACK!

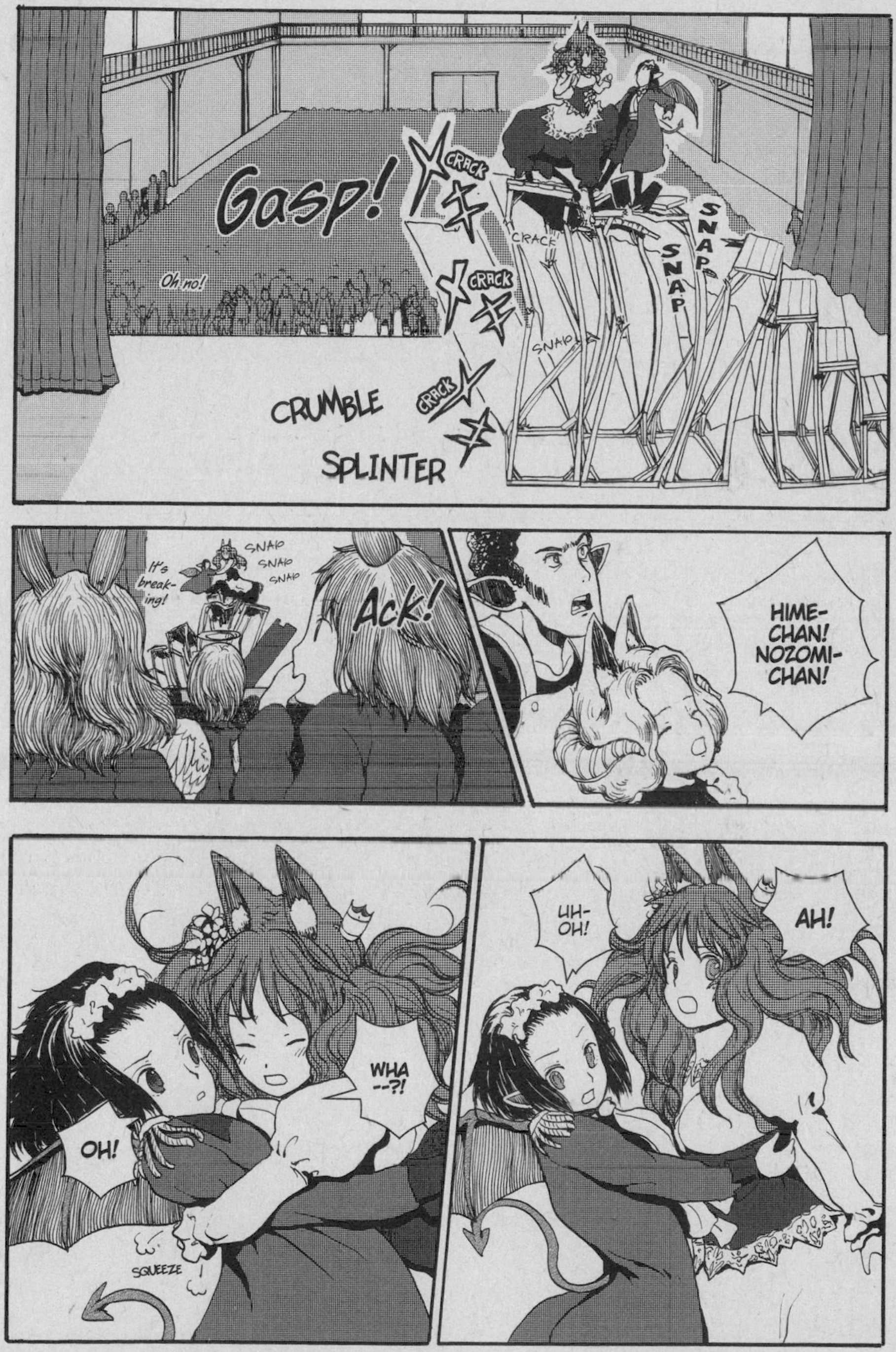

SNAP
SNAP
SNAP
CRACK
Gasp!
CRACK
SNAP
CRACK
Oh no!
CRACK
CRUMBLE
SPLINTER
HIME-CHAN! NOZOMI-CHAN!
Ack!
SNAP SNAP SNAP
It's breaking!
AH!
UH-OH!
WHA--?!
OH!
SQUEEZE

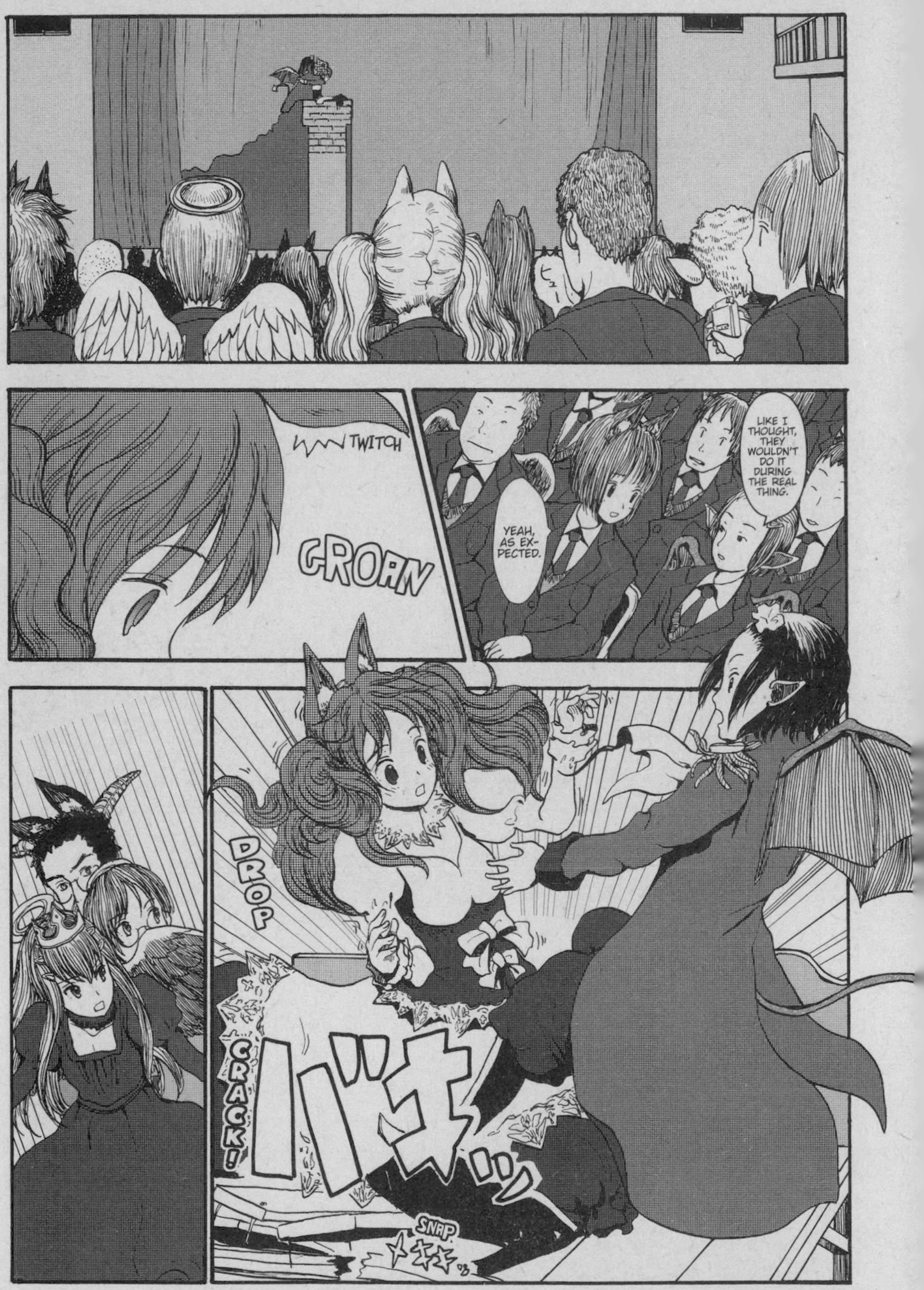
LIKE I THOUGHT, THEY WOULDN'T DO IT DURING THE REAL THING.
YEAH, AS EXPECTED.
TWITCH
GROAN
DROP
CRACK!
SNAP

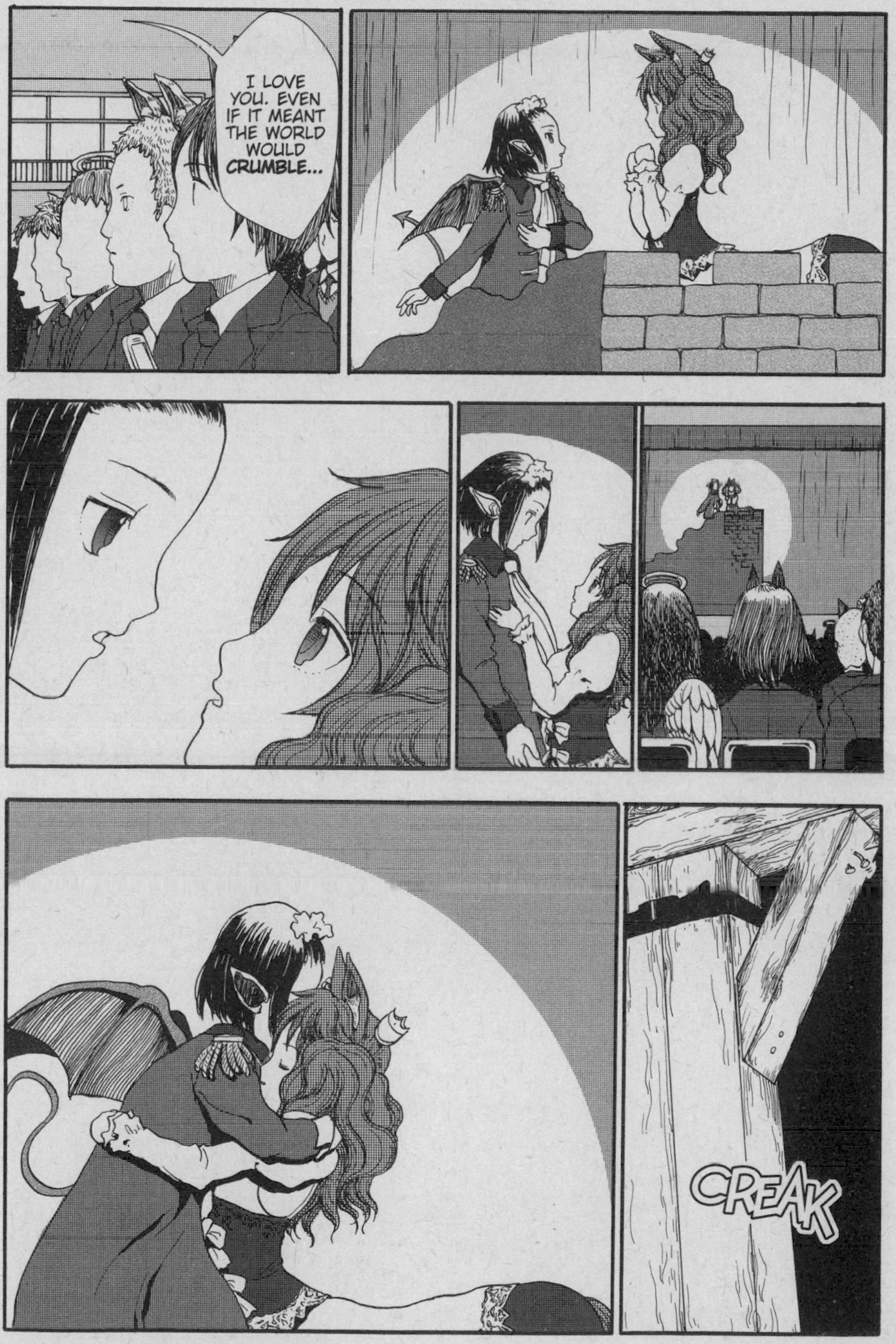
I LOVE YOU. EVEN IF IT MEANT THE WORLD WOULD CRUMBLE...
CREAK

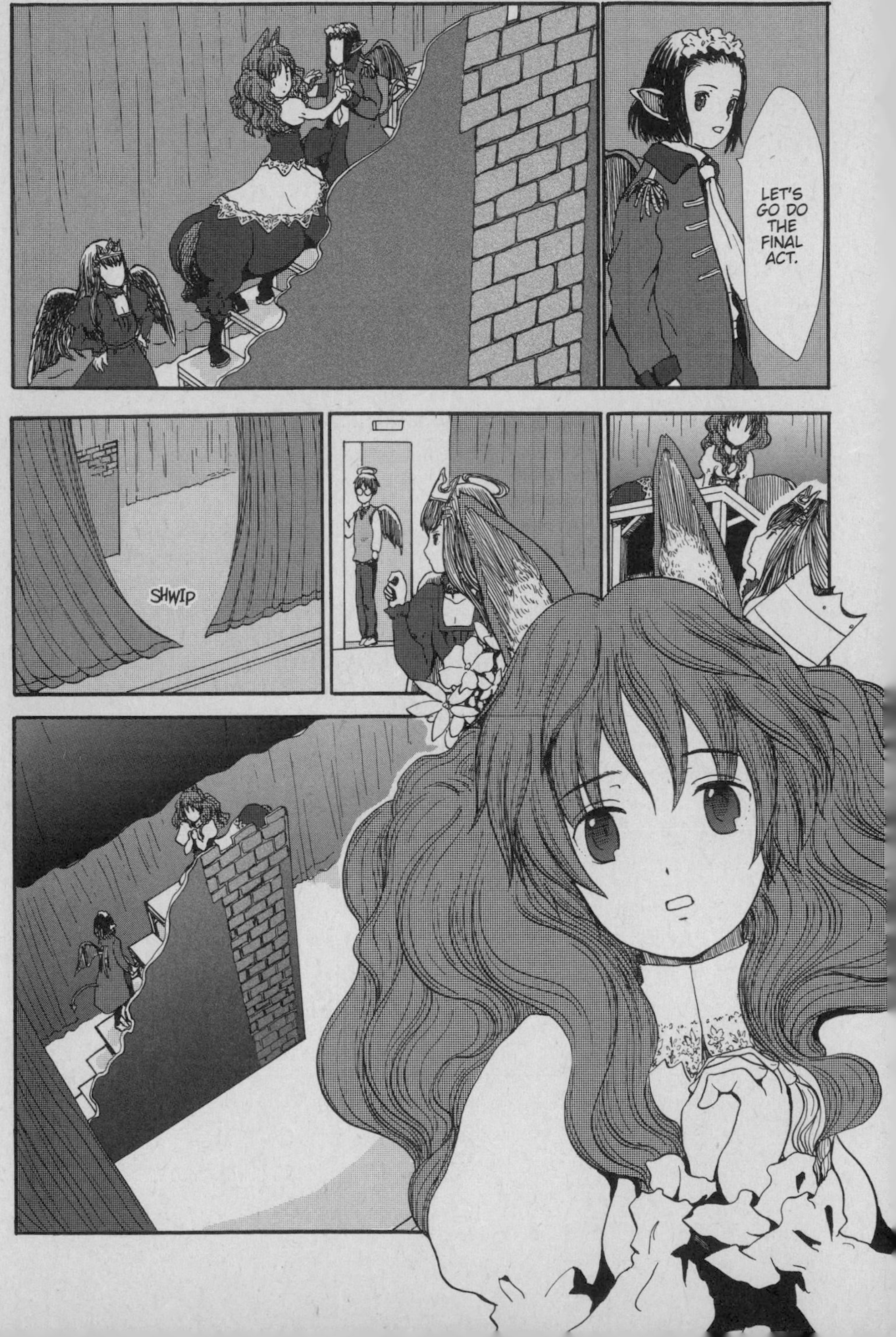
LET'S GO DO THE FINAL ACT.
SHWIP

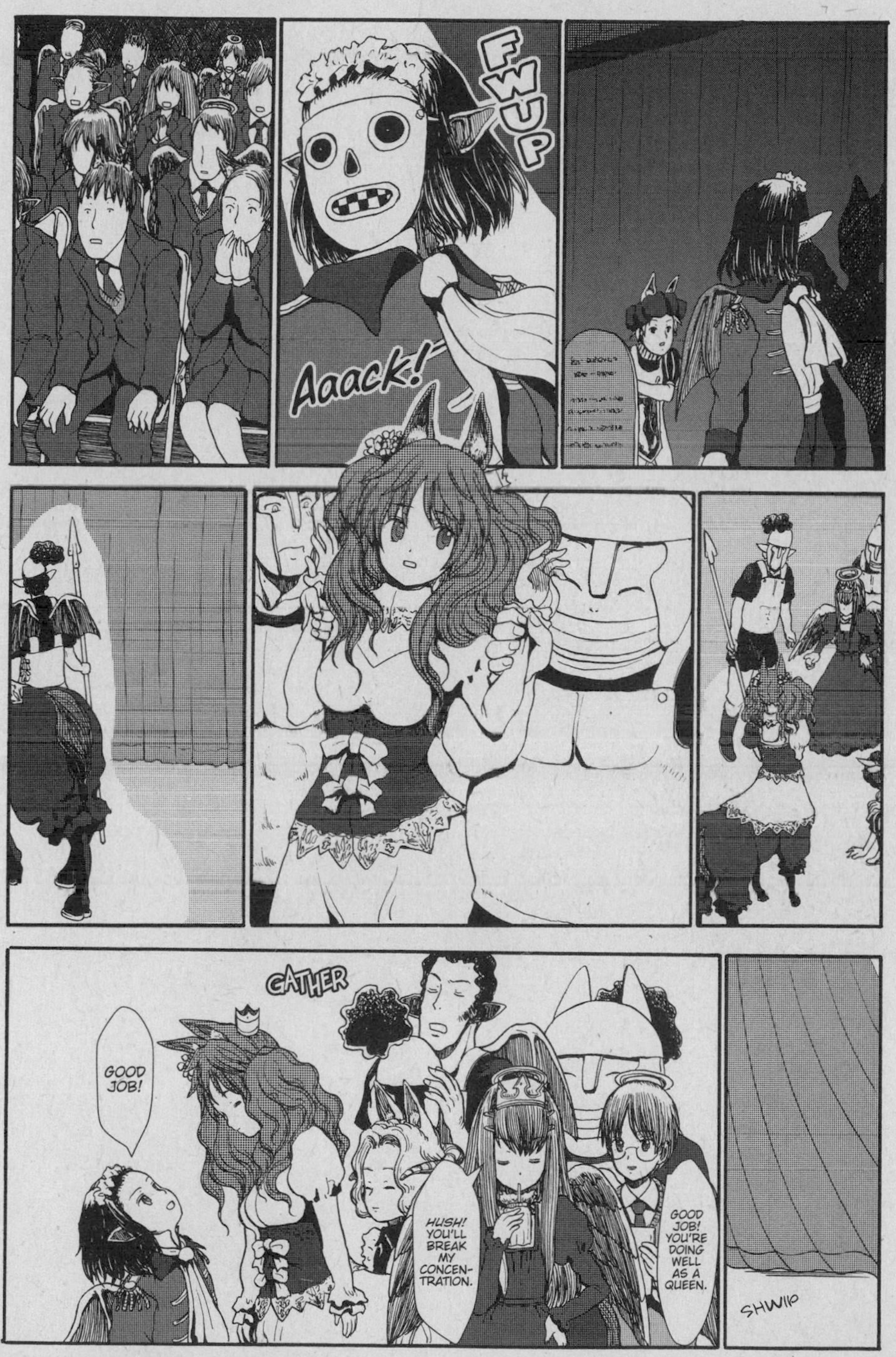
FWUP
Aaack!
SHWIP
GOOD JOB! YOU'RE DOING WELL AS A QUEEN.
HUSH! YOU'LL BREAK MY CONCEN-TRATION.
GATHER
GOOD JOB!

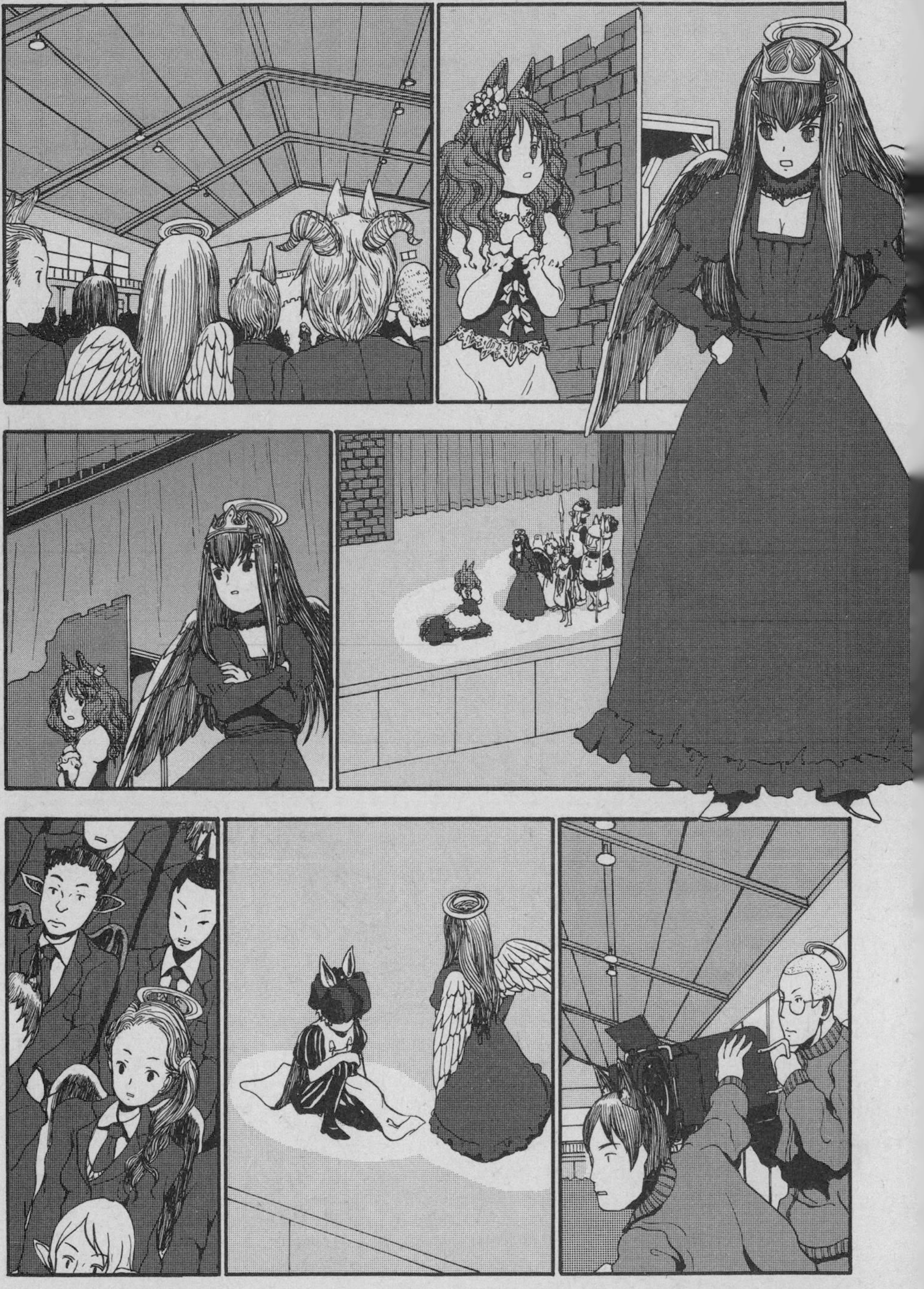

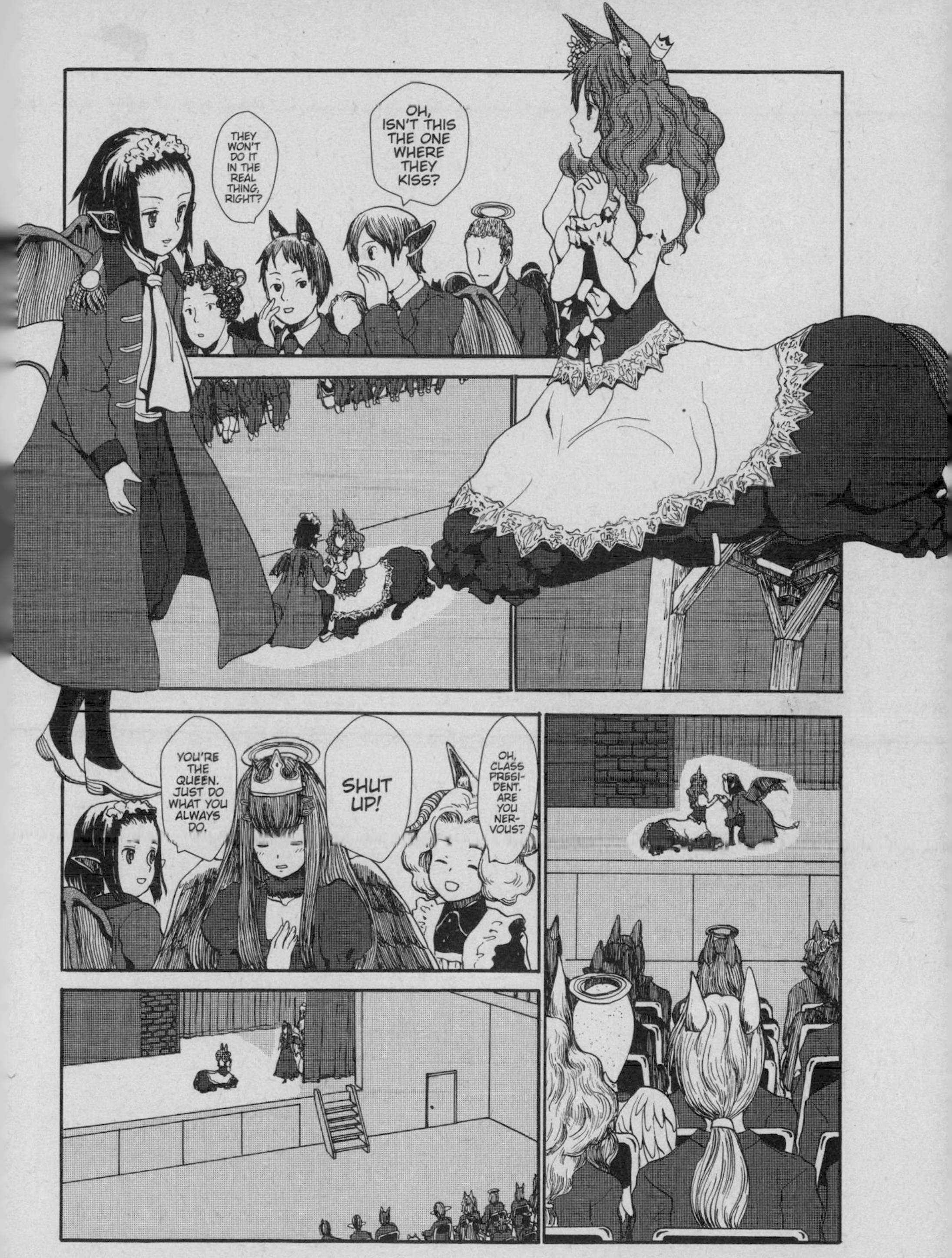
OH, ISN'T THIS THE ONE WHERE THEY KISS?
THEY WON'T DO IT IN THE REAL THING, RIGHT?
OH, CLASS PRESIDENT. ARE YOU NERVOUS?
SHUT UP!
YOU'RE THE QUEEN. JUST DO WHAT YOU ALWAYS DO.

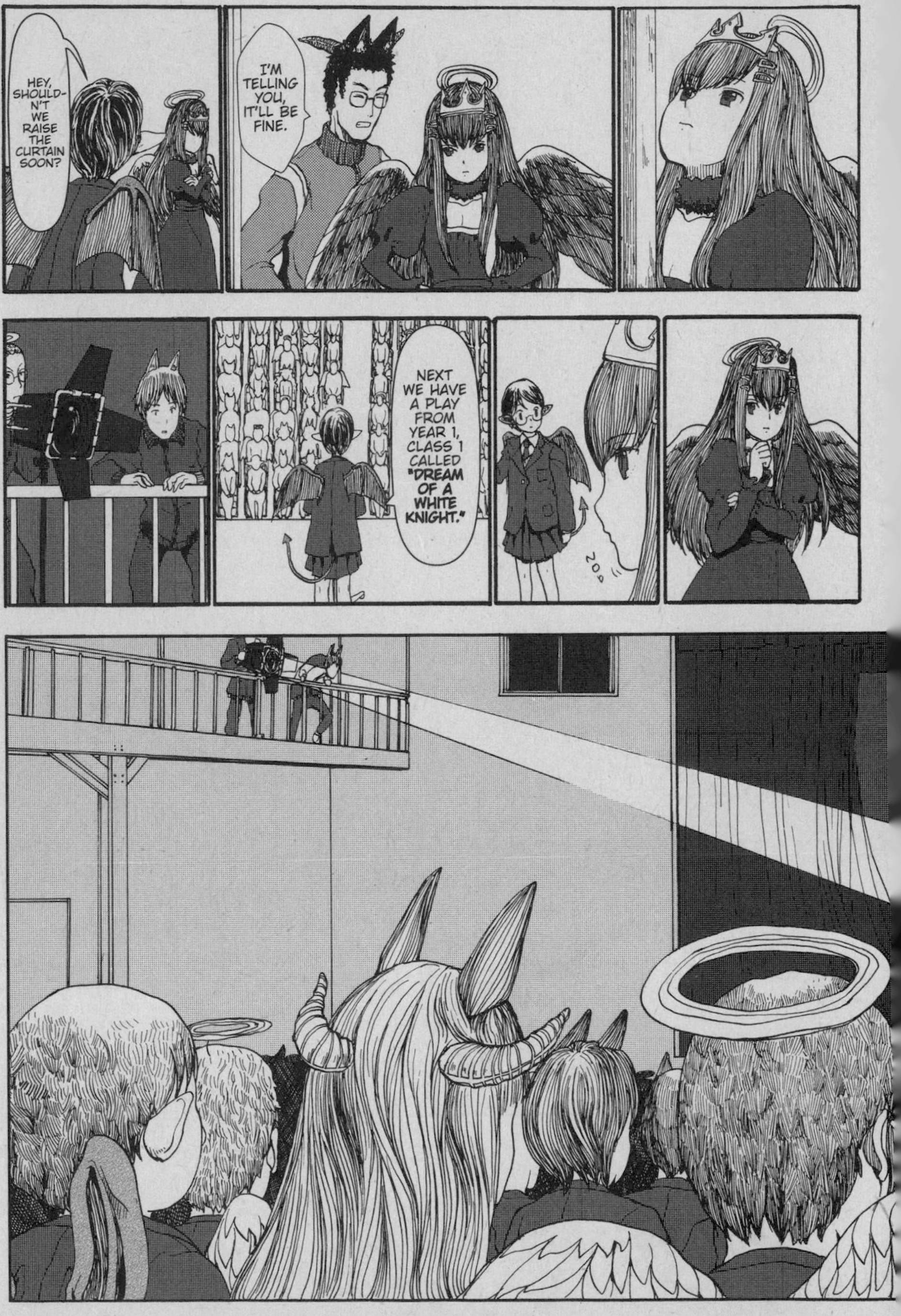
HEY, SHOULDN'T WE RAISE THE CURTAIN SOON?
I'M TELLING YOU, IT'LL BE FINE.
NEXT WE HAVE A PLAY FROM YEAR 1, CLASS 1 CALLED "DREAM OF A WHITE KNIGHT."
NOD

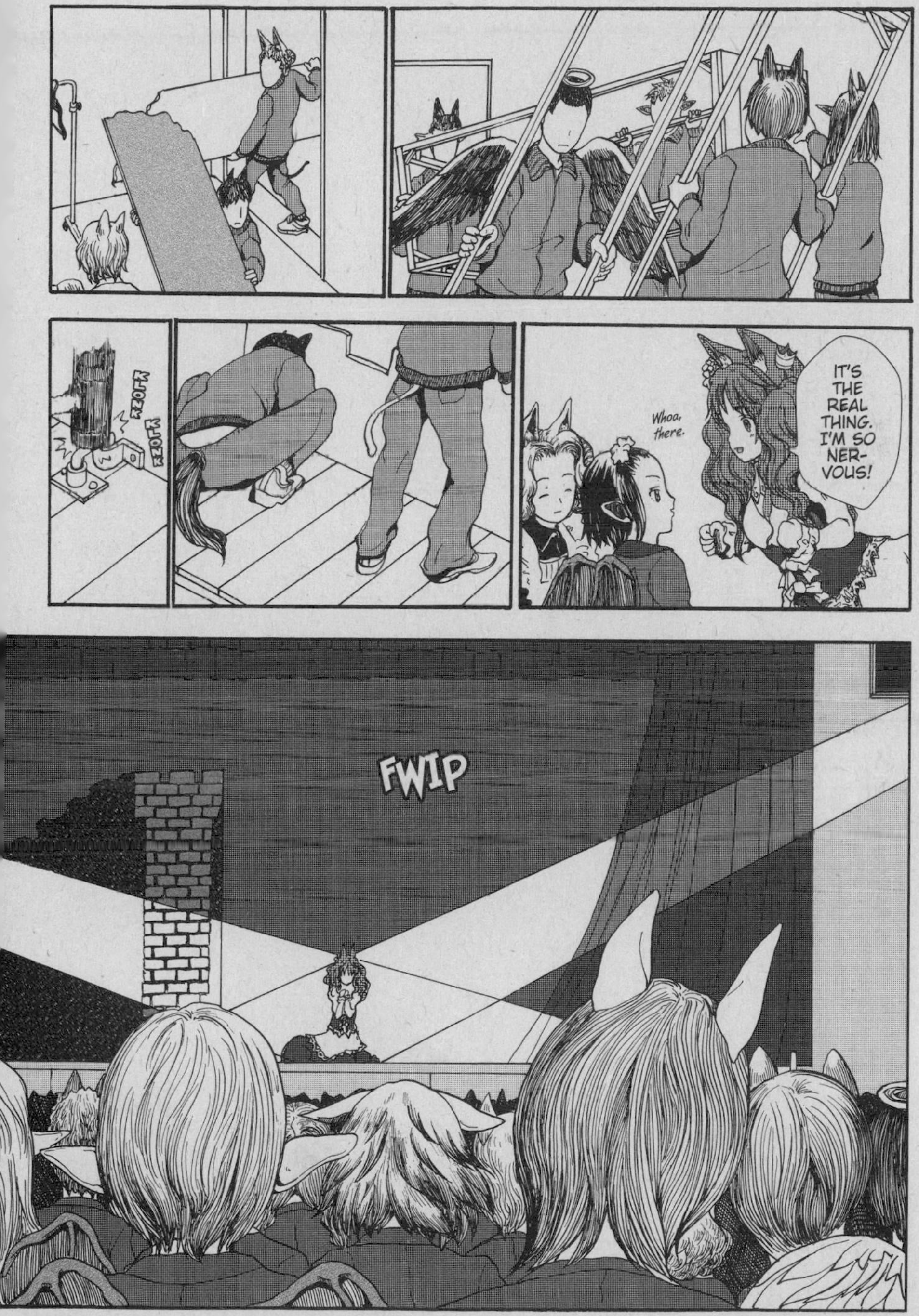
IT'S THE REAL THING. I'M SO NER-VOUS!
Whoa, there.
KLONK
KLONK
FWIP

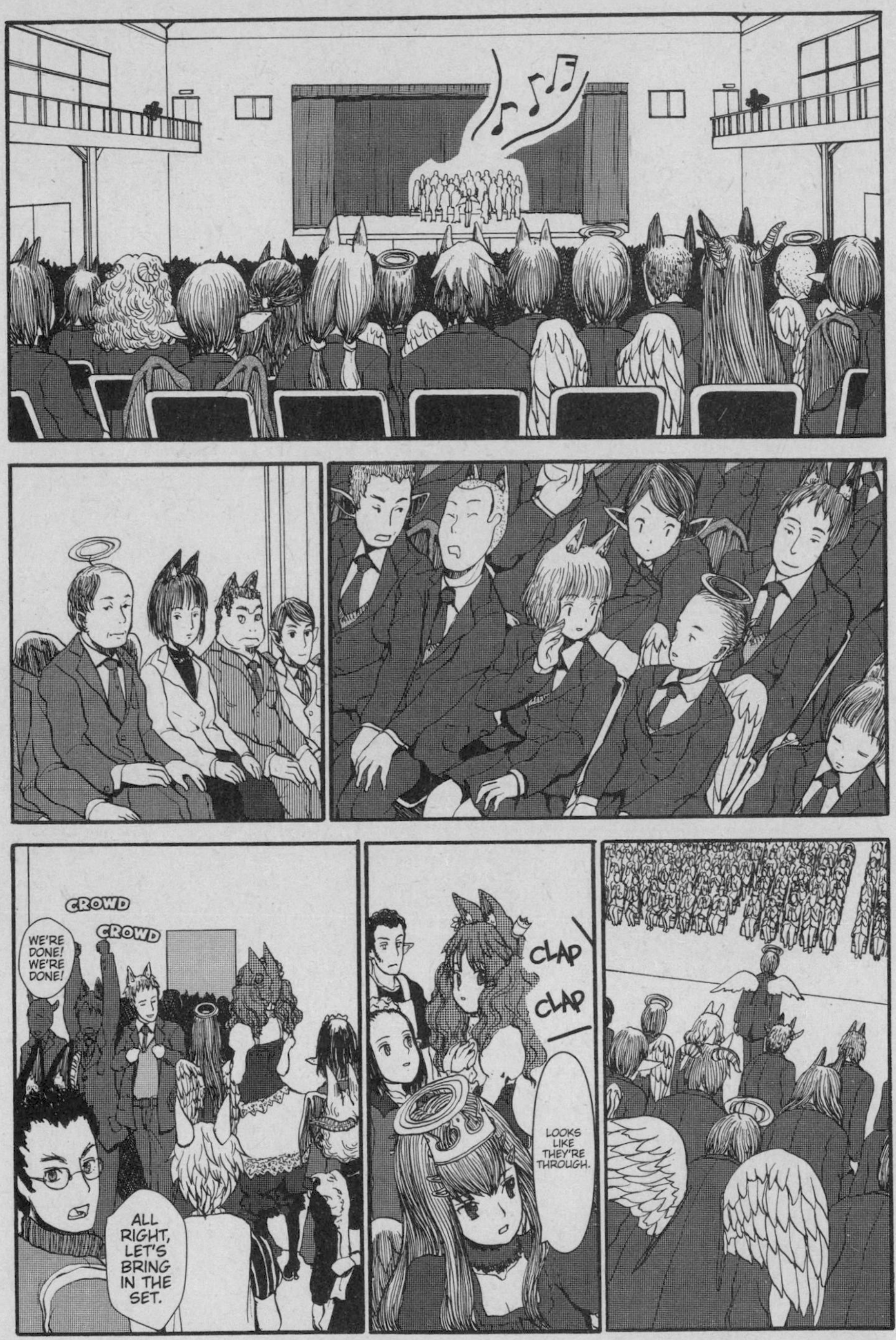
CLAP
CLAP
LOOKS LIKE THEY'RE THROUGH.
CROWD
CROWD
WE'RE DONE! WE'RE DONE!
ALL RIGHT, LET'S BRING IN THE SET.

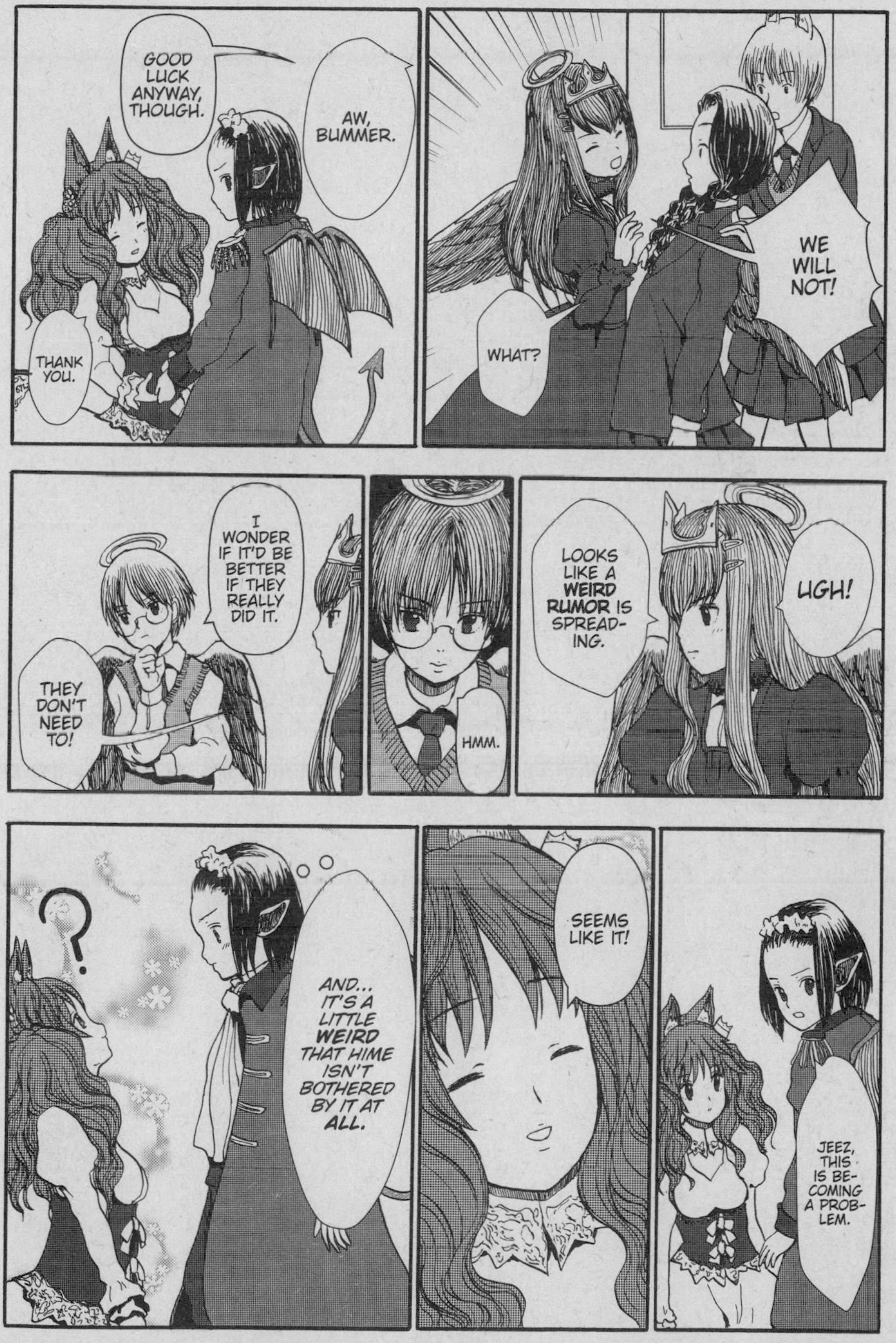
WE WILL NOT!
WHAT?
AW, BUMMER.
GOOD LUCK ANYWAY, THOUGH.
THANK YOU.
UGH!
LOOKS LIKE A WEIRD RUMOR IS SPREAD-ING.
HMM.
I WONDER IF IT'D BE BETTER IF THEY REALLY DID IT.
THEY DON'T NEED TO!
JEEZ, THIS IS BE-COMING A PROB-LEM.
SEEMS LIKE IT!
AND... IT'S A LITTLE WEIRD THAT HIME ISN'T BOTHERED BY IT AT ALL.

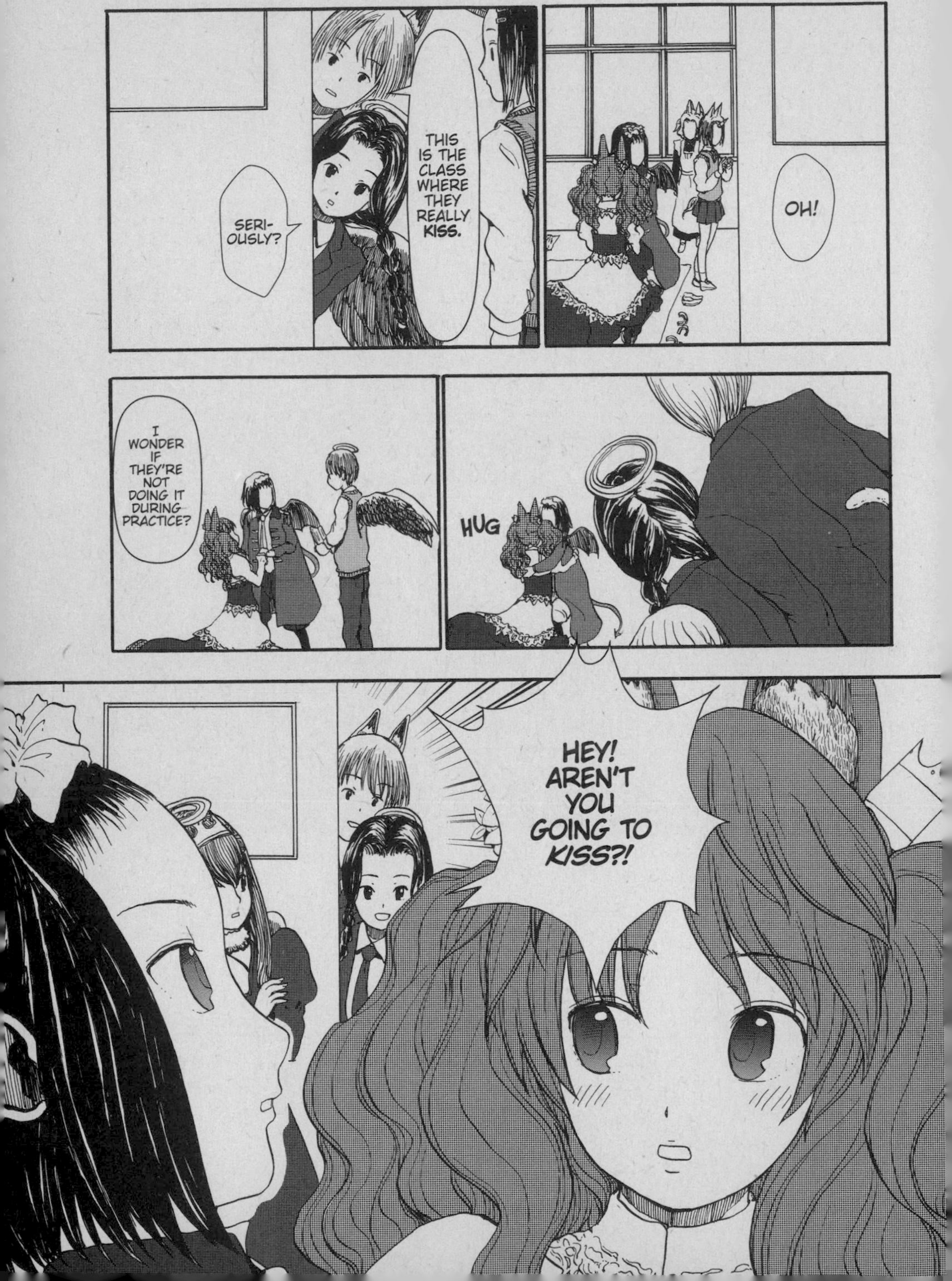
OH!
THIS IS THE CLASS WHERE THEY REALLY KISS.
SERI-OUSLY?
HUG
I WONDER IF THEY'RE NOT DOING IT DURING PRACTICE?
HEY! AREN'T YOU GOING TO KISS?!

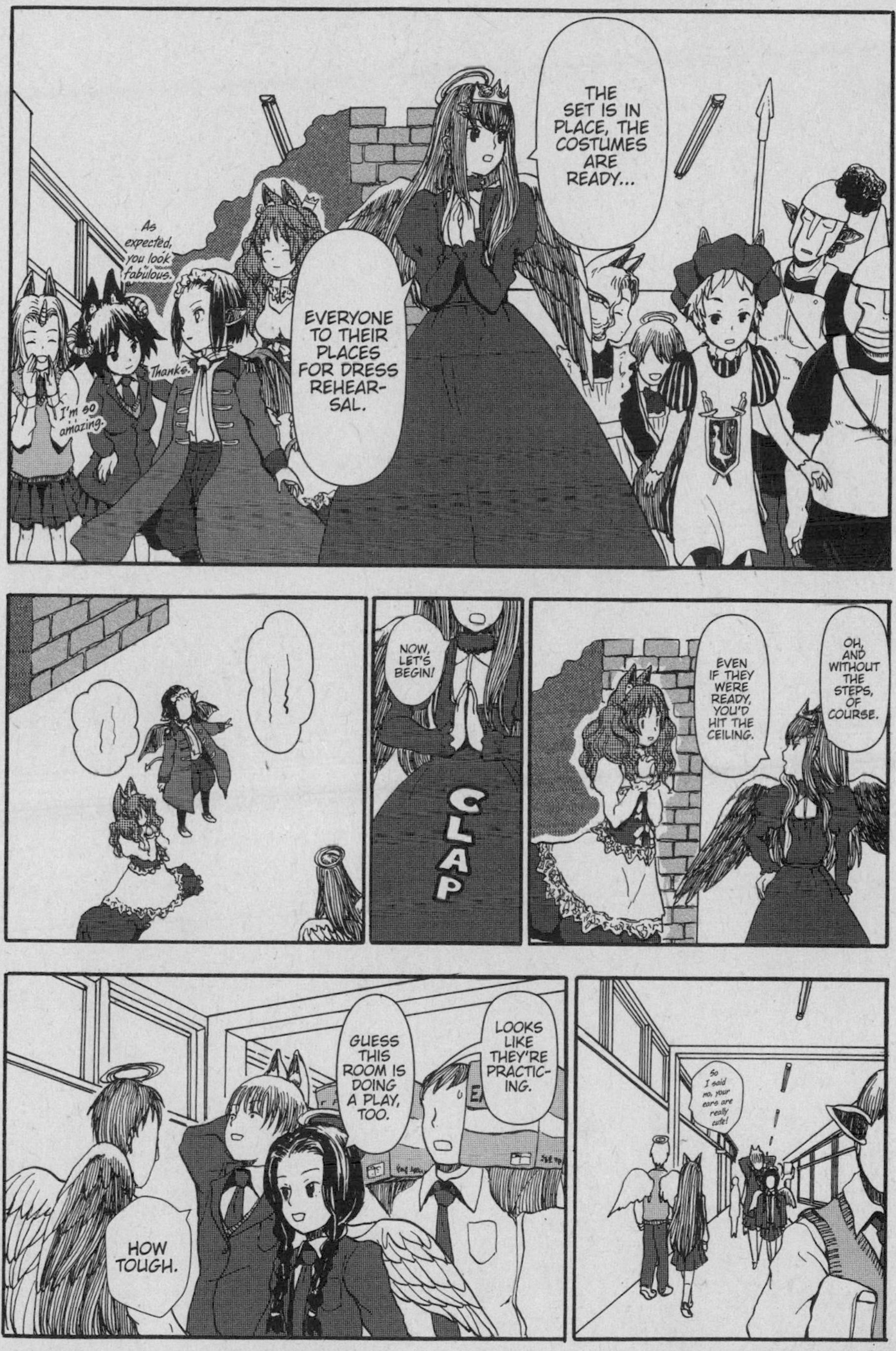
THE SET IS IN PLACE, THE COSTUMES ARE READY...
EVERYONE TO THEIR PLACES FOR DRESS REHEAR-SAL.
As expected, you look fabulous.
Thanks.
I'm so amazing.
OH, AND WITHOUT THE STEPS, OF COURSE.
EVEN IF THEY WERE READY, YOU'D HIT THE CEILING.
NOW, LET'S BEGIN!
CLAP
So I said no, your ears are really cute!
LOOKS LIKE THEY'RE PRACTIC-ING.
GUESS THIS ROOM IS DOING A PLAY, TOO.
HOW TOUGH.

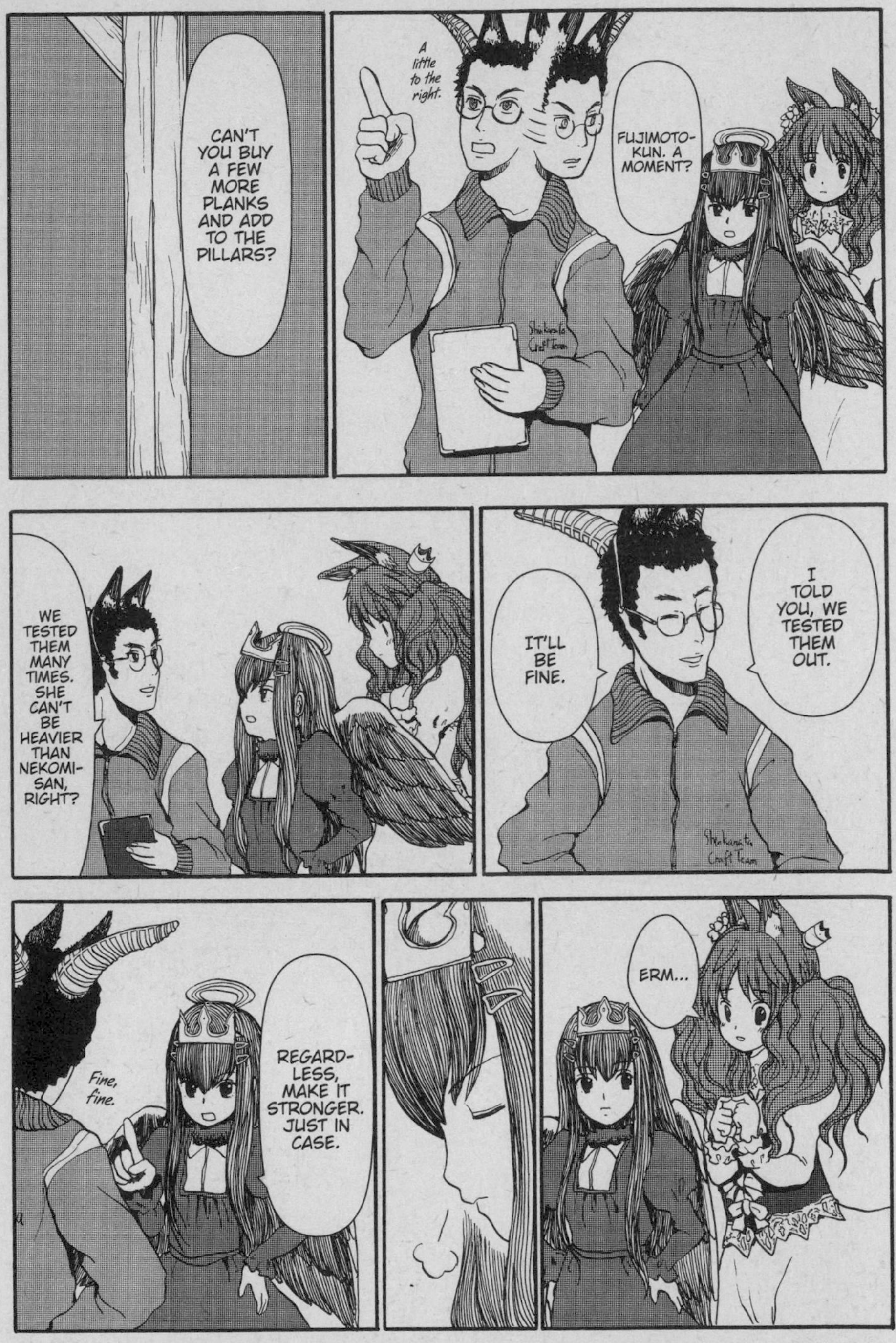
FUJIMOTO-KUN. A MOMENT?
A little to the right.
Shikanata Craft Team
CAN'T YOU BUY A FEW MORE PLANKS AND ADD TO THE PILLARS?
I TOLD YOU, WE TESTED THEM OUT.
IT'LL BE FINE.
Shikanata Craft Team
WE TESTED THEM MANY TIMES. SHE CAN'T BE HEAVIER THAN NEKOMI-SAN, RIGHT?
ERM...
REGARD-LESS, MAKE IT STRONGER. JUST IN CASE.
Fine, fine.

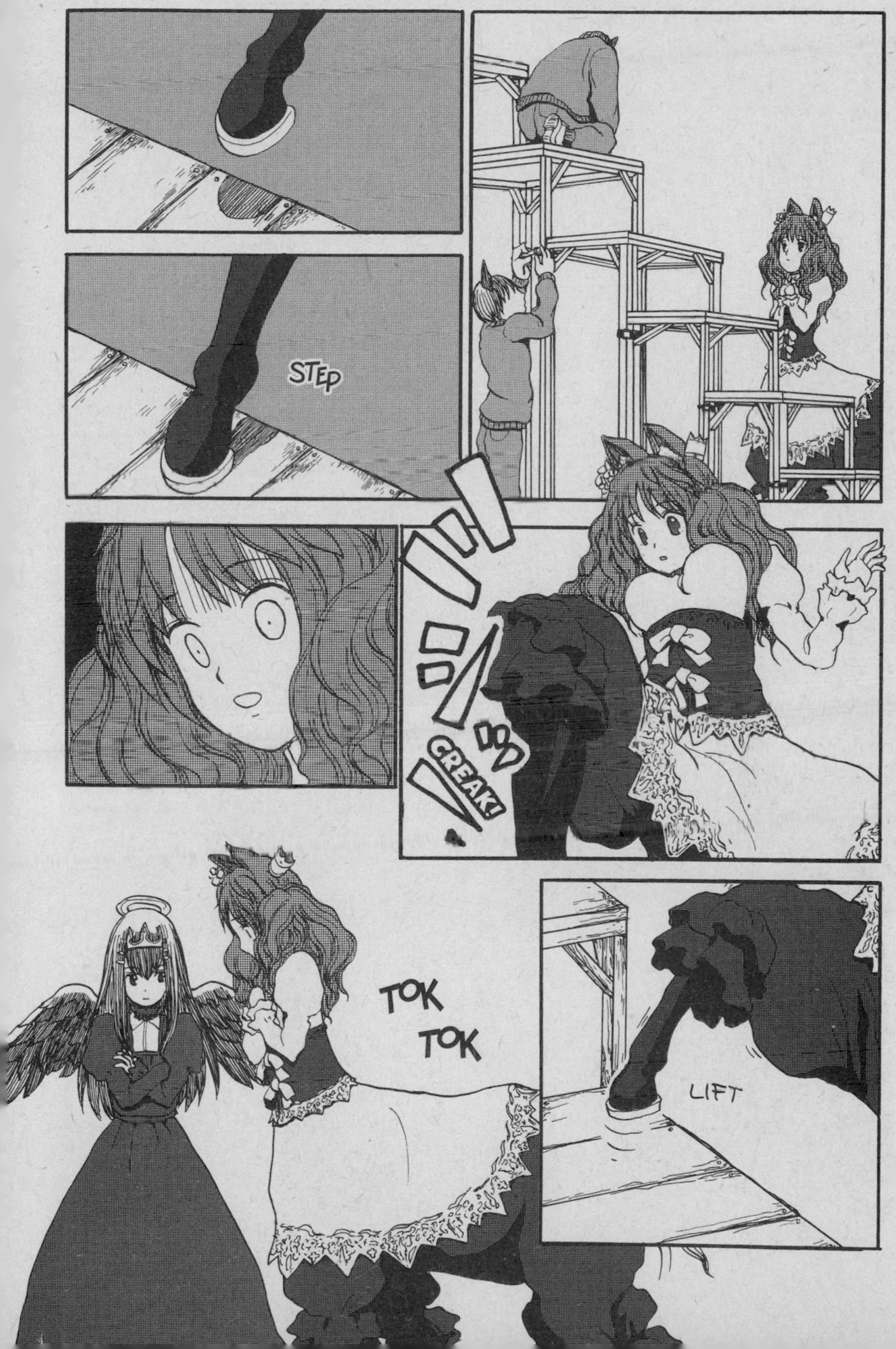
STEP
CREAK!
TOK
TOK
LIFT

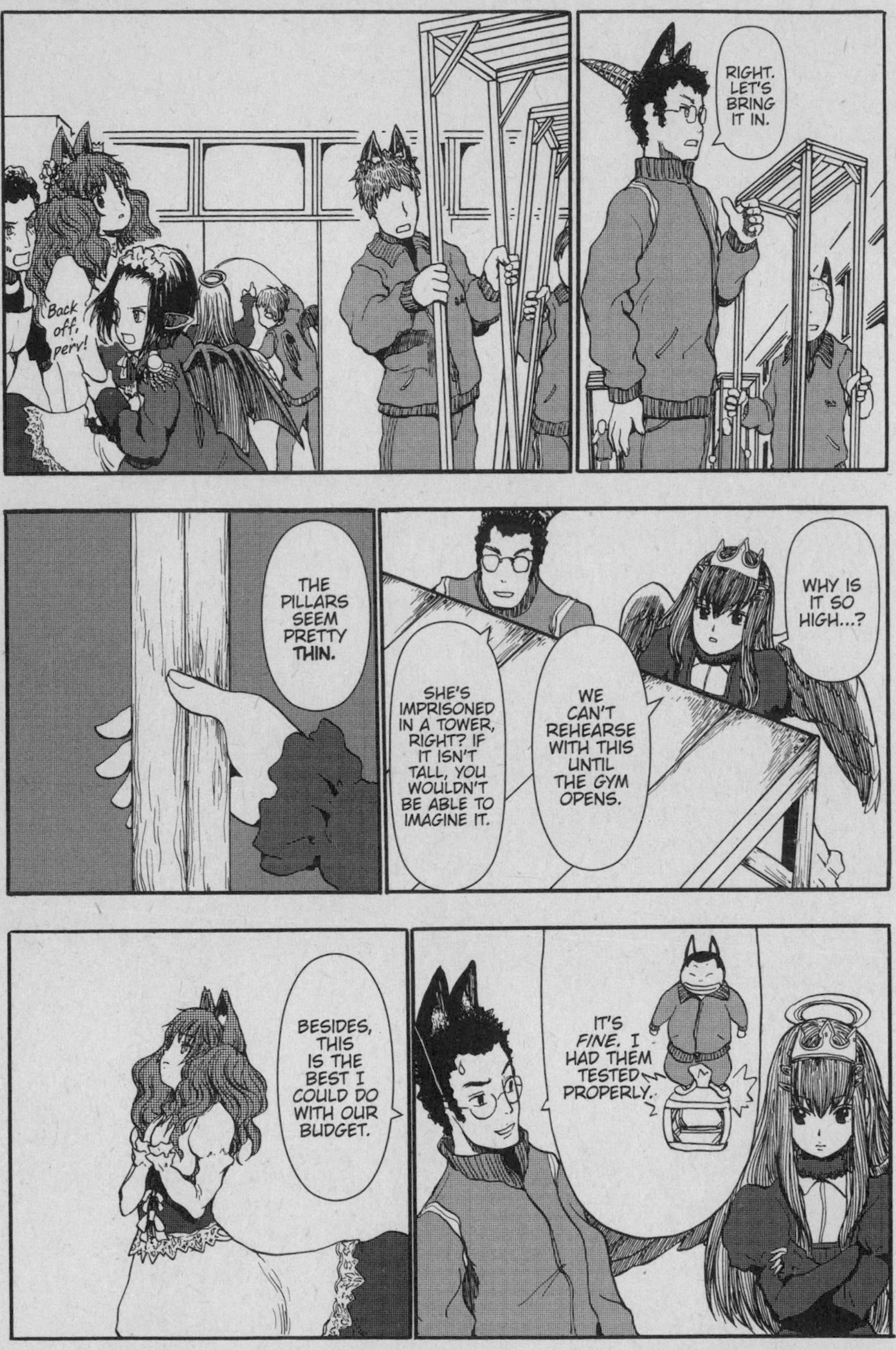
RIGHT. LET'S BRING IT IN.
Back off, perv!
WHY IS IT SO HIGH...?
WE CAN'T REHEARSE WITH THIS UNTIL THE GYM OPENS.
SHE'S IMPRISONED IN A TOWER, RIGHT? IF IT ISN'T TALL, YOU WOULDN'T BE ABLE TO IMAGINE IT.
THE PILLARS SEEM PRETTY THIN.
IT'S FINE. I HAD THEM TESTED PROPERLY.
BESIDES, THIS IS THE BEST I COULD DO WITH OUR BUDGET.

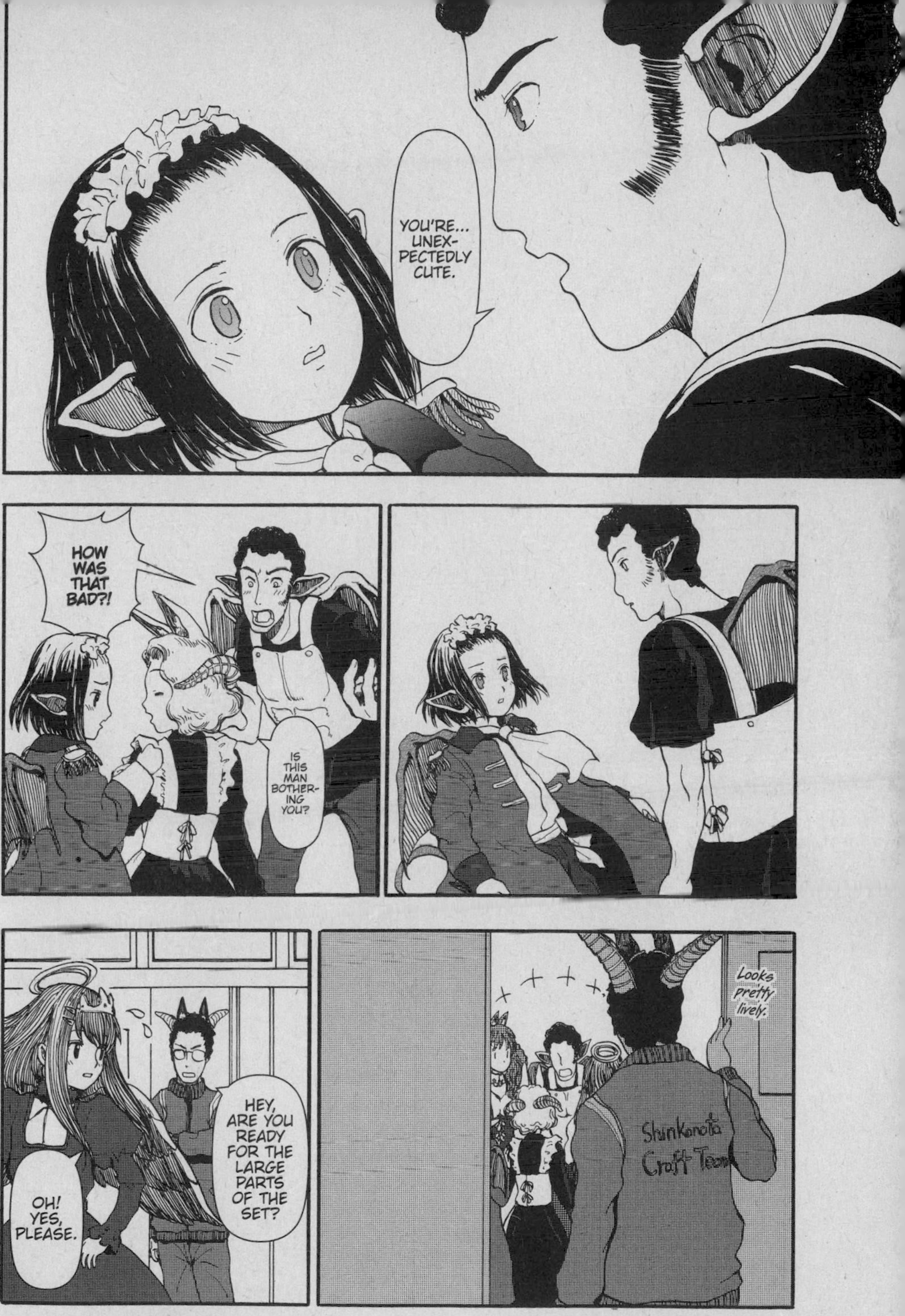
YOU'RE... UNEXPECTEDLY CUTE.
IS THIS MAN BOTHERING YOU?
HOW WAS THAT BAD?!
Looks pretty lively.
Shinkonota Craft Team
HEY, ARE YOU READY FOR THE LARGE PARTS OF THE SET?
OH! YES, PLEASE.

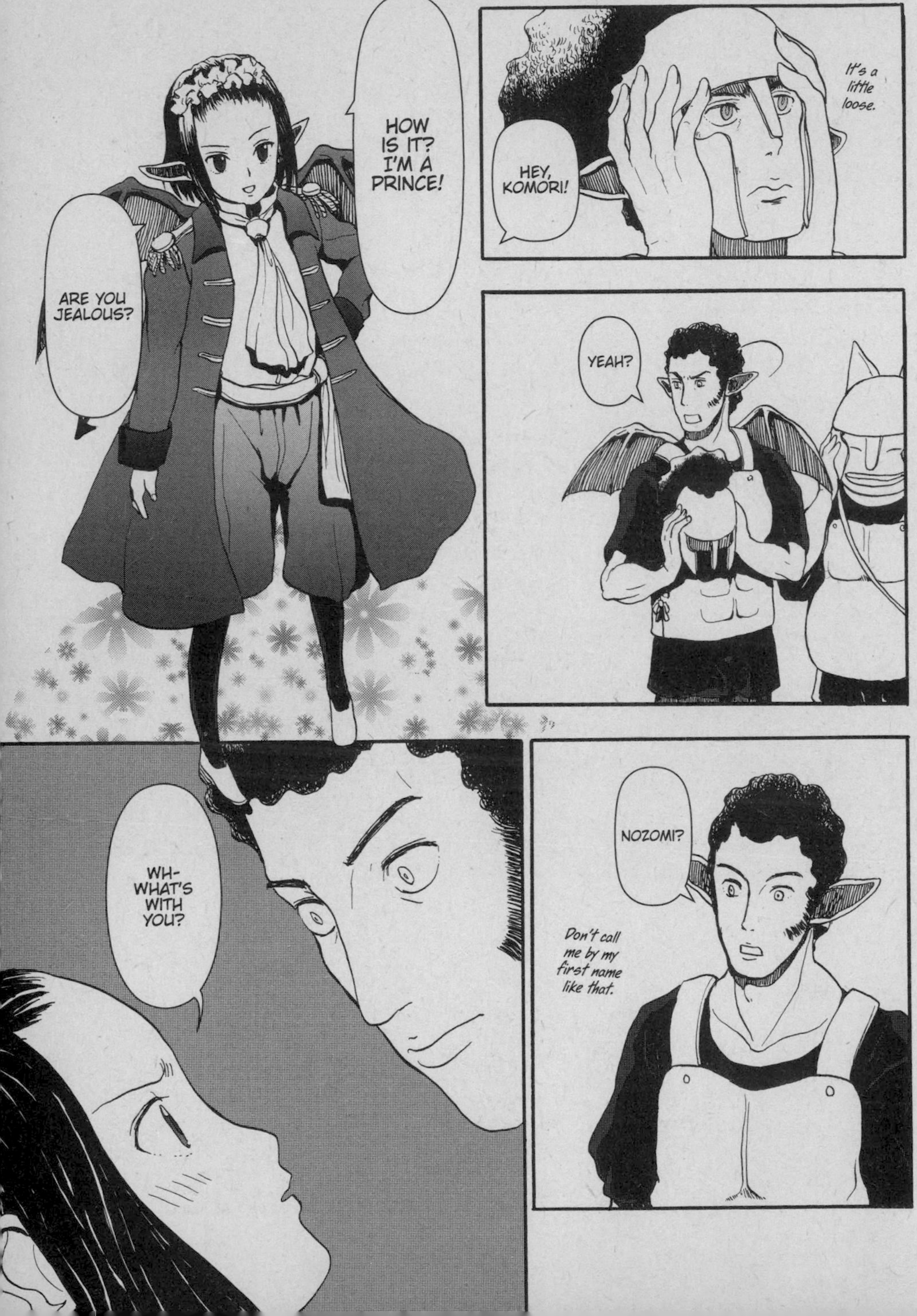
HEY, KOMORI!
It's a little loose.
YEAH?
HOW IS IT? I'M A PRINCE!
ARE YOU JEALOUS?
NOZOMI?
Don't call me by my first name like that.
WH-WHAT'S WITH YOU?

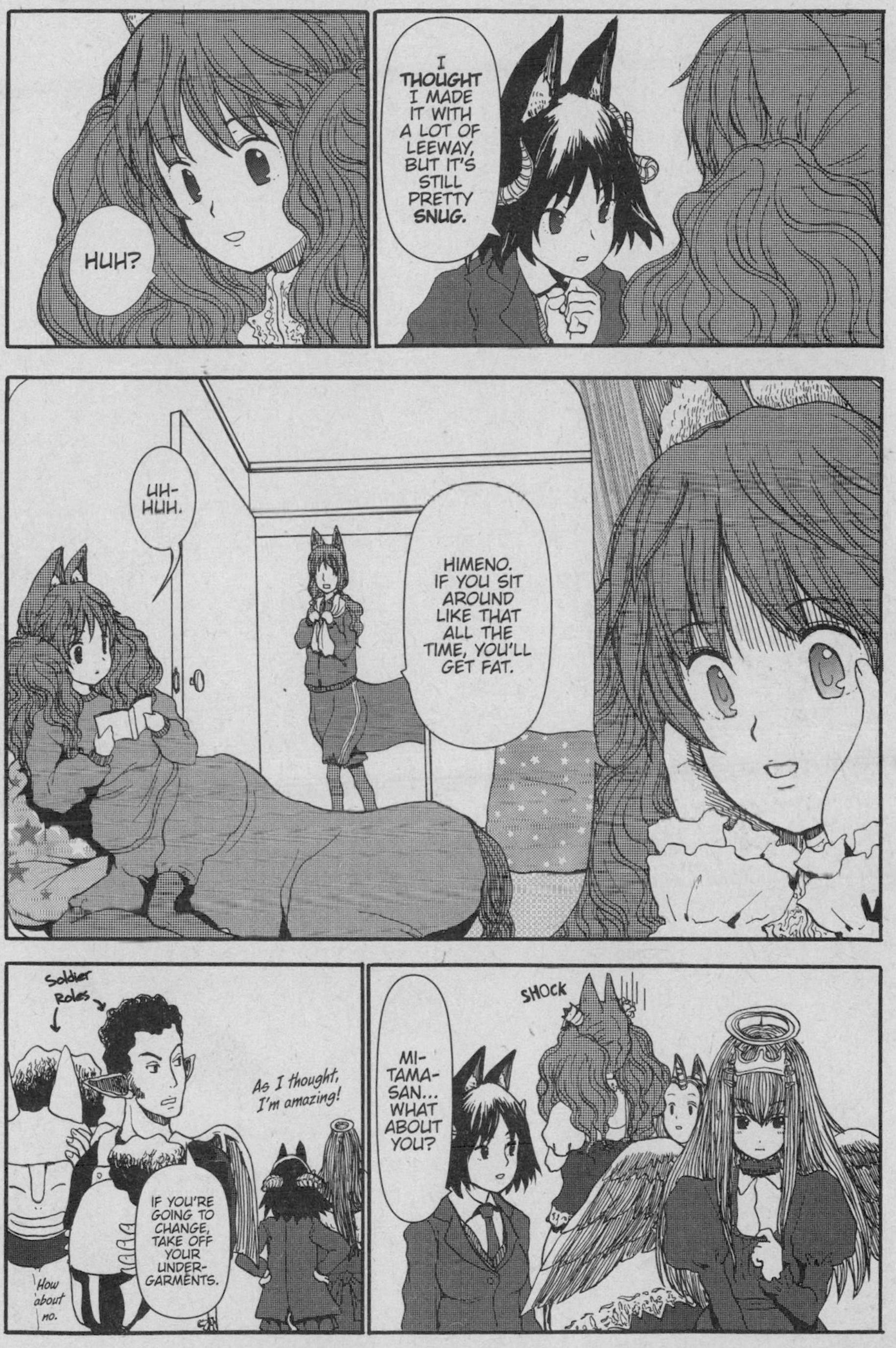
I THOUGHT I MADE IT WITH A LOT OF LEEWAY, BUT IT'S STILL PRETTY SNUG.
HUH?
HIMENO. IF YOU SIT AROUND LIKE THAT ALL THE TIME, YOU'LL GET FAT.
UH-HUH.
SHOCK
MI-TAMA-SAN... WHAT ABOUT YOU?
Soldier Roles
As I thought, I'm amazing!
IF YOU'RE GOING TO CHANGE, TAKE OFF YOUR UNDER-GARMENTS.
How about no.

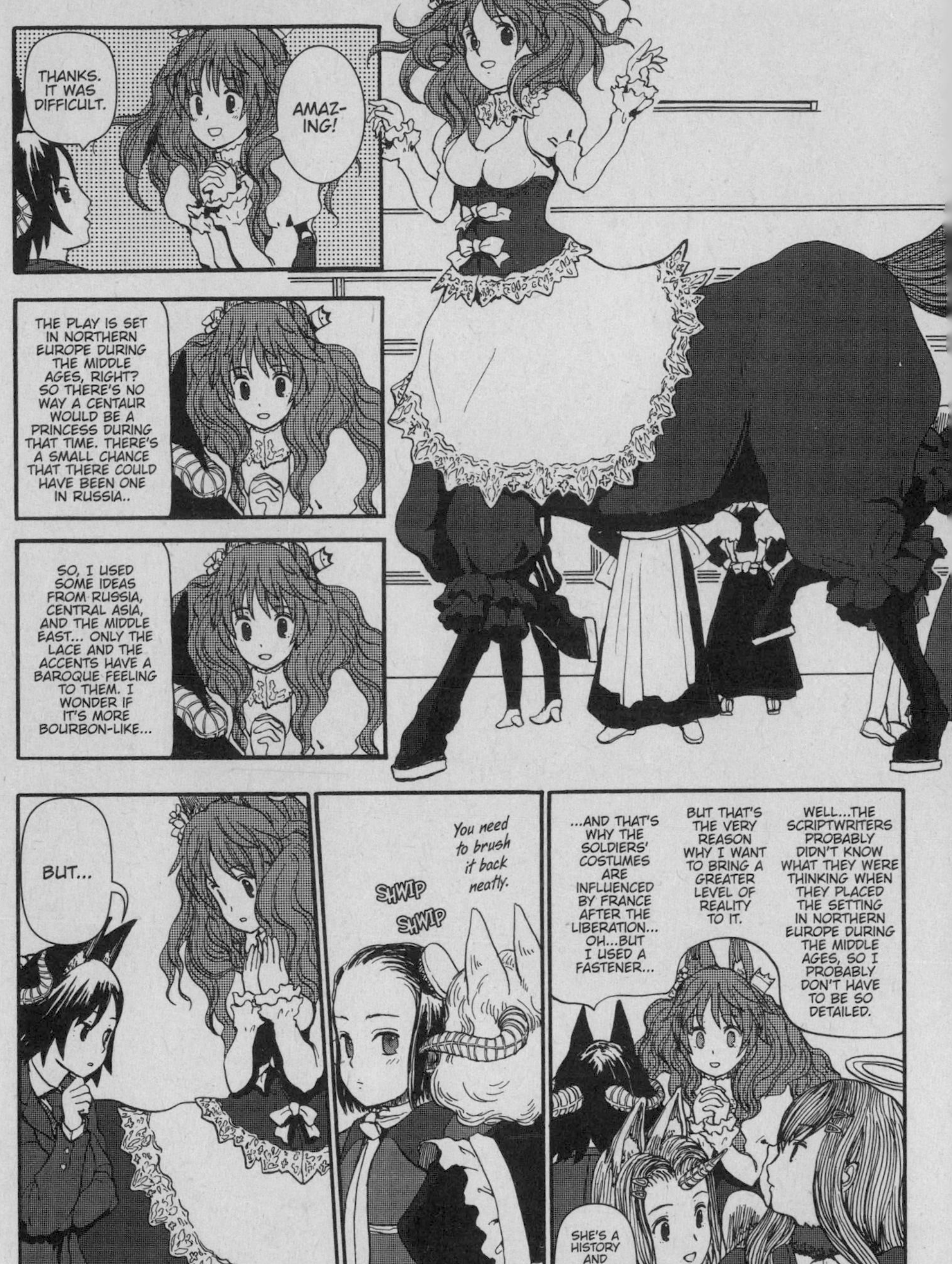
AMAZ-ING!
THANKS. IT WAS DIFFICULT.
THE PLAY IS SET IN NORTHERN EUROPE DURING THE MIDDLE AGES, RIGHT? SO THERE'S NO WAY A CENTAUR WOULD BE A PRINCESS DURING THAT TIME. THERE'S A SMALL CHANCE THAT THERE COULD HAVE BEEN ONE IN RUSSIA..
SO, I USED SOME IDEAS FROM RUSSIA, CENTRAL ASIA, AND THE MIDDLE EAST... ONLY THE LACE AND THE ACCENTS HAVE A BAROQUE FEELING TO THEM. I WONDER IF IT'S MORE BOURBON-LIKE...
WELL...THE SCRIPTWRITERS PROBABLY DIDN'T KNOW WHAT THEY WERE THINKING WHEN THEY PLACED THE SETTING IN NORTHERN EUROPE DURING THE MIDDLE AGES, SO I PROBABLY DON'T HAVE TO BE SO DETAILED.
BUT THAT'S THE VERY REASON WHY I WANT TO BRING A GREATER LEVEL OF REALITY TO IT.
...AND THAT'S WHY THE SOLDIERS' COSTUMES ARE INFLUENCED BY FRANCE AFTER THE LIBERATION... OH...BUT I USED A FASTENER...
SHE'S A HISTORY AND COSTUME GEEK. THIS TALK COULD TAKE ALL DAY.
You need to brush it back neatly.
SHWIP
SHWIP
BUT...

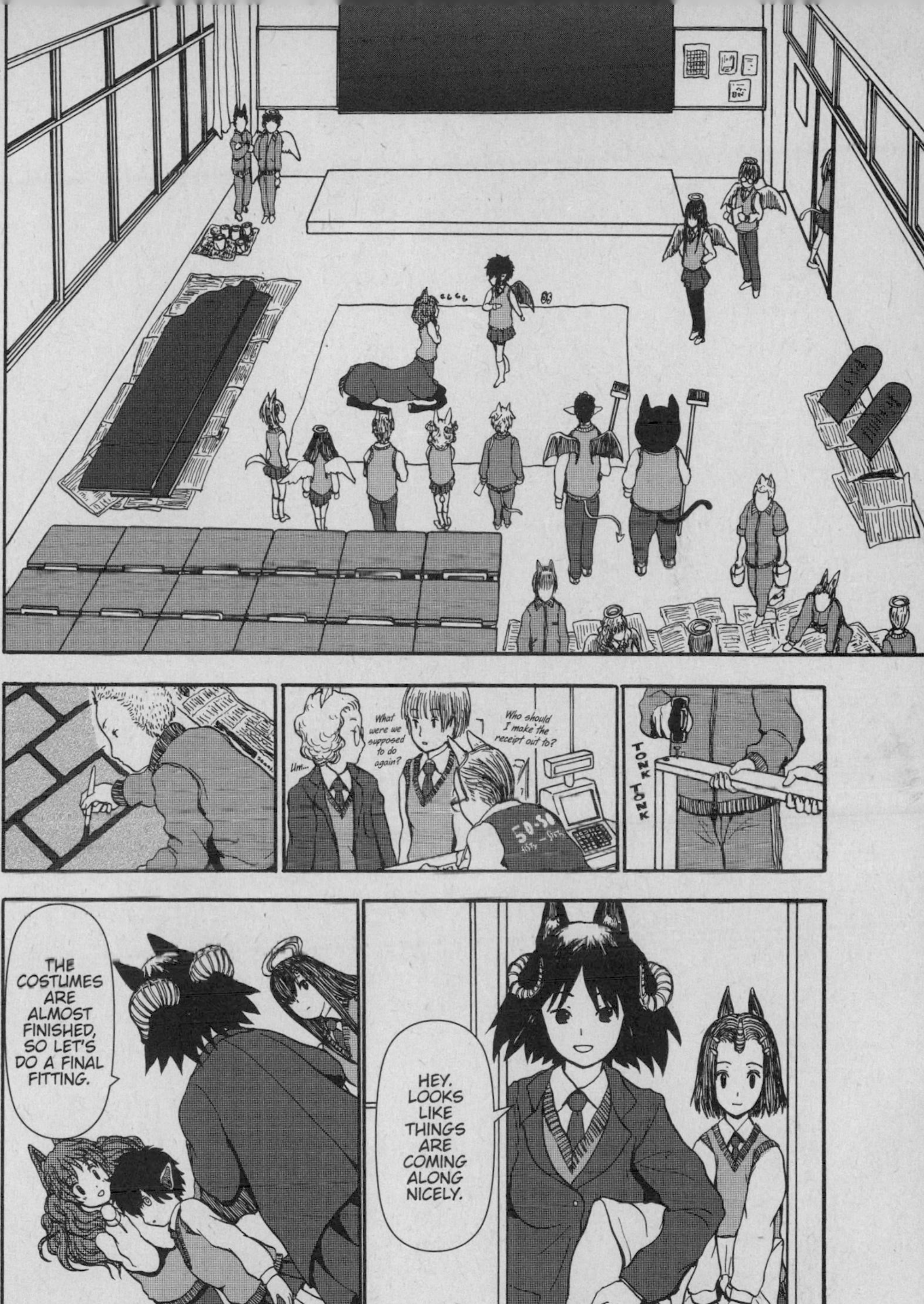
TONK TONK
Who should I make the receipt out to?
What were we supposed to do again?
Um...
HEY. LOOKS LIKE THINGS ARE COMING ALONG NICELY.
THE COSTUMES ARE ALMOST FINISHED, SO LET'S DO A FINAL FITTING.

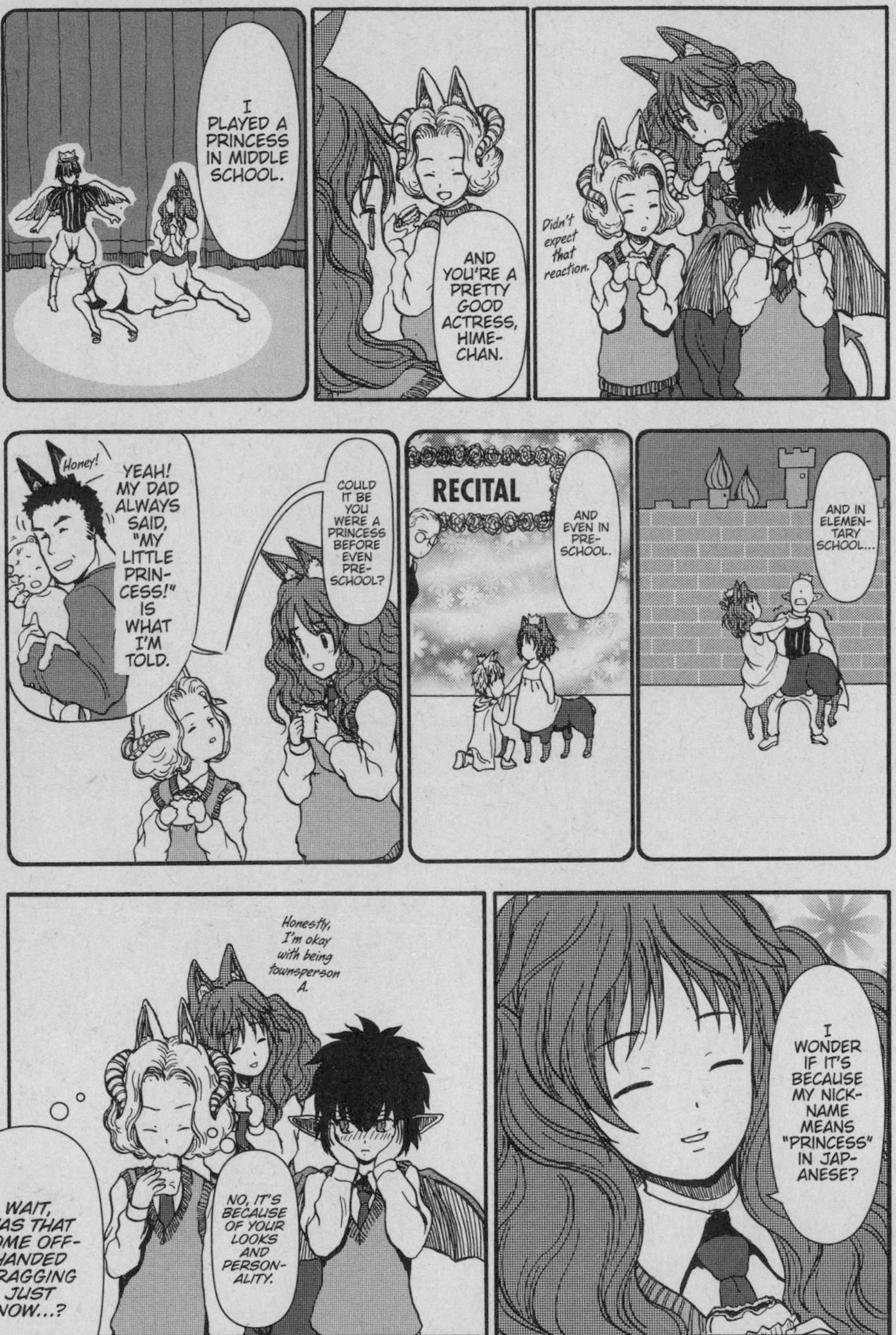
Didn't expect that reaction.
AND YOU'RE A PRETTY GOOD ACTRESS, HIME-CHAN.
I PLAYED A PRINCESS IN MIDDLE SCHOOL.
AND IN ELEMENTARY SCHOOL...
RECITAL
AND EVEN IN PRE-SCHOOL.
COULD IT BE YOU WERE A PRINCESS BEFORE EVEN PRE-SCHOOL?
Honey!
YEAH! MY DAD ALWAYS SAID, "MY LITTLE PRIN-CESS!" IS WHAT I'M TOLD.
I WONDER IF IT'S BECAUSE MY NICK-NAME MEANS "PRINCESS" IN JAP-ANESE?
Honestly, I'm okay with being townsperson A.
NO, IT'S BECAUSE OF YOUR LOOKS AND PERSON-ALITY.
WAIT, WAS THAT SOME OFF-HANDED BRAGGING JUST NOW...?

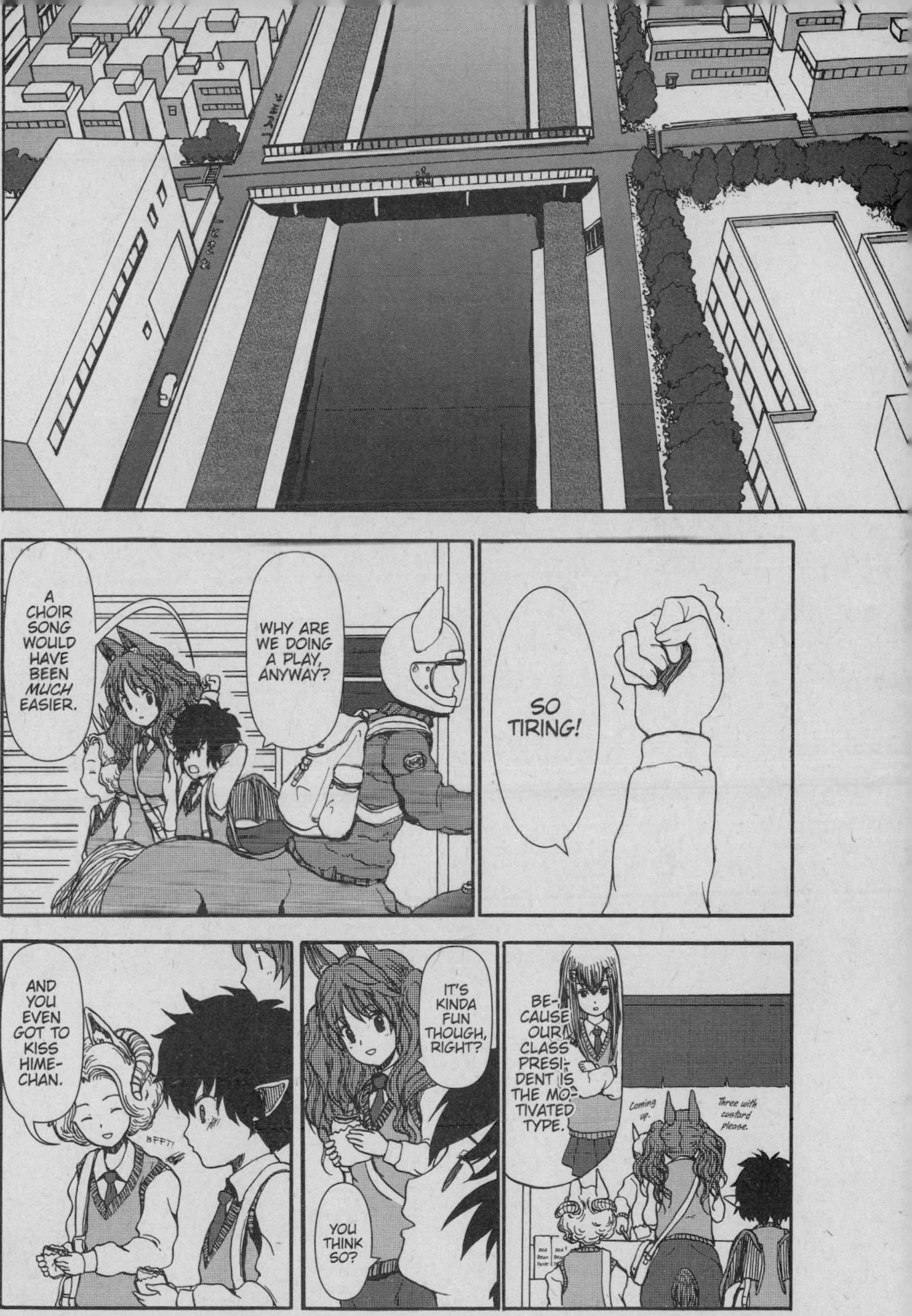
SO TIRING!
WHY ARE WE DOING A PLAY, ANYWAY?
A CHOIR SONG WOULD HAVE BEEN *MUCH* EASIER.
BE-CAUSE OUR CLASS PRESI-DENT IS THE MO-TIVATED TYPE.
Three with custard please.
Coming up.
IT'S KINDA FUN THOUGH, RIGHT?
YOU THINK SO?
AND YOU EVEN GOT TO KISS HIME-CHAN.
BFFT!

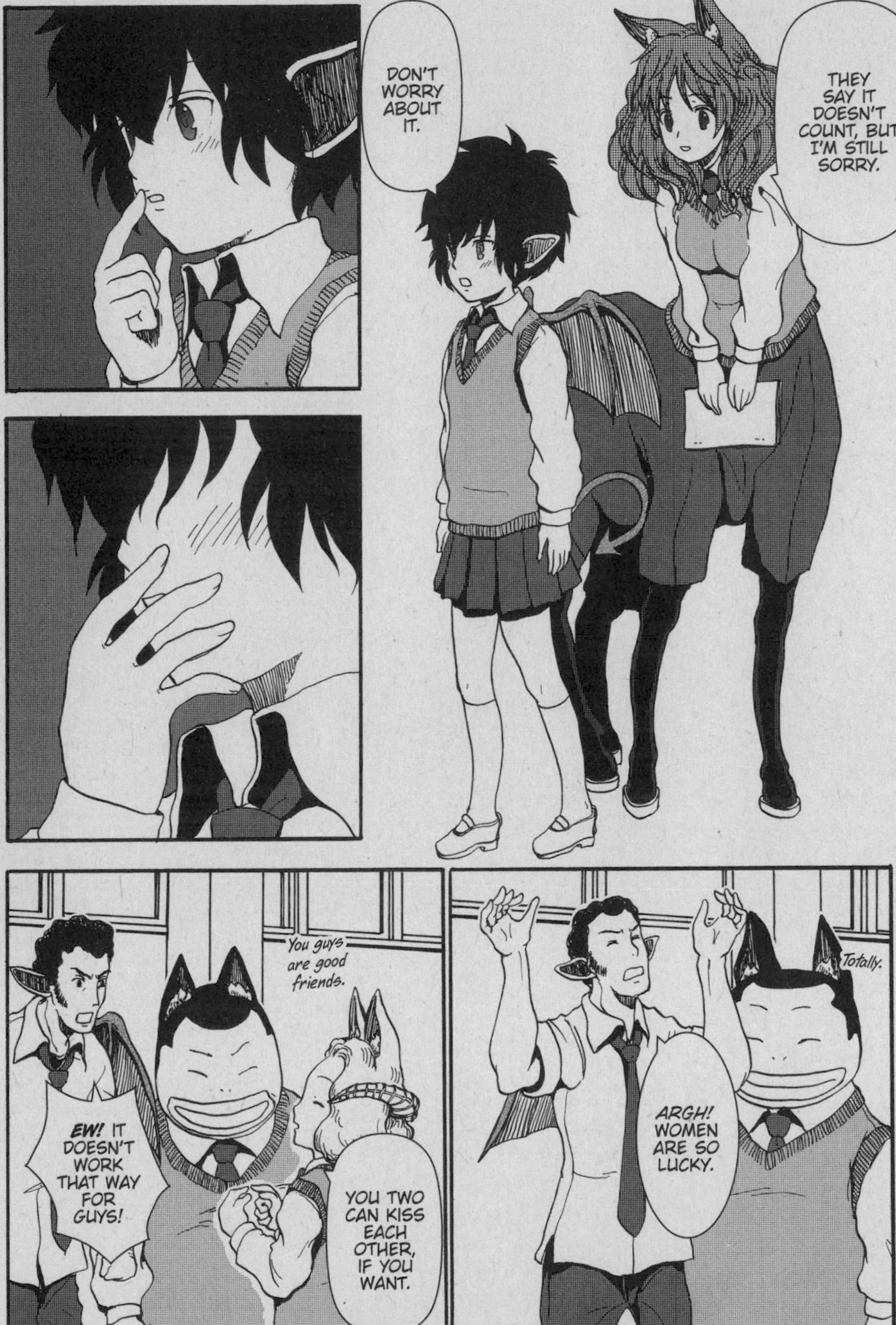
THEY SAY IT DOESN'T COUNT, BUT I'M STILL SORRY.
DON'T WORRY ABOUT IT.
YOU TWO CAN KISS EACH OTHER, IF YOU WANT.
EW! IT DOESN'T WORK THAT WAY FOR GUYS!
You guys are good friends.
ARGH! WOMEN ARE SO LUCKY.
Totally.

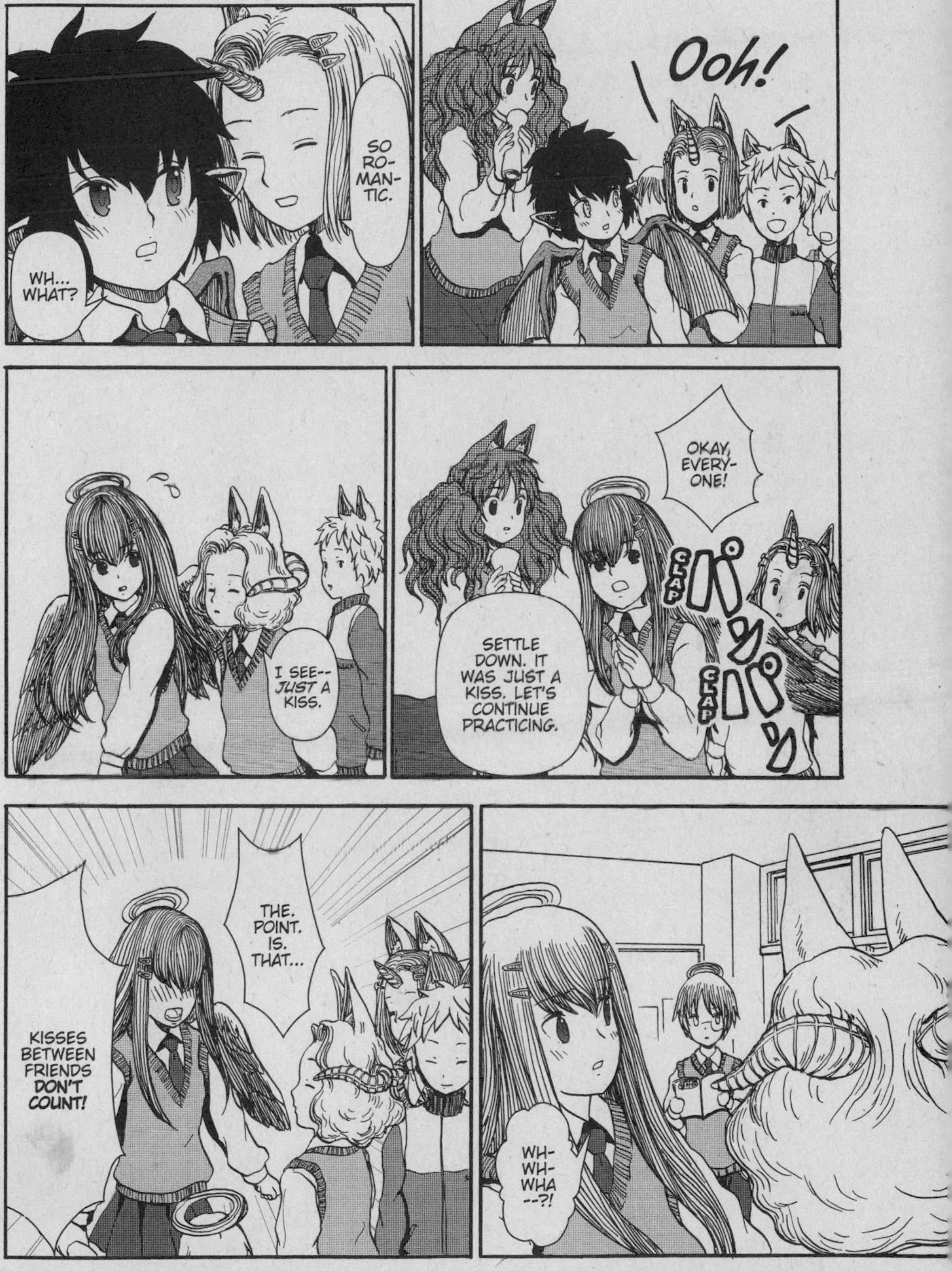
Ooh!
SO ROMANTIC.
WH... WHAT?
OKAY, EVERYONE!
CLAP
CLAP
パンパン
SETTLE DOWN. IT WAS JUST A KISS. LET'S CONTINUE PRACTICING.
I SEE-- *JUST* A KISS.
WH-WH-WHA--?!
THE. POINT. IS. THAT...
KISSES BETWEEN FRIENDS **DON'T COUNT!**

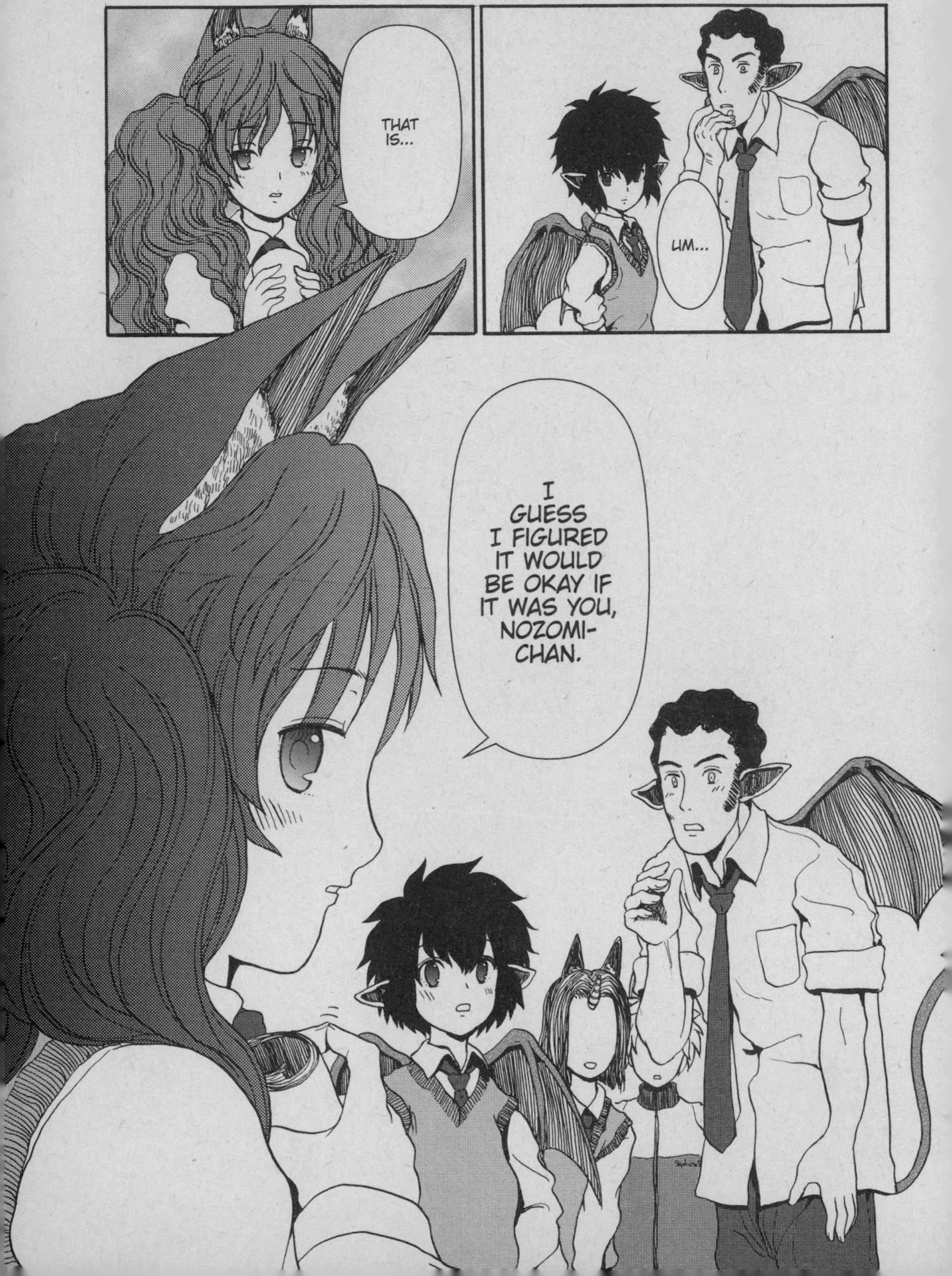
UM...
THAT IS...
I GUESS I FIGURED IT WOULD BE OKAY IF IT WAS YOU, NOZOMI-CHAN.

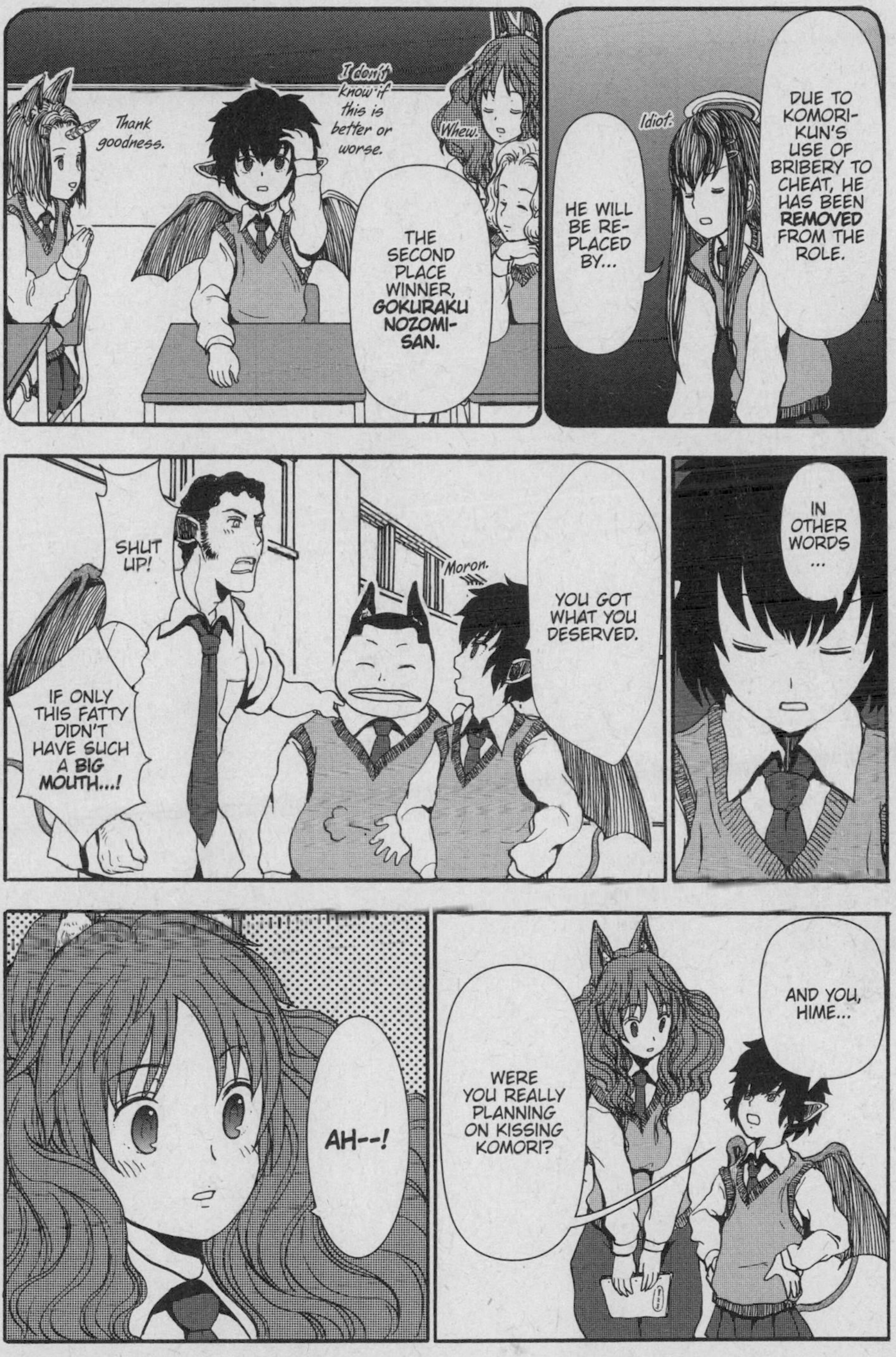
DUE TO KOMORI-KUN'S USE OF BRIBERY TO CHEAT, HE HAS BEEN REMOVED FROM THE ROLE.
Idiot.
HE WILL BE RE-PLACED BY...
THE SECOND PLACE WINNER, GOKURAKU NOZOMI-SAN.
Whew.
I don't know if this is better or worse.
Thank goodness.
IN OTHER WORDS...
YOU GOT WHAT YOU DESERVED.
Moron.
SHUT UP!
IF ONLY THIS FATTY DIDN'T HAVE SUCH A BIG MOUTH...!
AND YOU, HIME...
WERE YOU REALLY PLANNING ON KISSING KOMORI?
AH--!

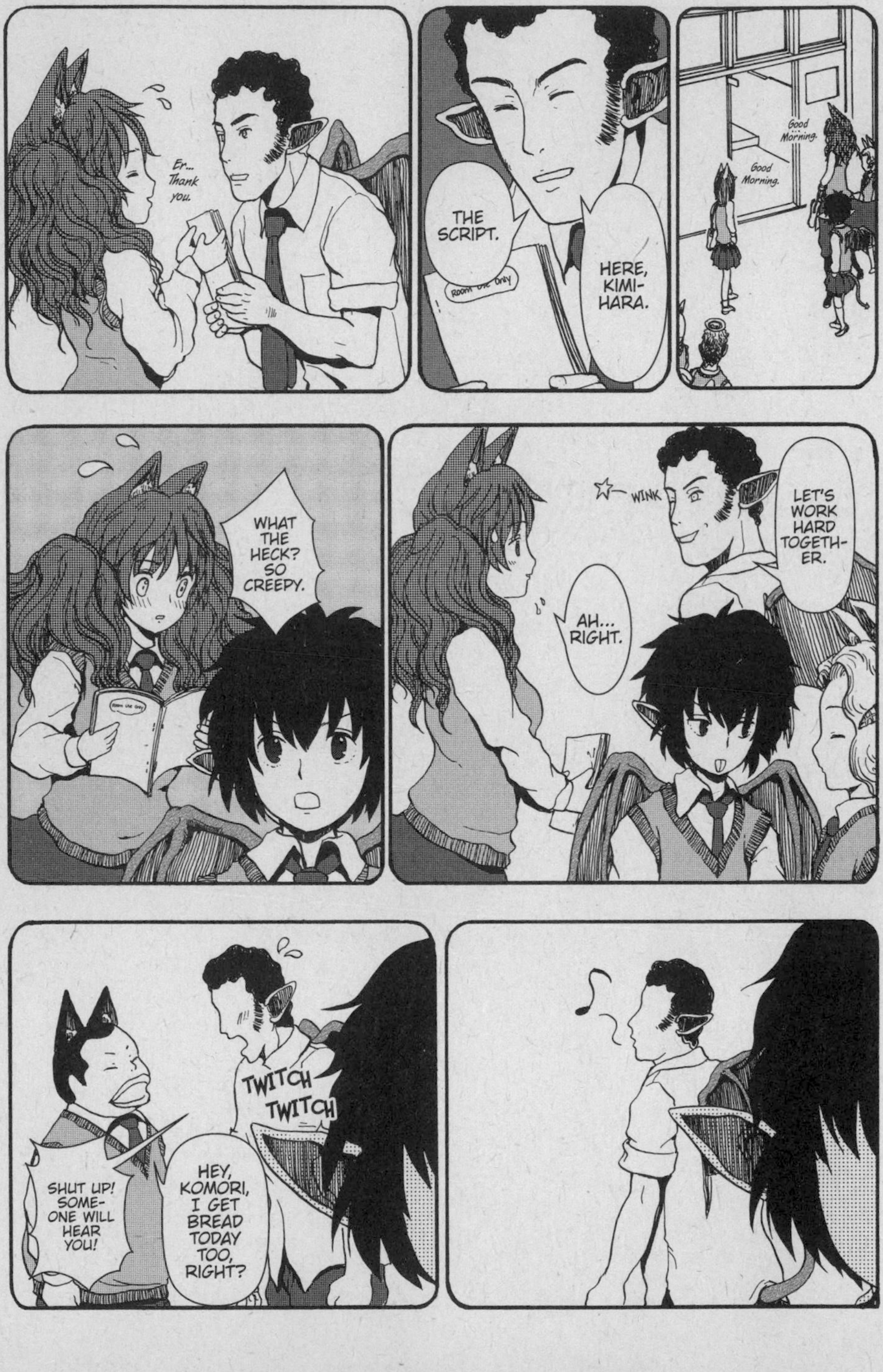
Good Morning.
Good Morning.
HERE, KIMI-HARA.
THE SCRIPT.
Er... Thank you.
WINK
LET'S WORK HARD TOGETH-ER.
AH... RIGHT.
WHAT THE HECK? SO CREEPY.
HEY, KOMORI, I GET BREAD TODAY TOO, RIGHT?
TWITCH TWITCH
SHUT UP! SOME-ONE WILL HEAR YOU!

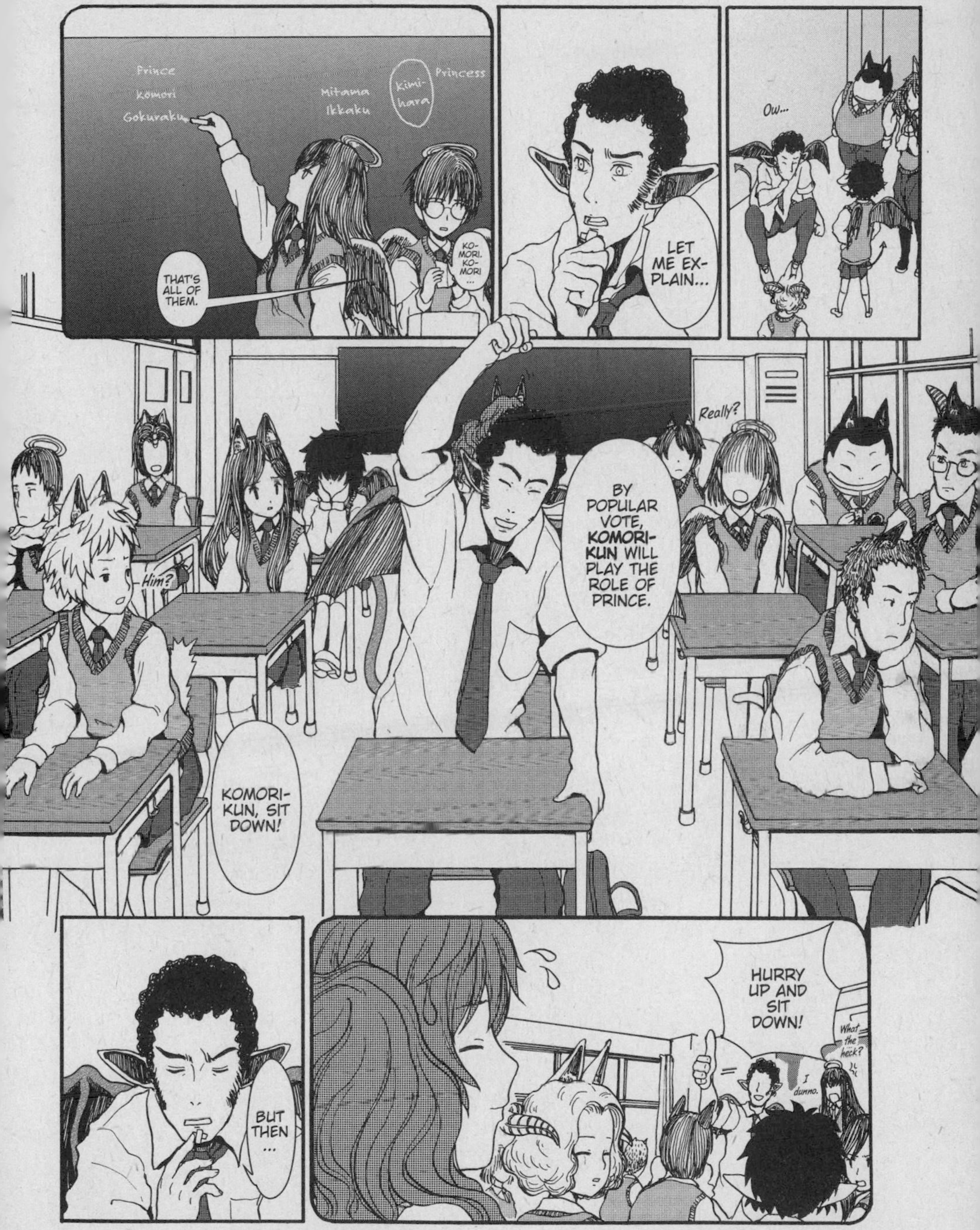
Ow...
LET ME EX-PLAIN...
Prince
Komori
Gokuraku
Princess
Mitama
Ikkaku
kimi-hara
KO-MORI. KO-MORI ...
THAT'S ALL OF THEM.
Really?
BY POPULAR VOTE, KOMORI-KUN WILL PLAY THE ROLE OF PRINCE.
Him?
KOMORI-KUN, SIT DOWN!
HURRY UP AND SIT DOWN!
What the heck?
I dunno.
BUT THEN ...

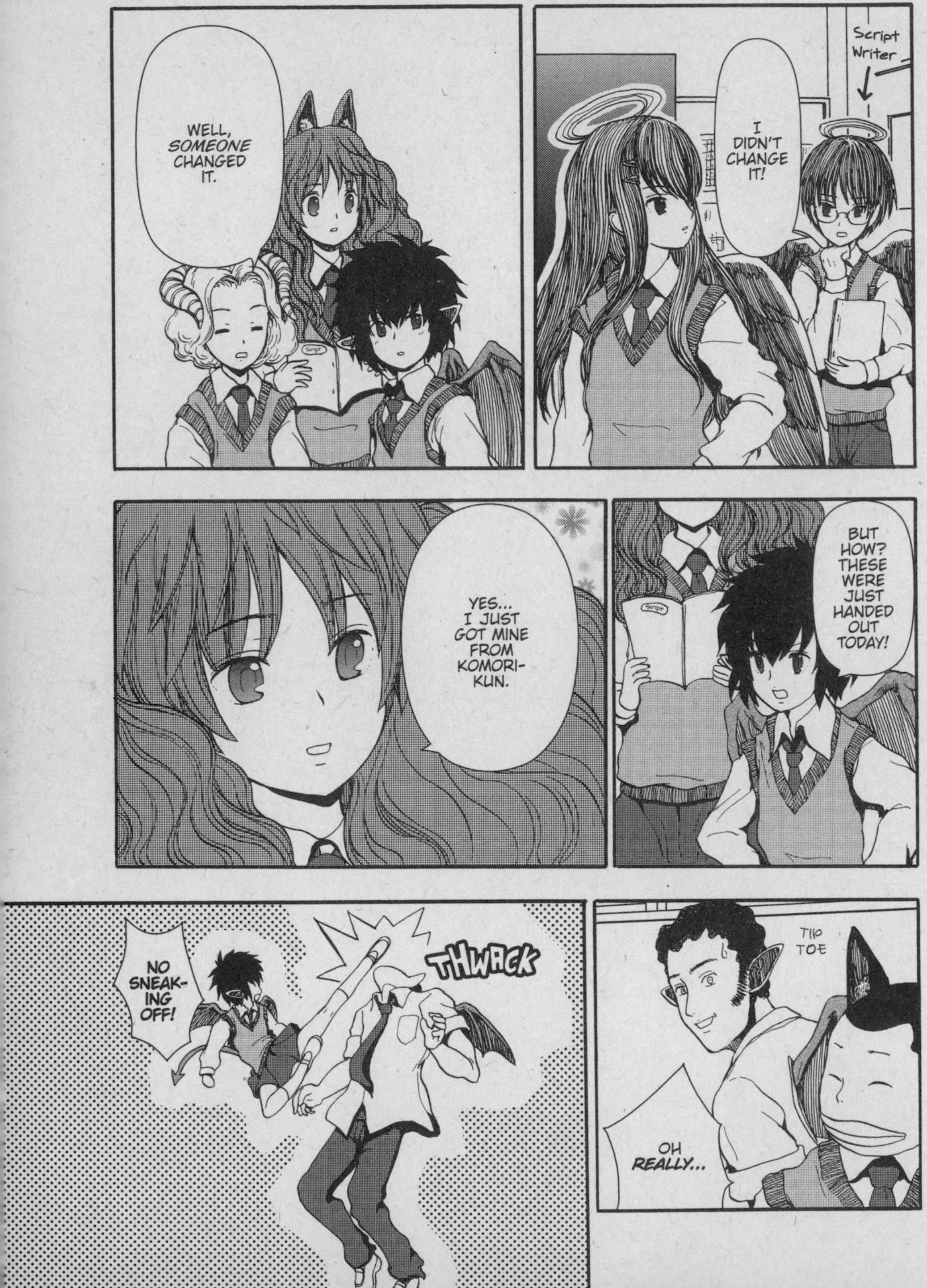
Script Writer
I DIDN'T CHANGE IT!
WELL, SOMEONE CHANGED IT.
BUT HOW? THESE WERE JUST HANDED OUT TODAY!
YES... I JUST GOT MINE FROM KOMORI-KUN.
TIP TOE
OH REALLY...
THWACK
NO SNEAKING OFF!

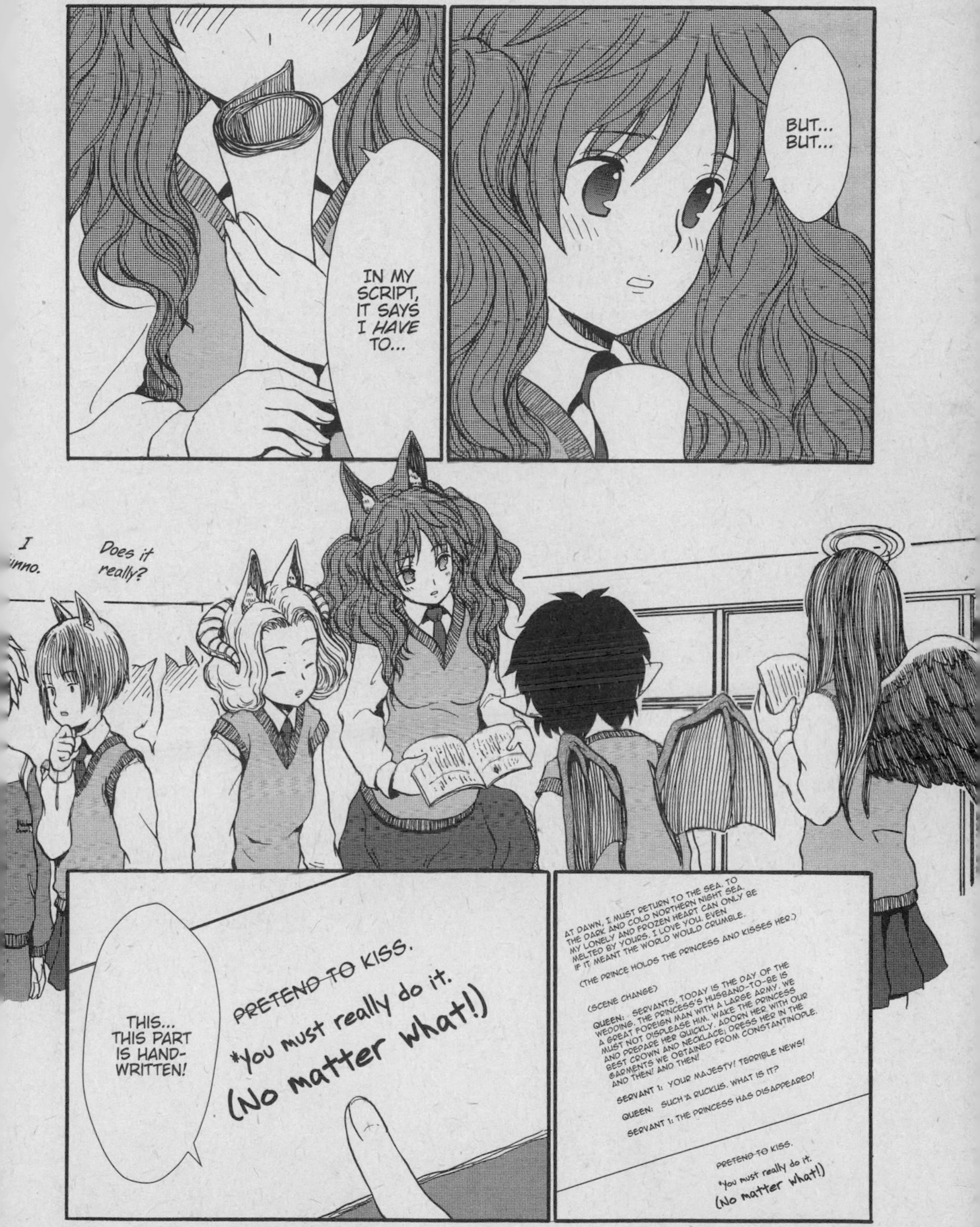

BUT... BUT...
IN MY SCRIPT, IT SAYS I HAVE TO...
Does it really?
I inno.
AT DAWN, I MUST RETURN TO THE SEA. TO THE DARK AND COLD NORTHERN NIGHT SEA. MY LONELY AND FROZEN HEART CAN ONLY BE MELTED BY YOURS. I LOVE YOU. EVEN IF IT MEANT THE WORLD WOULD CRUMBLE.
(THE PRINCE HOLDS THE PRINCESS AND KISSES HER.)
(SCENE CHANGE)
QUEEN: SERVANTS, TODAY IS THE DAY OF THE WEDDING. THE PRINCESS'S HUSBAND-TO-BE IS A GREAT FOREIGN MAN WITH A LARGE ARMY. WE MUST NOT DISPLEASE HIM. WAKE THE PRINCESS AND PREPARE HER QUICKLY. ADORN HER WITH OUR BEST CROWN AND NECKLACE; DRESS HER IN THE GARMENTS WE OBTAINED FROM CONSTANTINOPLE. AND THEN! AND THEN!
SERVANT 1: YOUR MAJESTY! TERRIBLE NEWS!
QUEEN: SUCH A RUCKUS. WHAT IS IT?
SERVANT 1: THE PRINCESS HAS DISAPPEARED!
~~PRETEND TO~~ KISS.
*You must really do it.
(No matter what!)
~~PRETEND TO~~ KISS.
*You must really do it.
(No matter what!)
THIS... THIS PART IS HAND-WRITTEN!

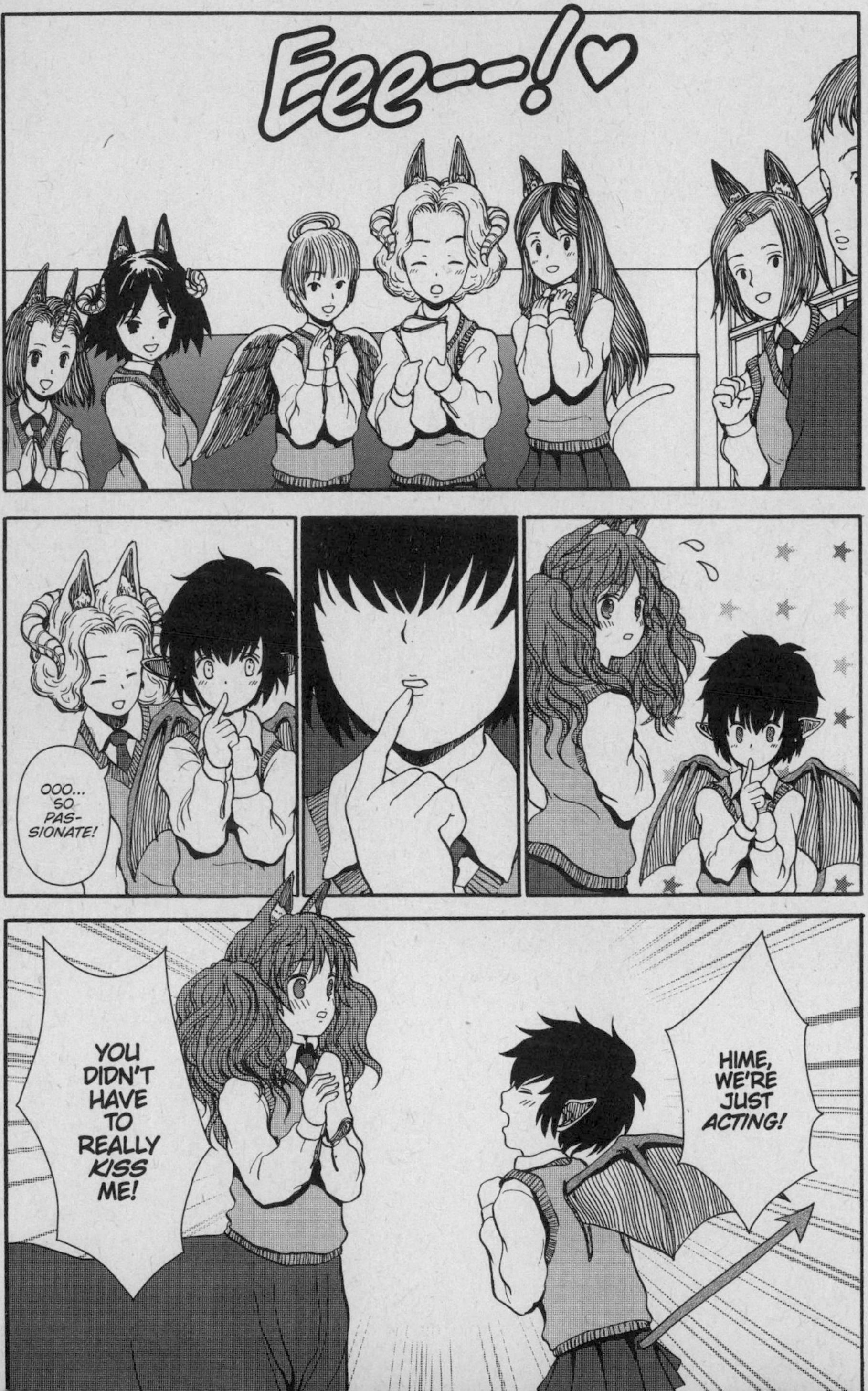
Eee---!♡
OOO... SO PAS-SIONATE!
HIME, WE'RE JUST ACTING!
YOU DIDN'T HAVE TO REALLY KISS ME!

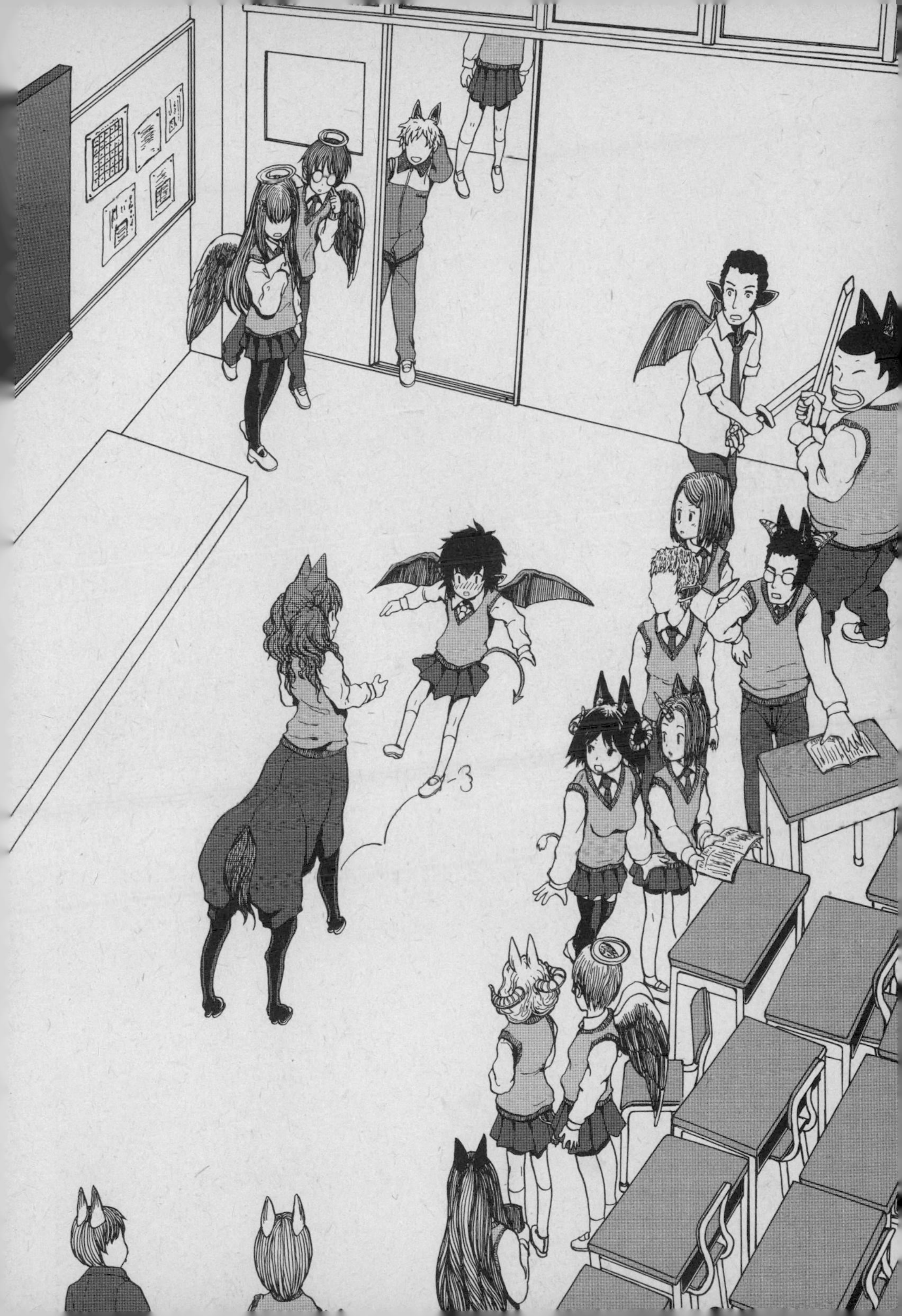

CHAPTER 1

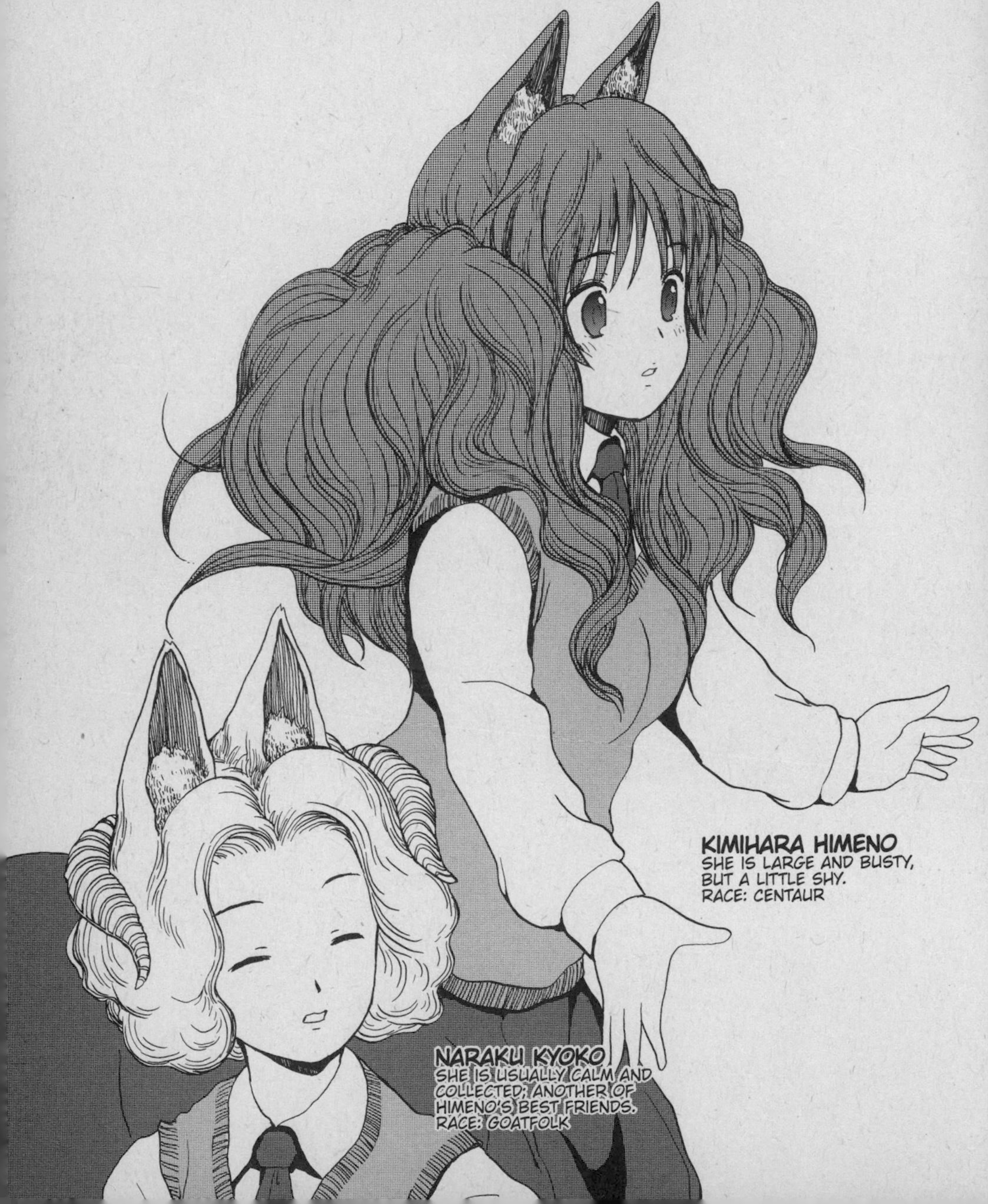
KIMIHARA HIMENO
SHE IS LARGE AND BUSTY, BUT A LITTLE SHY.
RACE: CENTAUR
NARAKU KYOKO
SHE IS USUALLY CALM AND COLLECTED; ANOTHER OF HIMENO'S BEST FRIENDS.
RACE: GOATFOLK

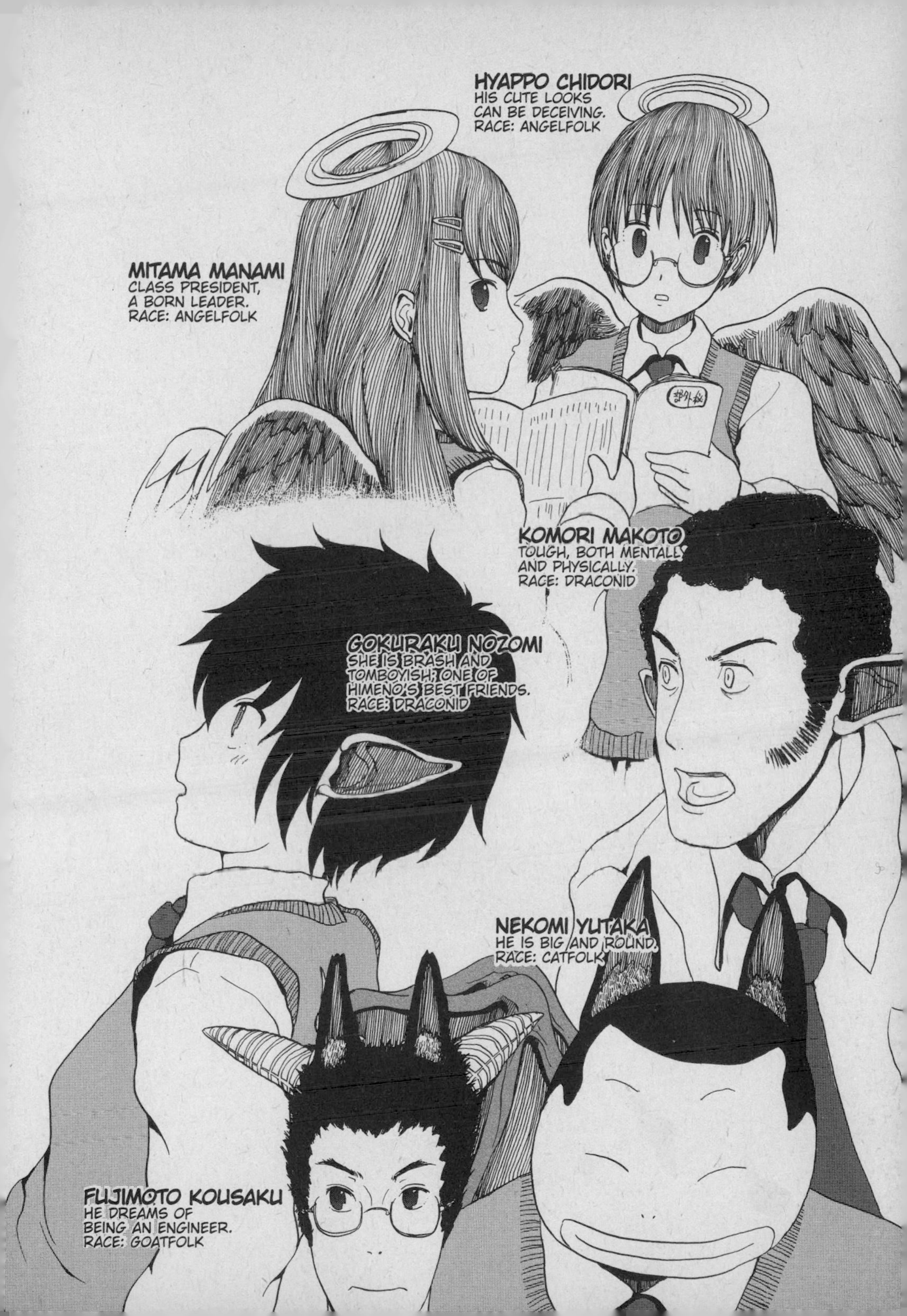
HYAPPO CHIDORI
HIS CUTE LOOKS CAN BE DECEIVING. RACE: ANGELFOLK
MITAMA MANAMI
CLASS PRESIDENT, A BORN LEADER. RACE: ANGELFOLK
KOMORI MAKOTO
TOUGH, BOTH MENTALLY AND PHYSICALLY. RACE: DRACONID
GOKURAKU NOZOMI
SHE IS BRASH AND TOMBOYISH; ONE OF HIMENO'S BEST FRIENDS. RACE: DRACONID
NEKOMI YUTAKA
HE IS BIG AND ROUND. RACE: CATFOLK
FUJIMOTO KOUSAKU
HE DREAMS OF BEING AN ENGINEER. RACE: GOATFOLK

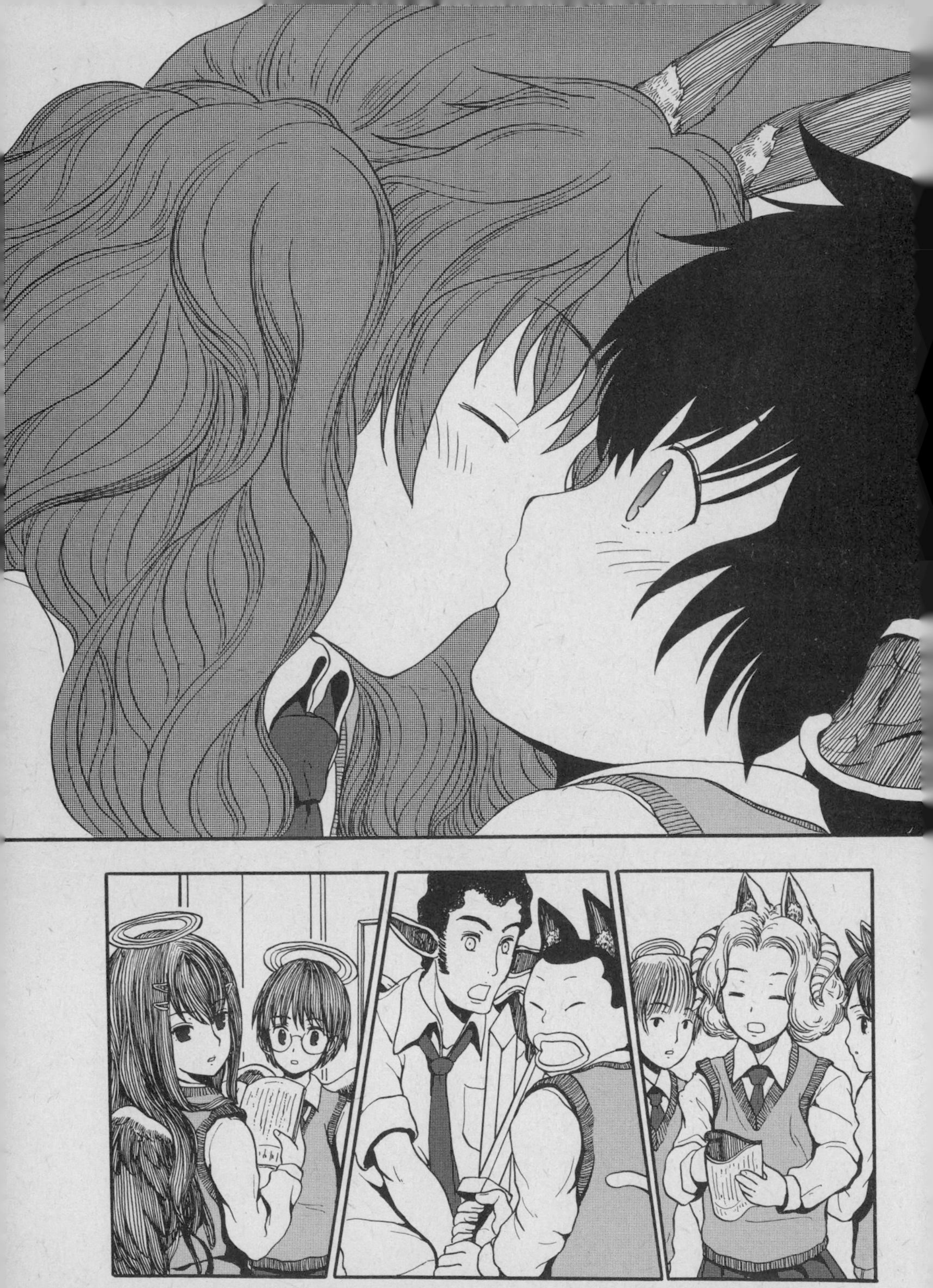

HOW ANGELFOLK UNDRESS

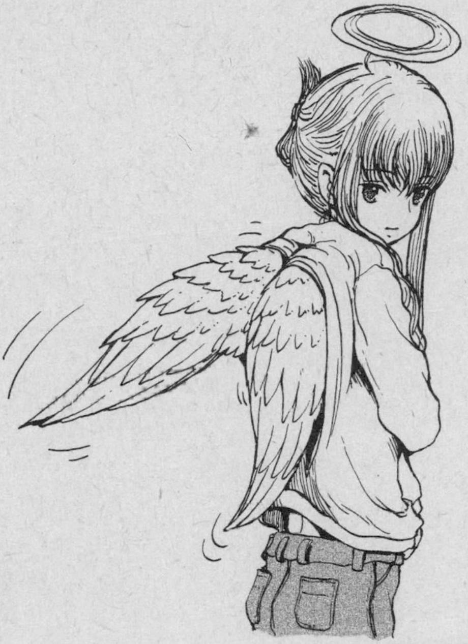

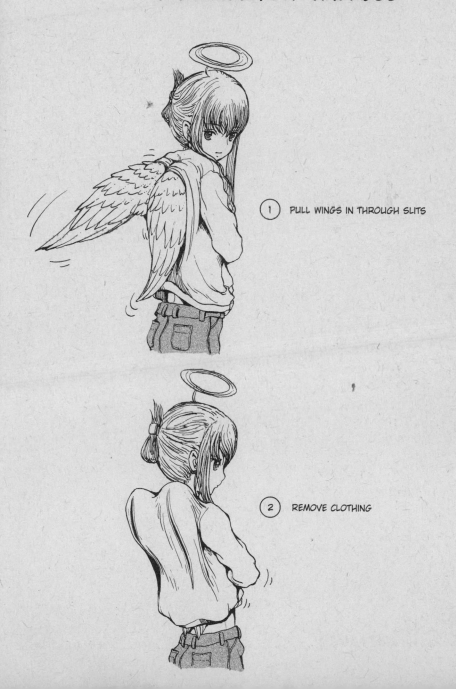

1. PULL WINGS IN THROUGH SLITS

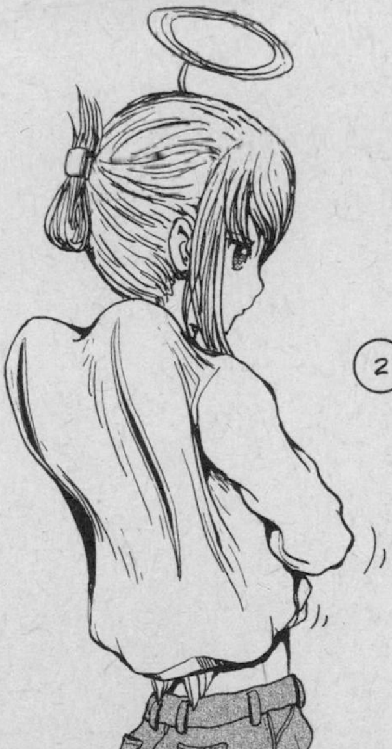

2. REMOVE CLOTHING

A Centaur's Life

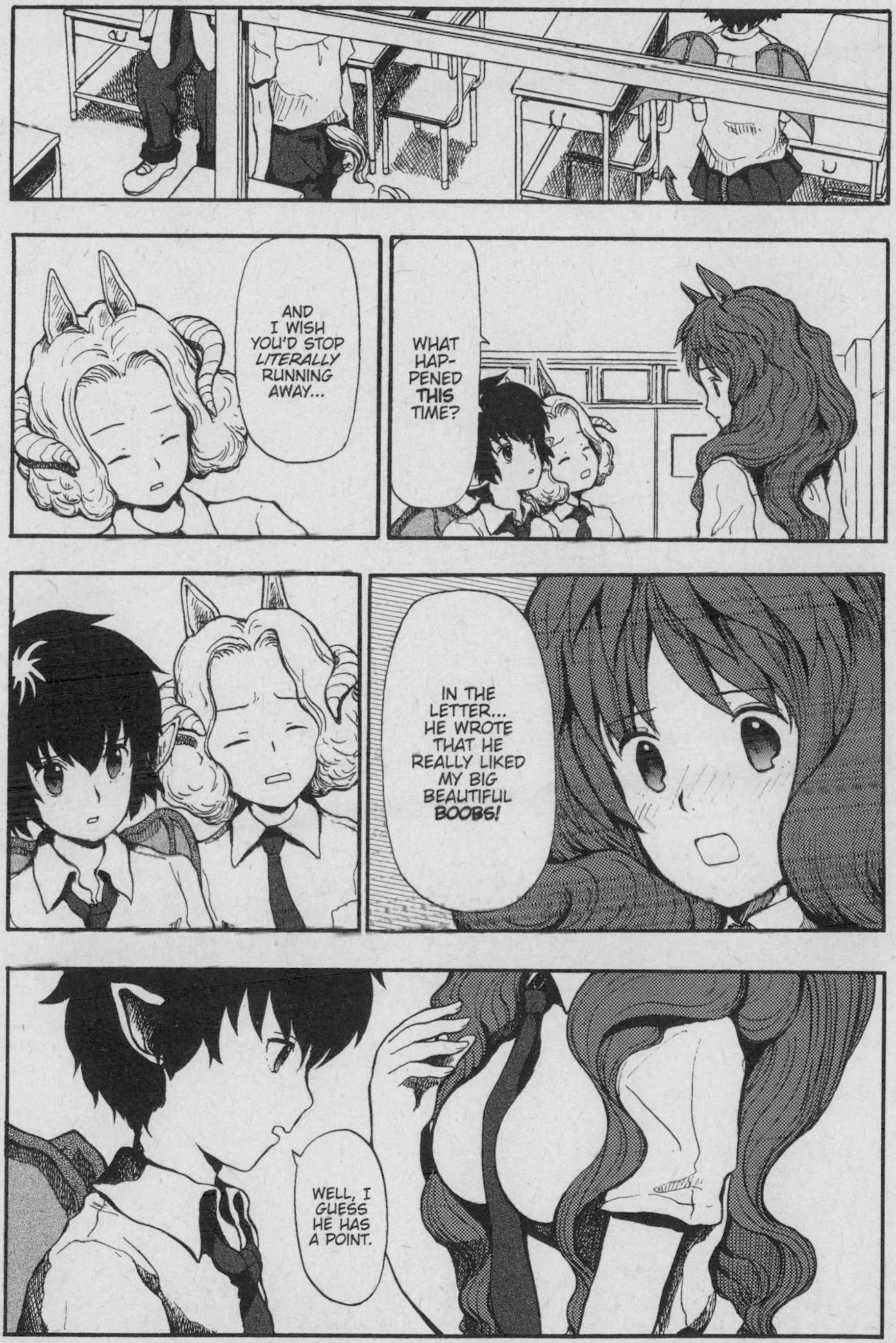
WHAT HAP-PENED THIS TIME?
AND I WISH YOU'D STOP *LITERALLY* RUNNING AWAY...
IN THE LETTER... HE WROTE THAT HE REALLY LIKED MY BIG BEAUTIFUL **BOOBS!**
WELL, I GUESS HE HAS A POINT.

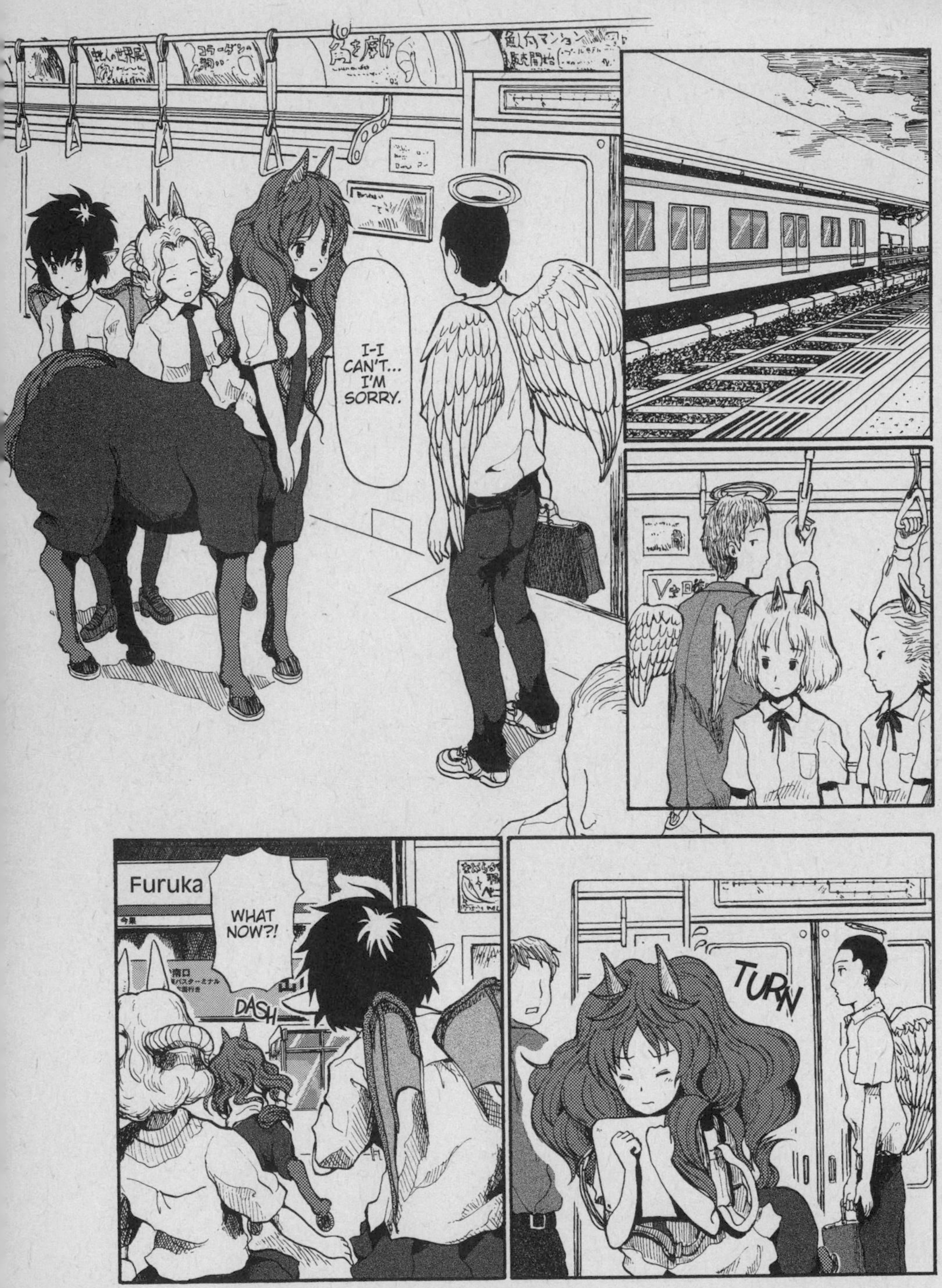
I-I CAN'T... I'M SORRY.
TURN
Furuka
WHAT NOW?!
DASH

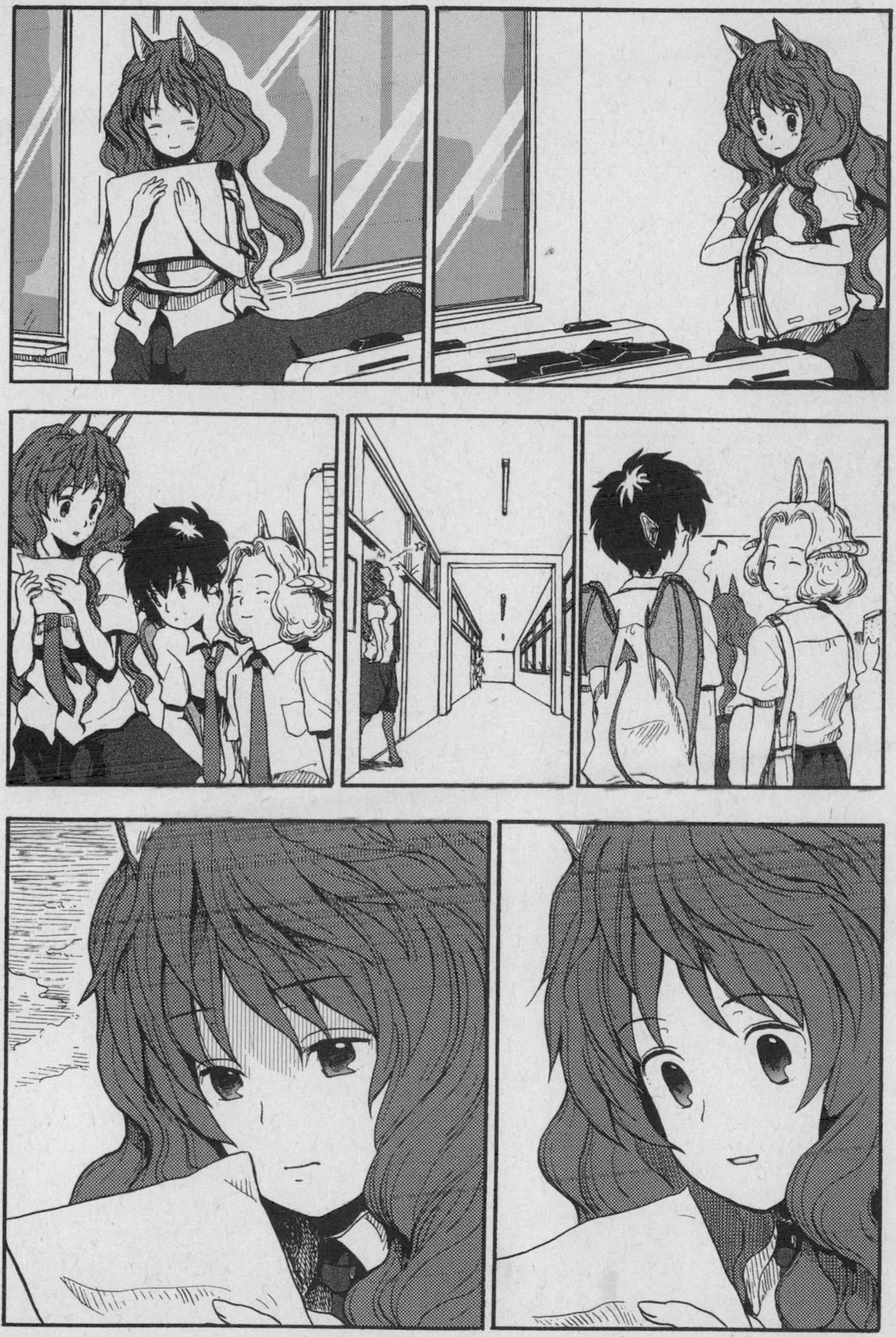

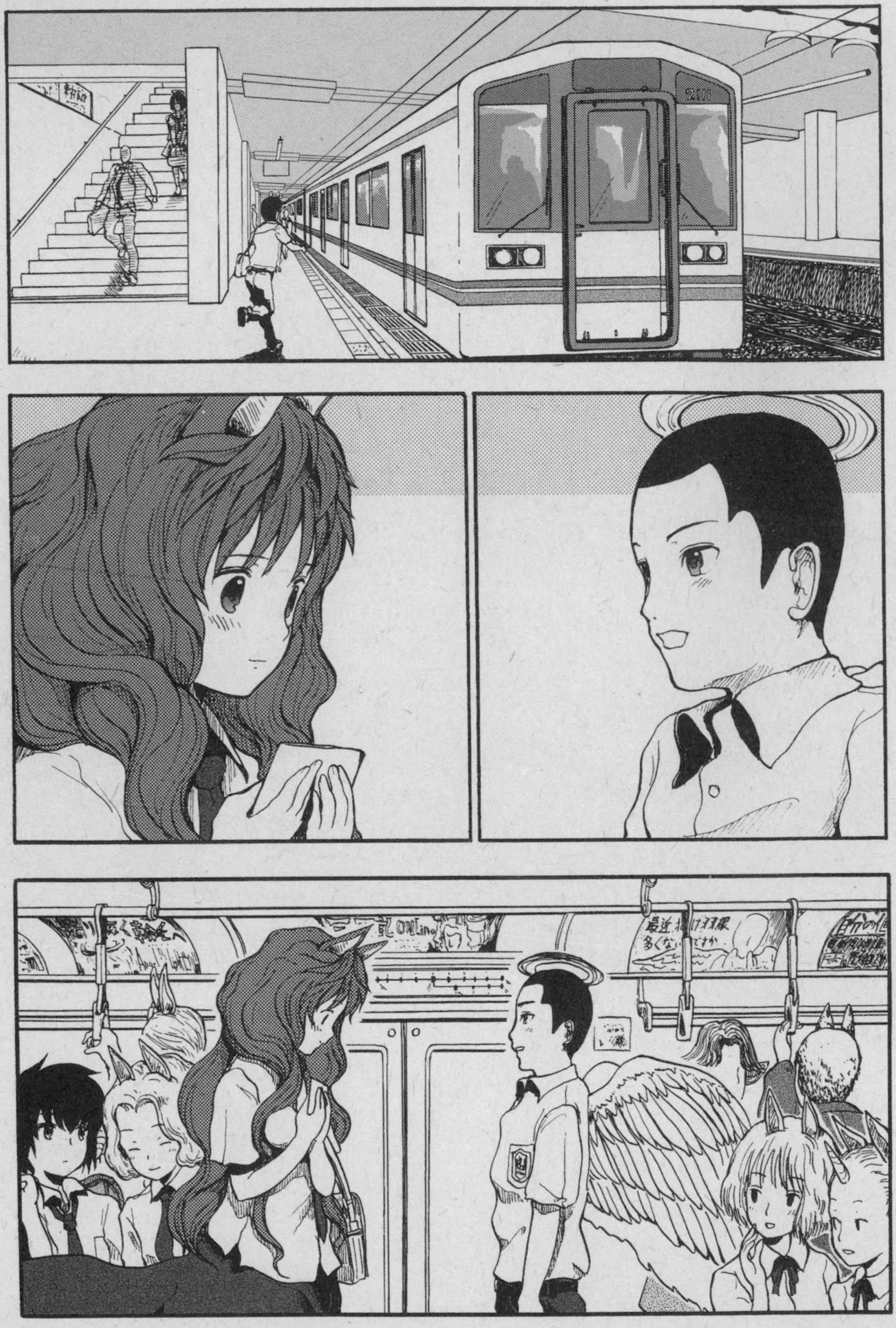

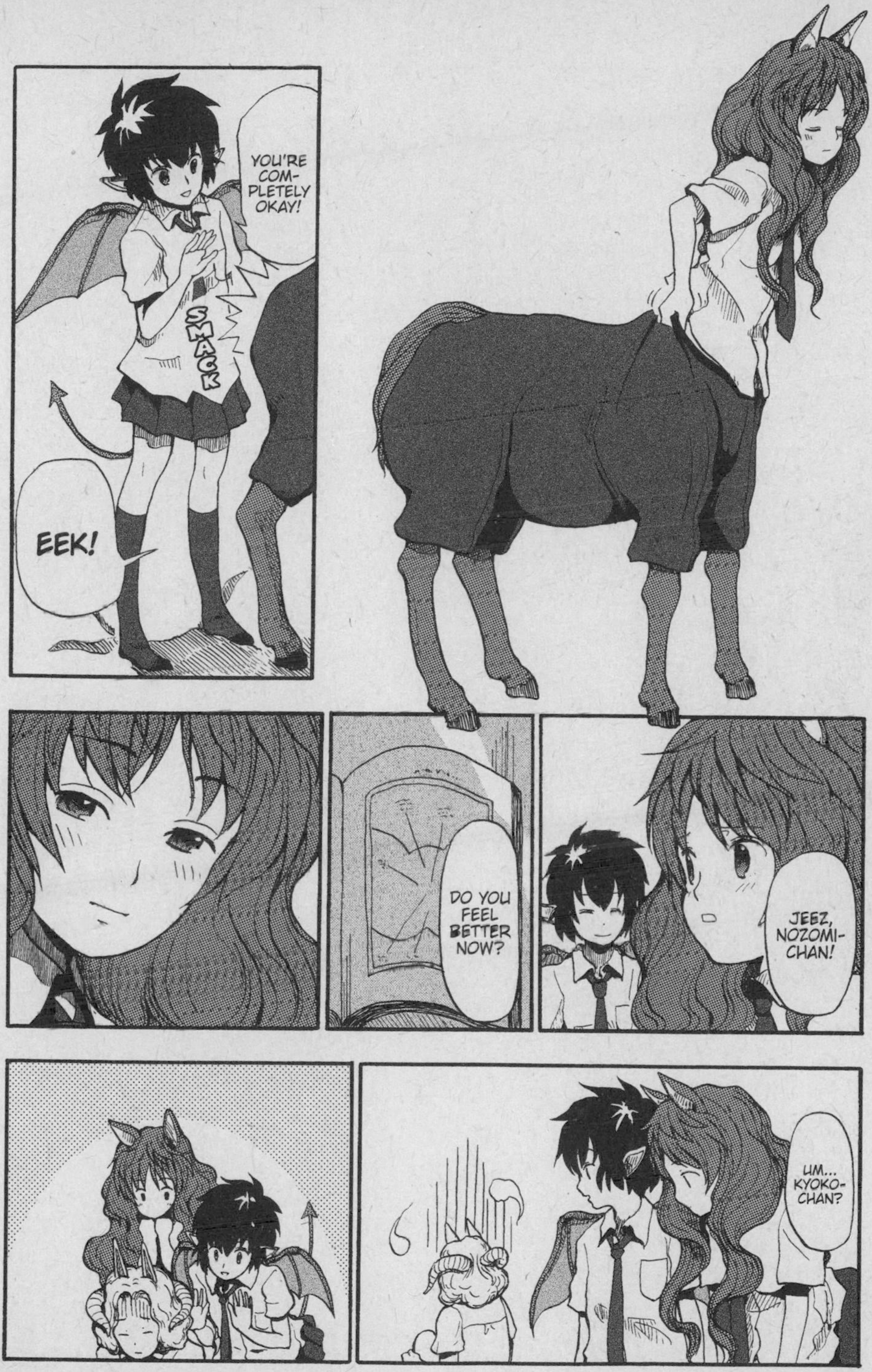
YOU'RE COM-PLETELY OKAY!
SMACK
EEK!
JEEZ, NOZOMI-CHAN!
DO YOU FEEL BETTER NOW?
UM... KYOKO-CHAN?

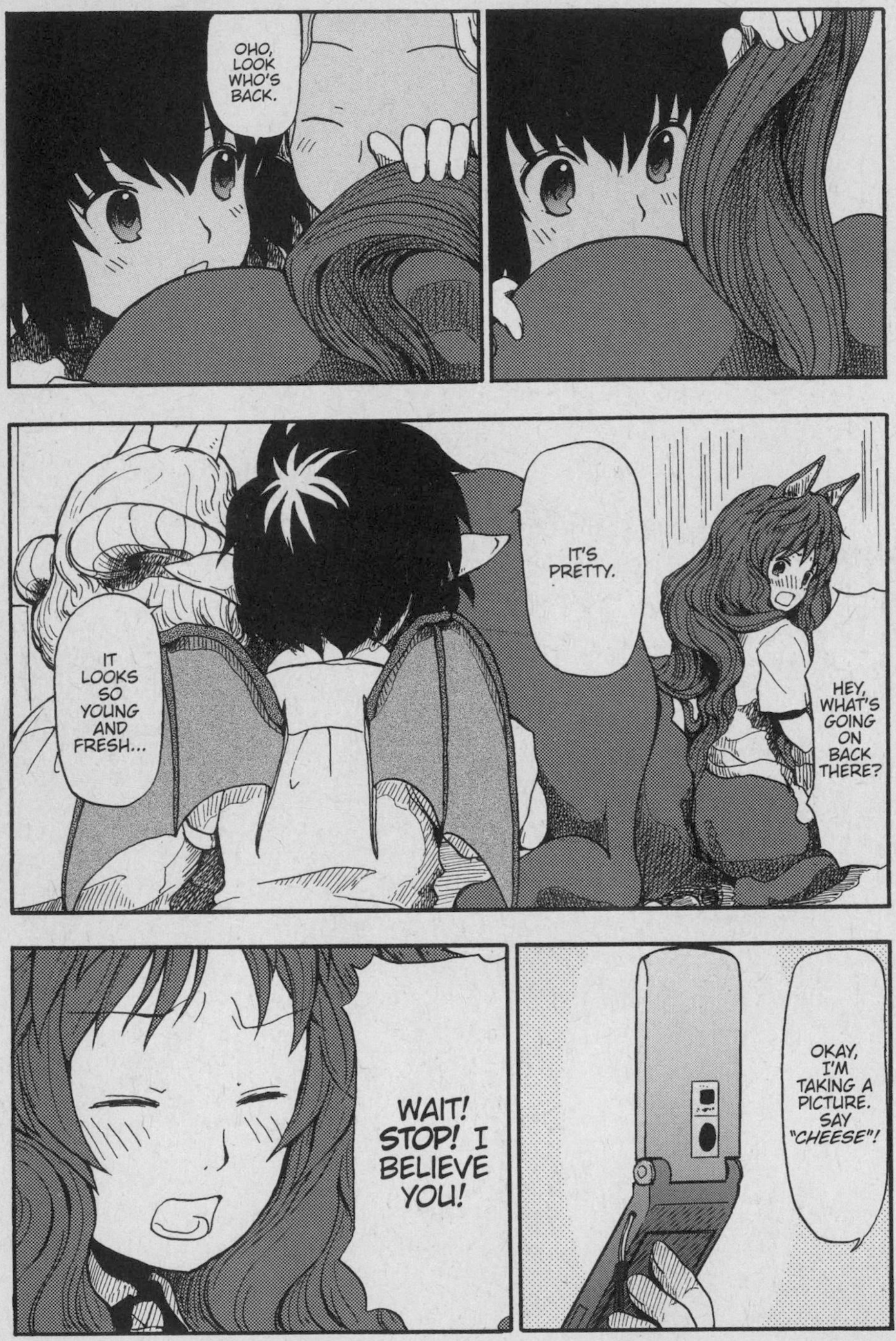
OHO, LOOK WHO'S BACK.
HEY, WHAT'S GOING ON BACK THERE?
IT'S PRETTY.
IT LOOKS SO YOUNG AND FRESH...
OKAY, I'M TAKING A PICTURE. SAY "CHEESE"!
WAIT! STOP! I BELIEVE YOU!

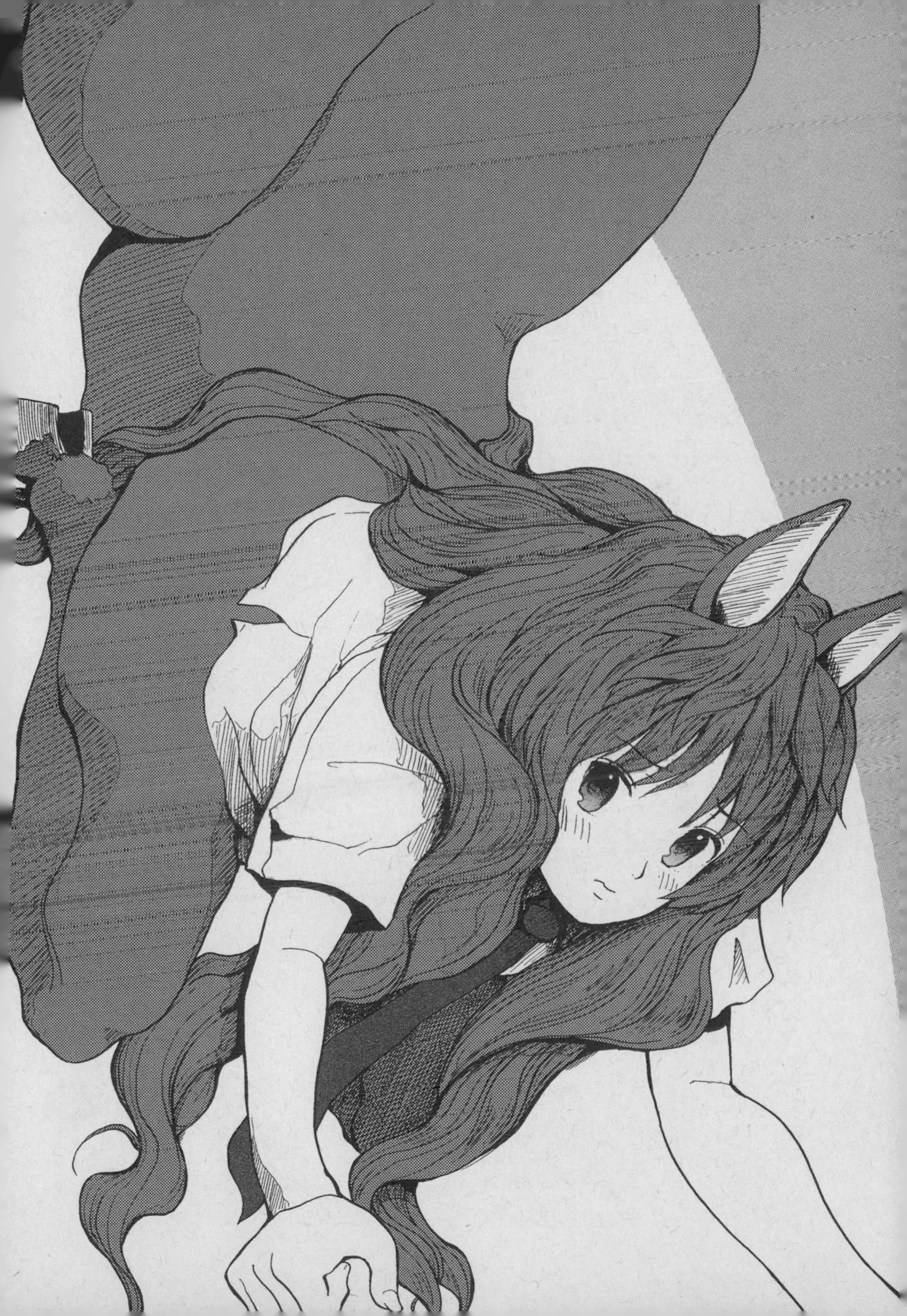

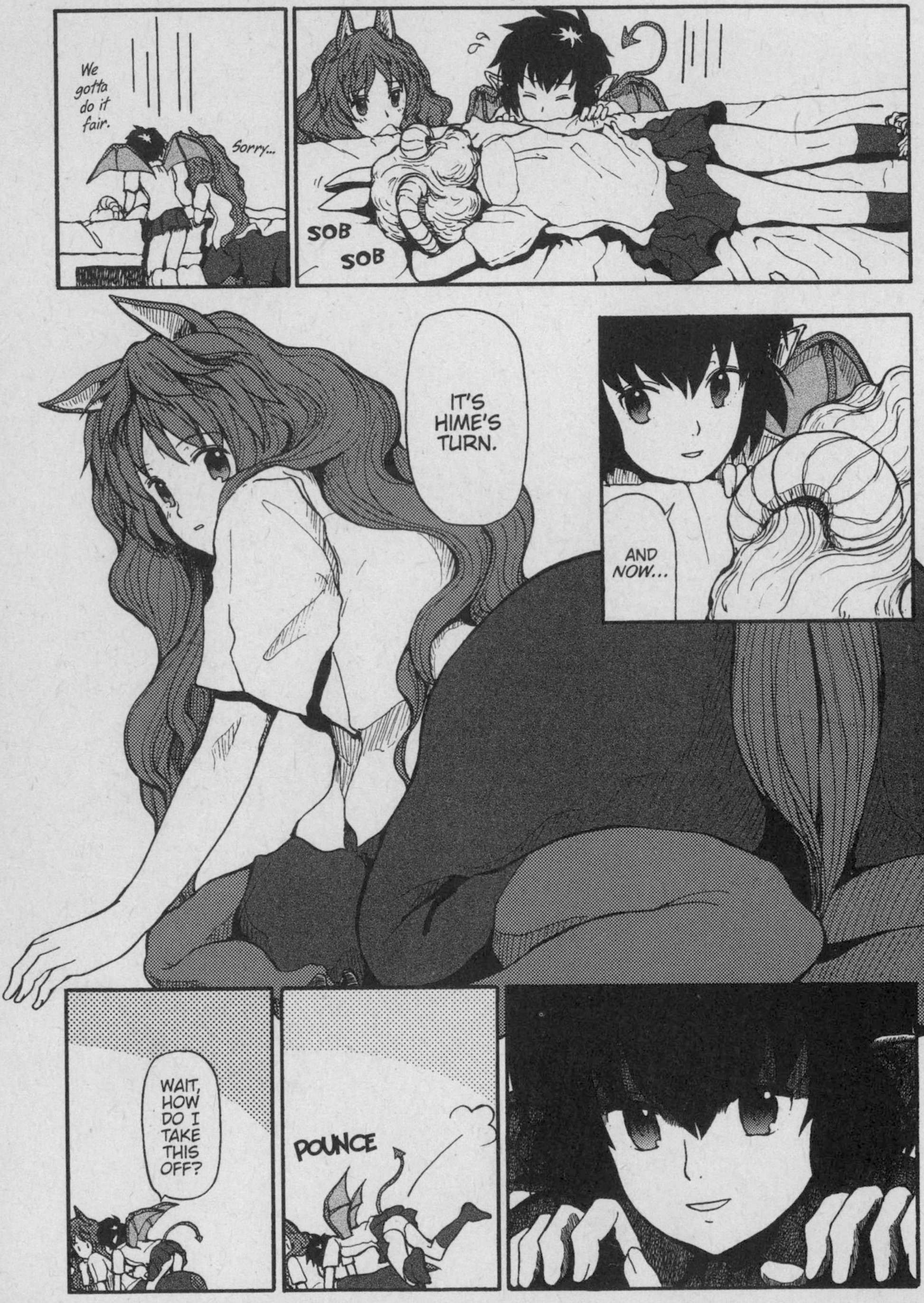
SOB
SOB
We gotta do it fair.
Sorry...
AND NOW...
IT'S HIME'S TURN.
POUNCE
WAIT, HOW DO I TAKE THIS OFF?

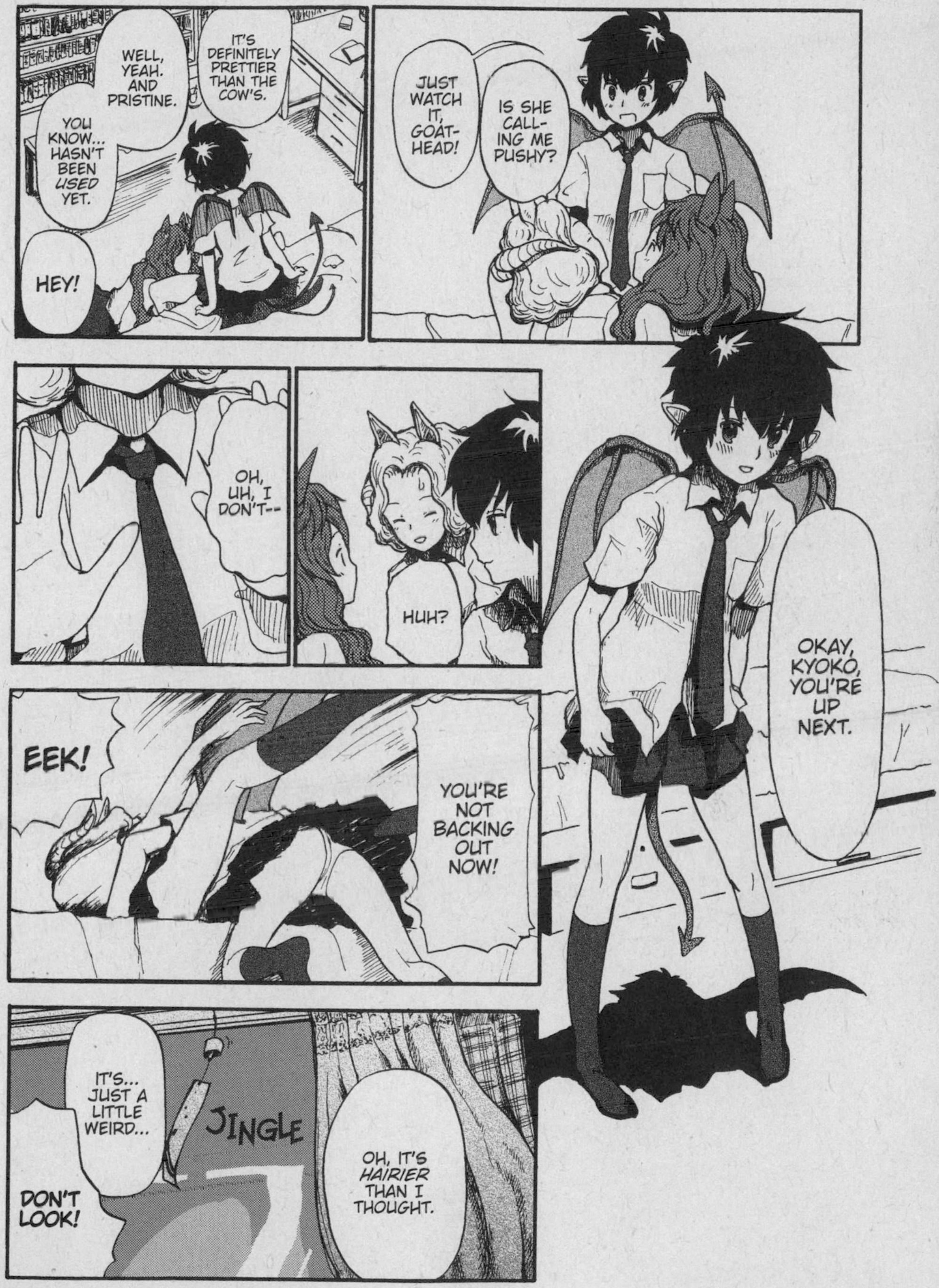
IS SHE CALLING ME PUSHY?
JUST WATCH IT, GOAT-HEAD!
IT'S DEFINITELY PRETTIER THAN THE COW'S.
WELL, YEAH. AND PRISTINE.
YOU KNOW... HASN'T BEEN *USED* YET.
HEY!
OKAY, KYOKO, YOU'RE UP NEXT.
HUH?
OH, UH, I DON'T--
YOU'RE NOT BACKING OUT NOW!
EEK!
OH, IT'S *HAIRIER* THAN I THOUGHT.
JINGLE
IT'S... JUST A LITTLE WEIRD...
DON'T LOOK!

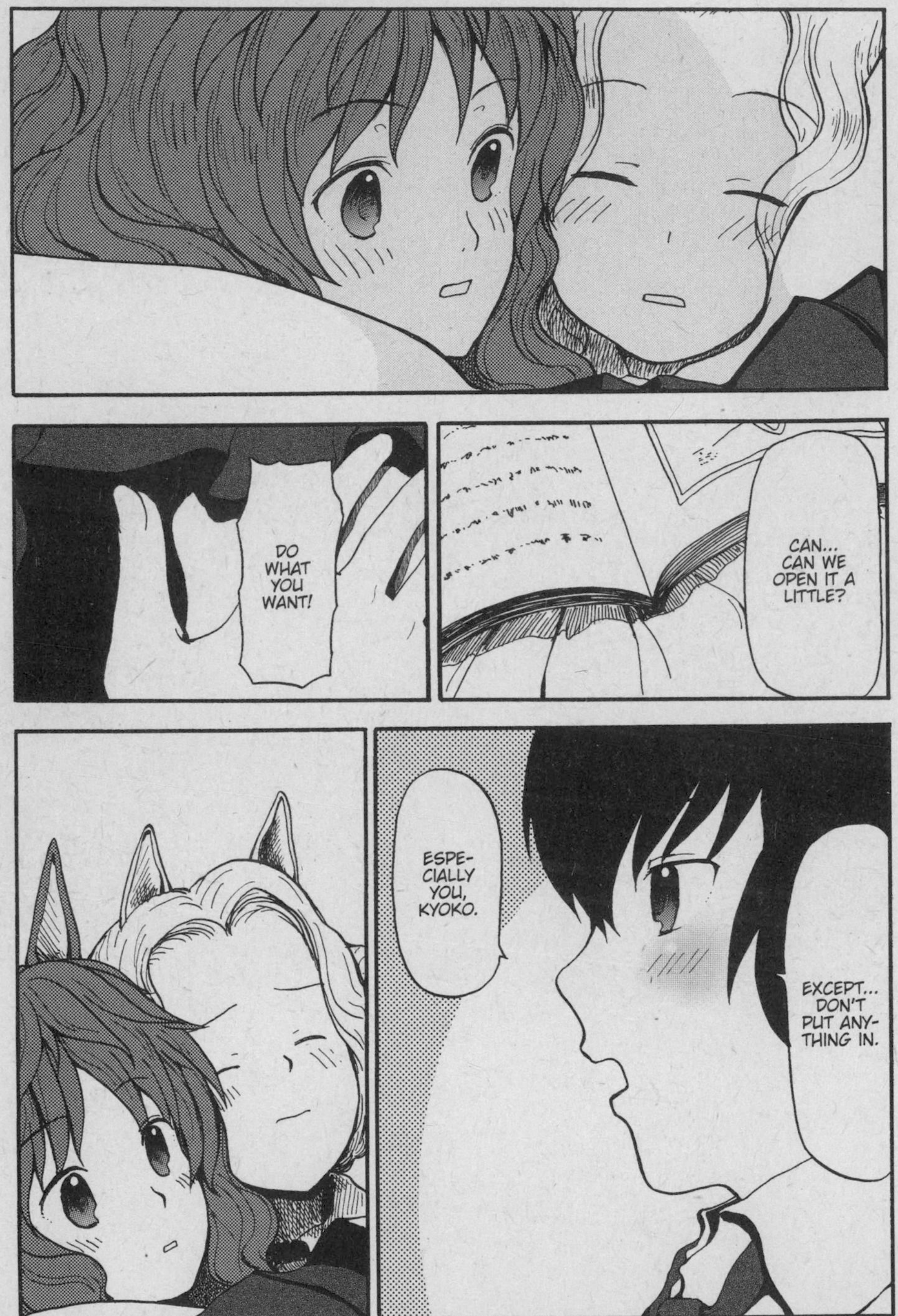
CAN... CAN WE OPEN IT A LITTLE?
DO WHAT YOU WANT!
EXCEPT... DON'T PUT ANYTHING IN.
ESPE-CIALLY YOU, KYOKO.

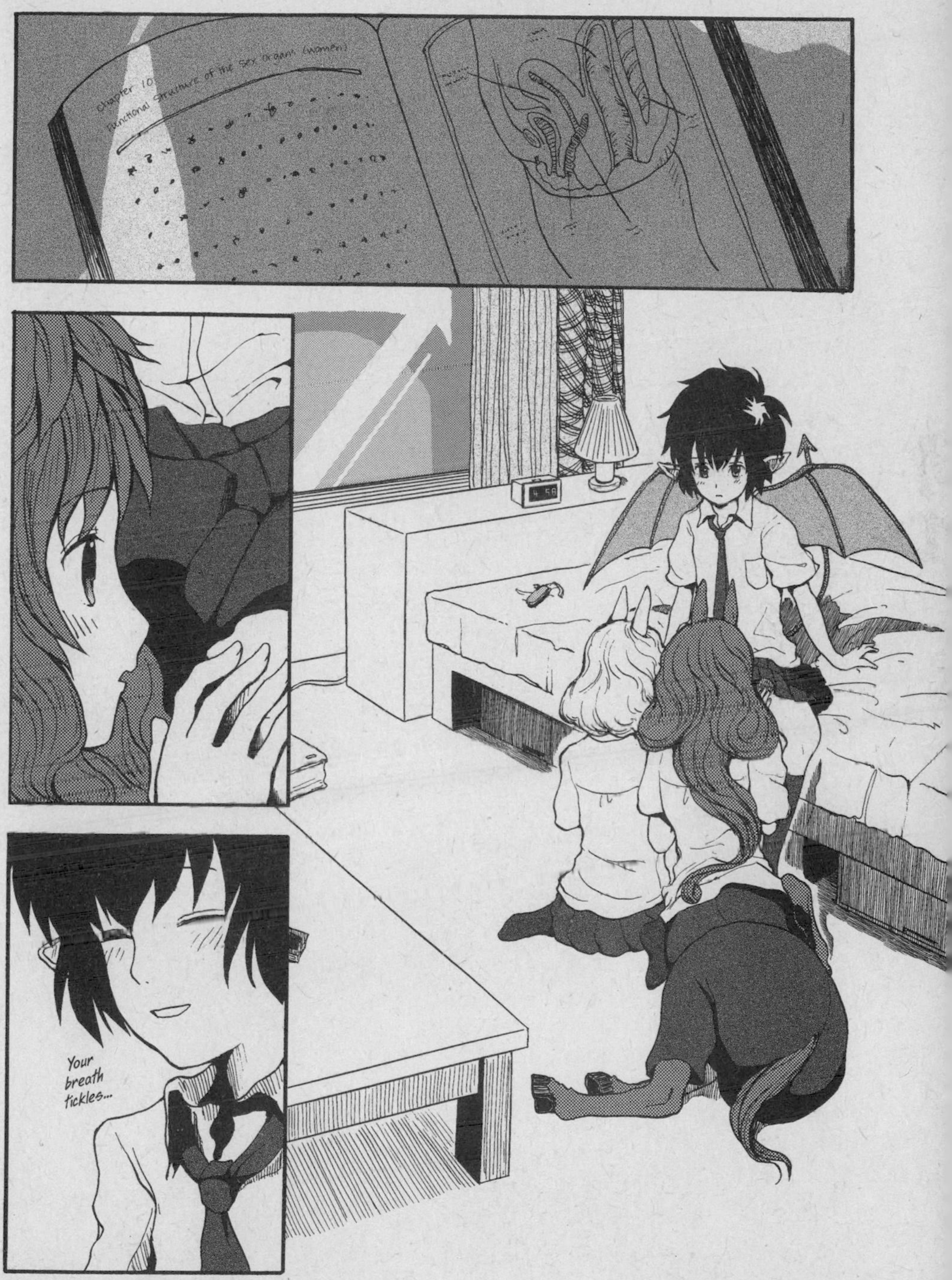
Chapter 10
Functional Structure of the Sex Organs (Women)
Your breath tickles...

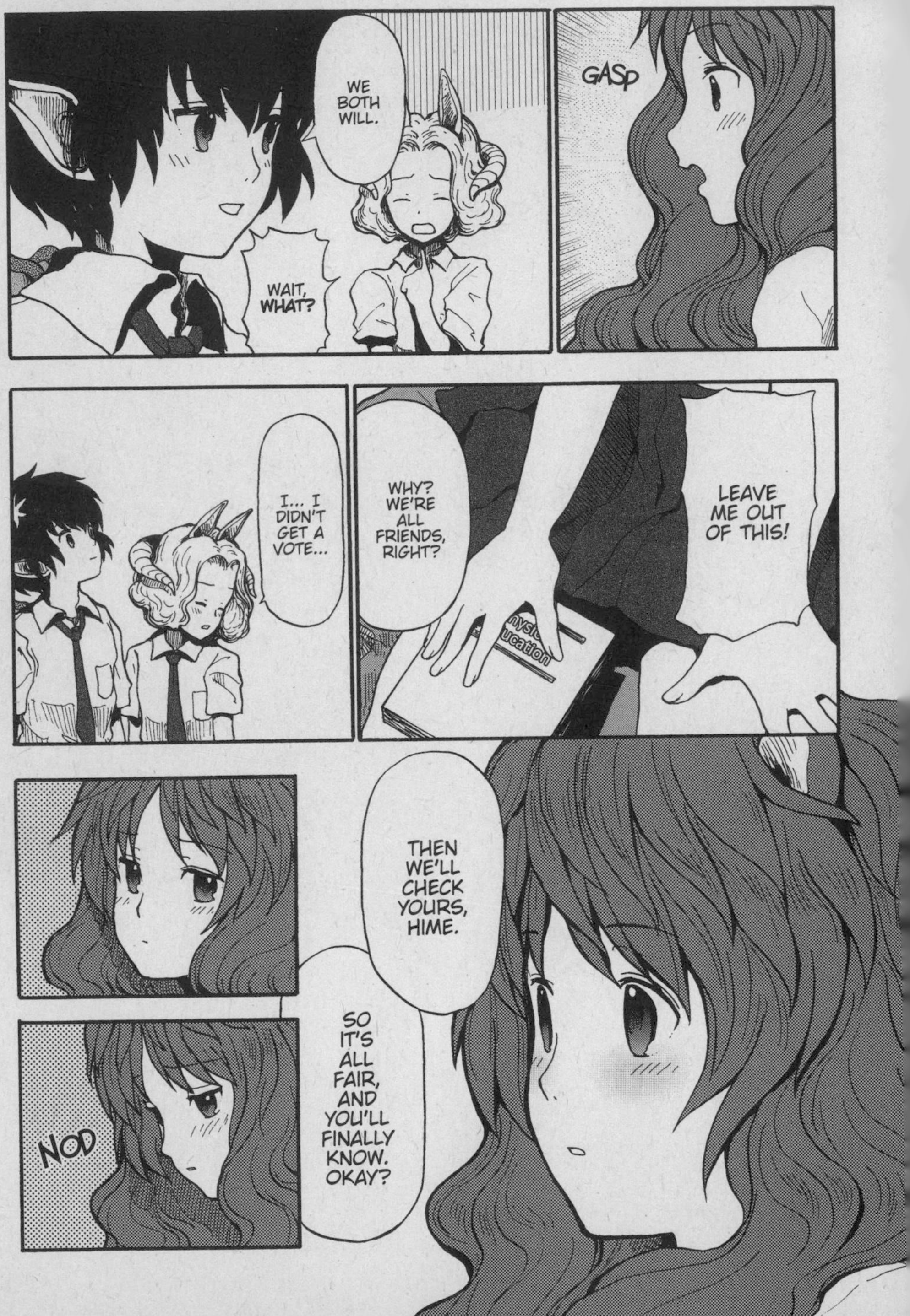
GASP
WE BOTH WILL.
WAIT, WHAT?
LEAVE ME OUT OF THIS!
WHY? WE'RE ALL FRIENDS, RIGHT?
I... I DIDN'T GET A VOTE...
THEN WE'LL CHECK YOURS, HIME.
SO IT'S ALL FAIR, AND YOU'LL FINALLY KNOW. OKAY?
NOD

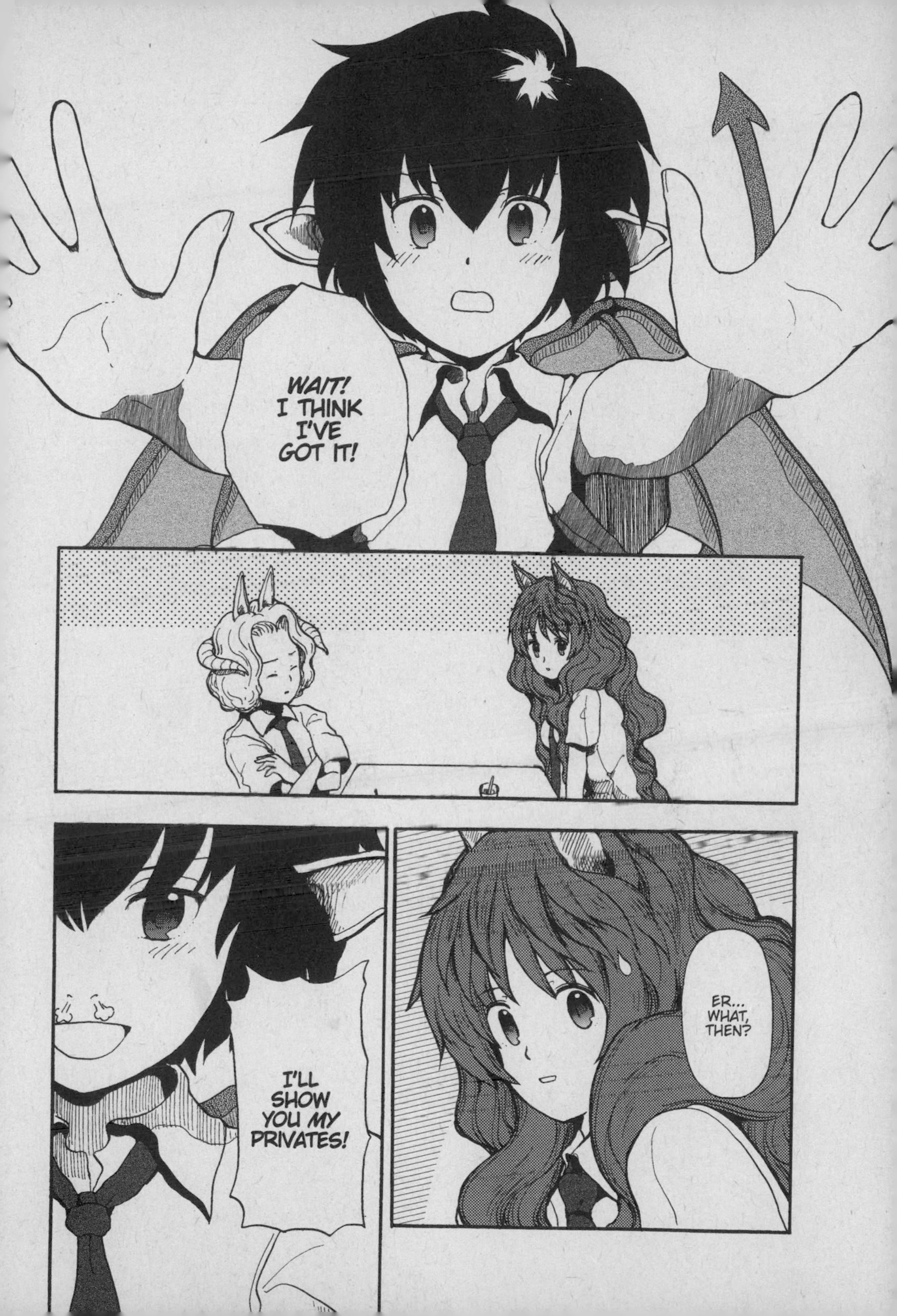
WAIT! I THINK I'VE GOT IT!
ER... WHAT, THEN?
I'LL SHOW YOU MY PRIVATES!

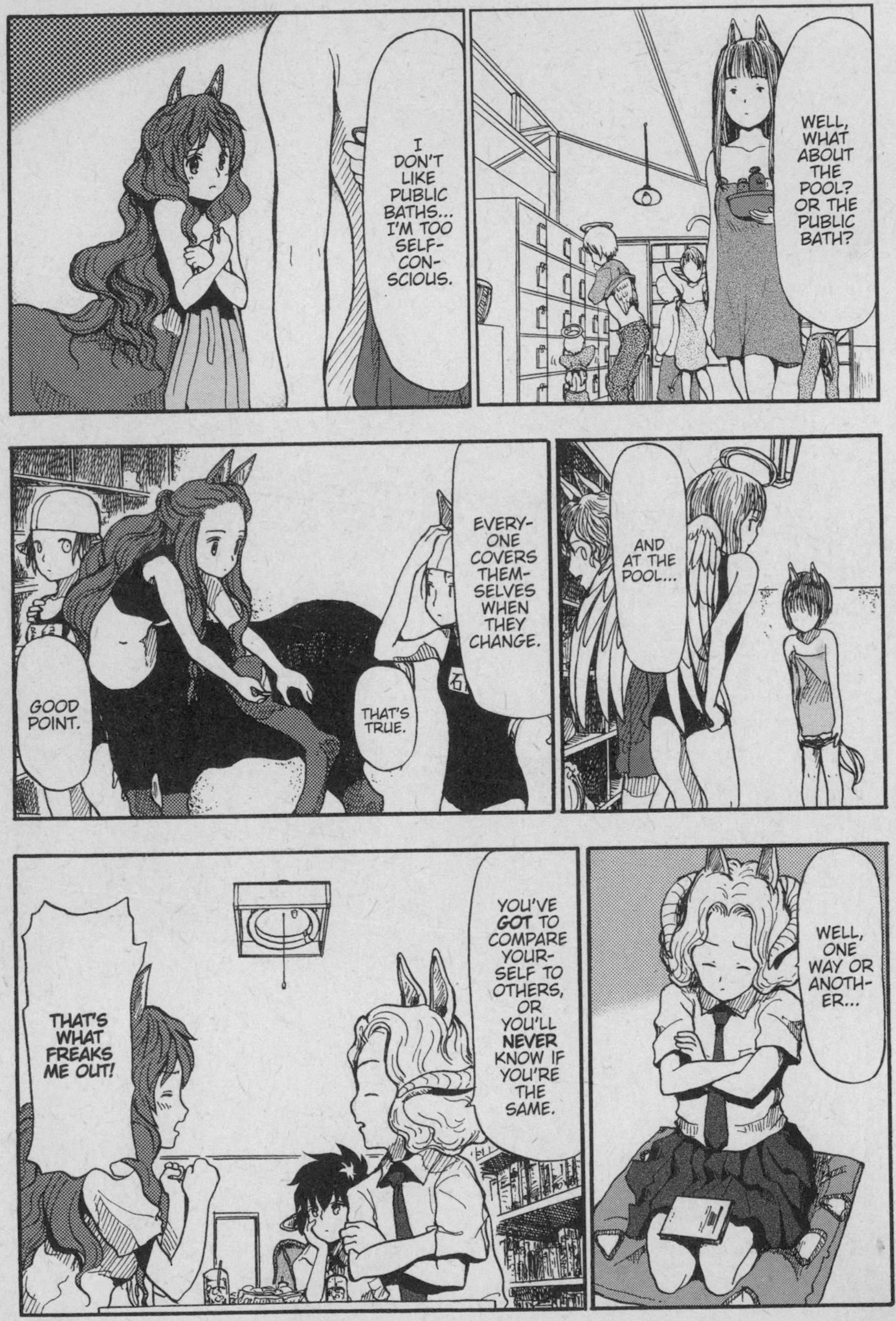
WELL, WHAT ABOUT THE POOL? OR THE PUBLIC BATH?
I DON'T LIKE PUBLIC BATHS... I'M TOO SELF-CONSCIOUS.
AND AT THE POOL...
EVERYONE COVERS THEMSELVES WHEN THEY CHANGE.
THAT'S TRUE.
GOOD POINT.
WELL, ONE WAY OR ANOTHER...
YOU'VE GOT TO COMPARE YOURSELF TO OTHERS, OR YOU'LL NEVER KNOW IF YOU'RE THE SAME.
THAT'S WHAT FREAKS ME OUT!

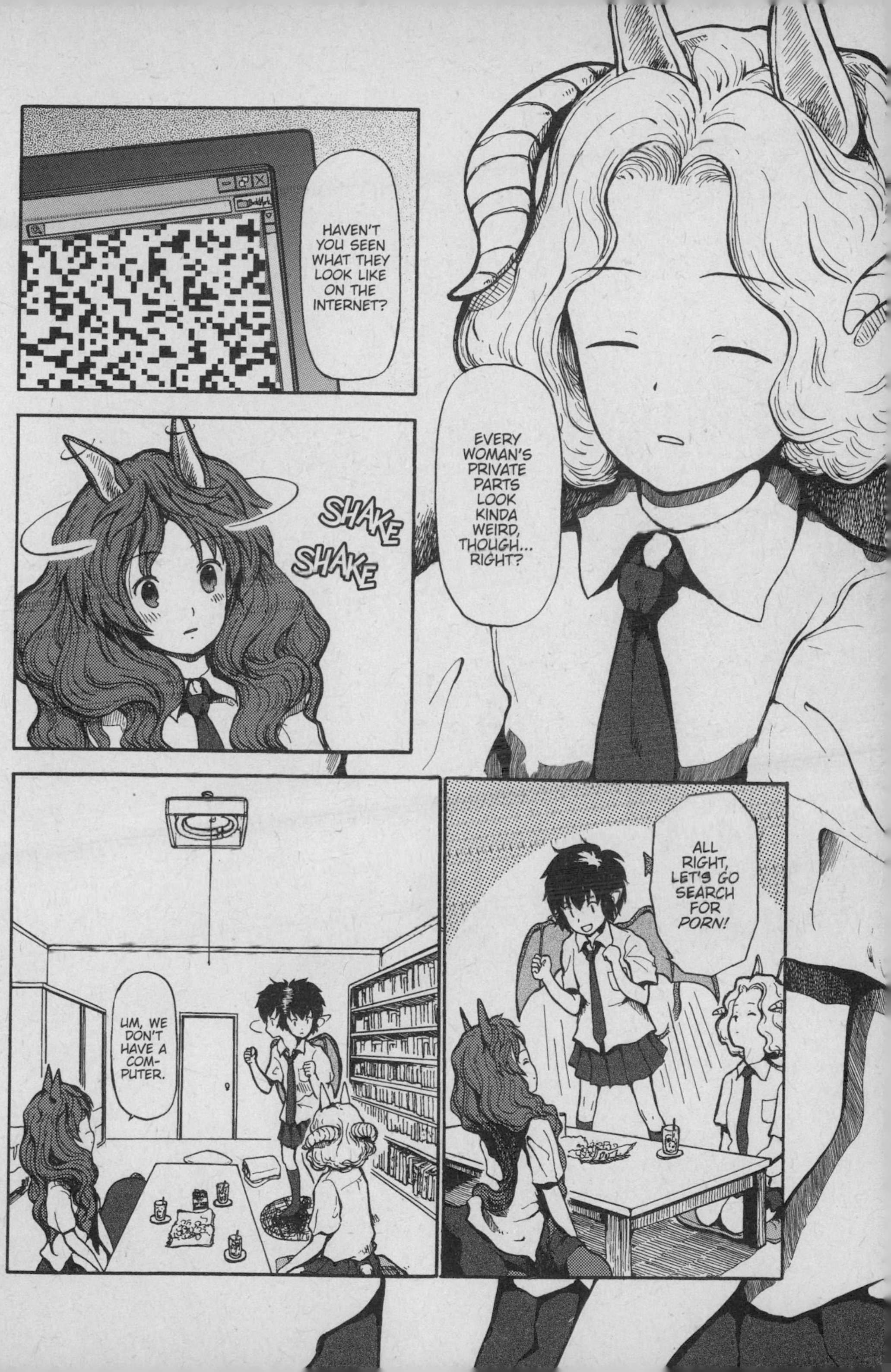
EVERY WOMAN'S PRIVATE PARTS LOOK KINDA WEIRD, THOUGH... RIGHT?
HAVEN'T YOU SEEN WHAT THEY LOOK LIKE ON THE INTERNET?
SHAKE
SHAKE
ALL RIGHT, LET'S GO SEARCH FOR *PORN!*
UM, WE DON'T HAVE A COM-PUTER.

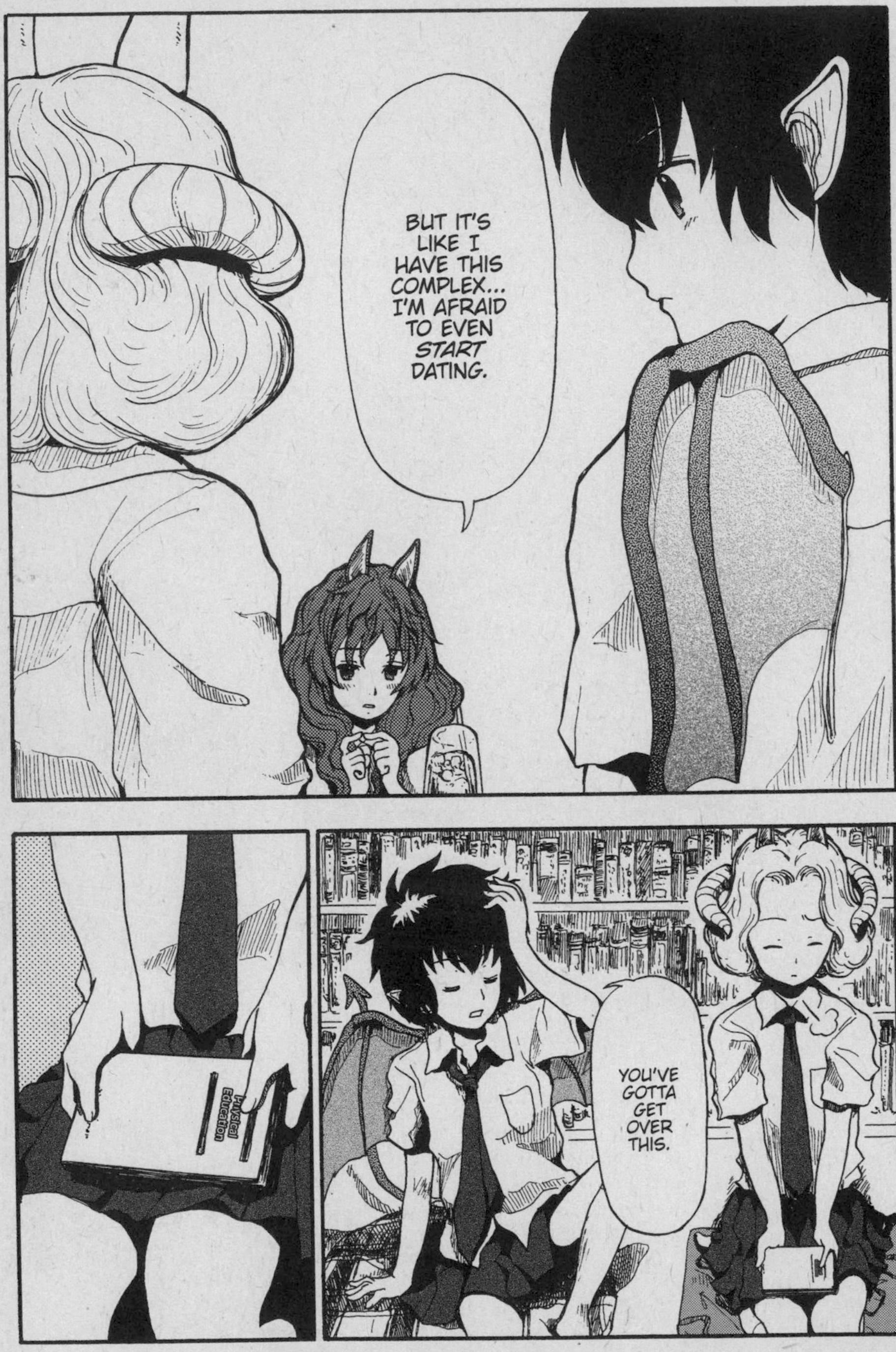
BUT IT'S LIKE I HAVE THIS COMPLEX... I'M AFRAID TO EVEN *START* DATING.
YOU'VE GOTTA GET OVER THIS.
Physical Education

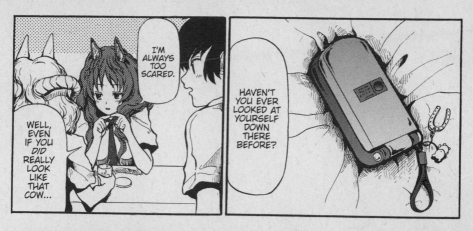

HAVEN'T YOU EVER LOOKED AT YOURSELF DOWN THERE BEFORE?
I'M ALWAYS TOO SCARED.
WELL, EVEN IF YOU *DID* REALLY LOOK LIKE THAT COW...
HERE'S THE THING...
BOYS ARE SO EXCITED ABOUT SEX...
THAT THEY PROBABLY DON'T EVEN *CARE*.
nysics
uage 1
Math 1
al Education
alth and
FLIP
AND BE-SIDES...
YOU'RE NOT EVEN *DATING* YET!
SHUT
Physical Education

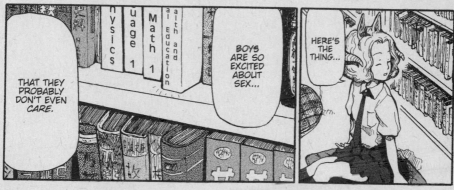

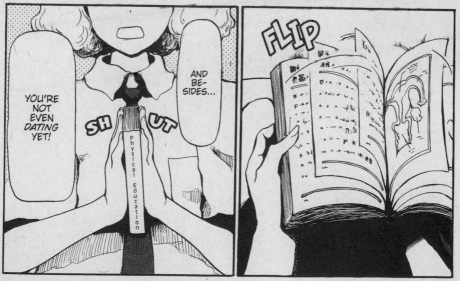

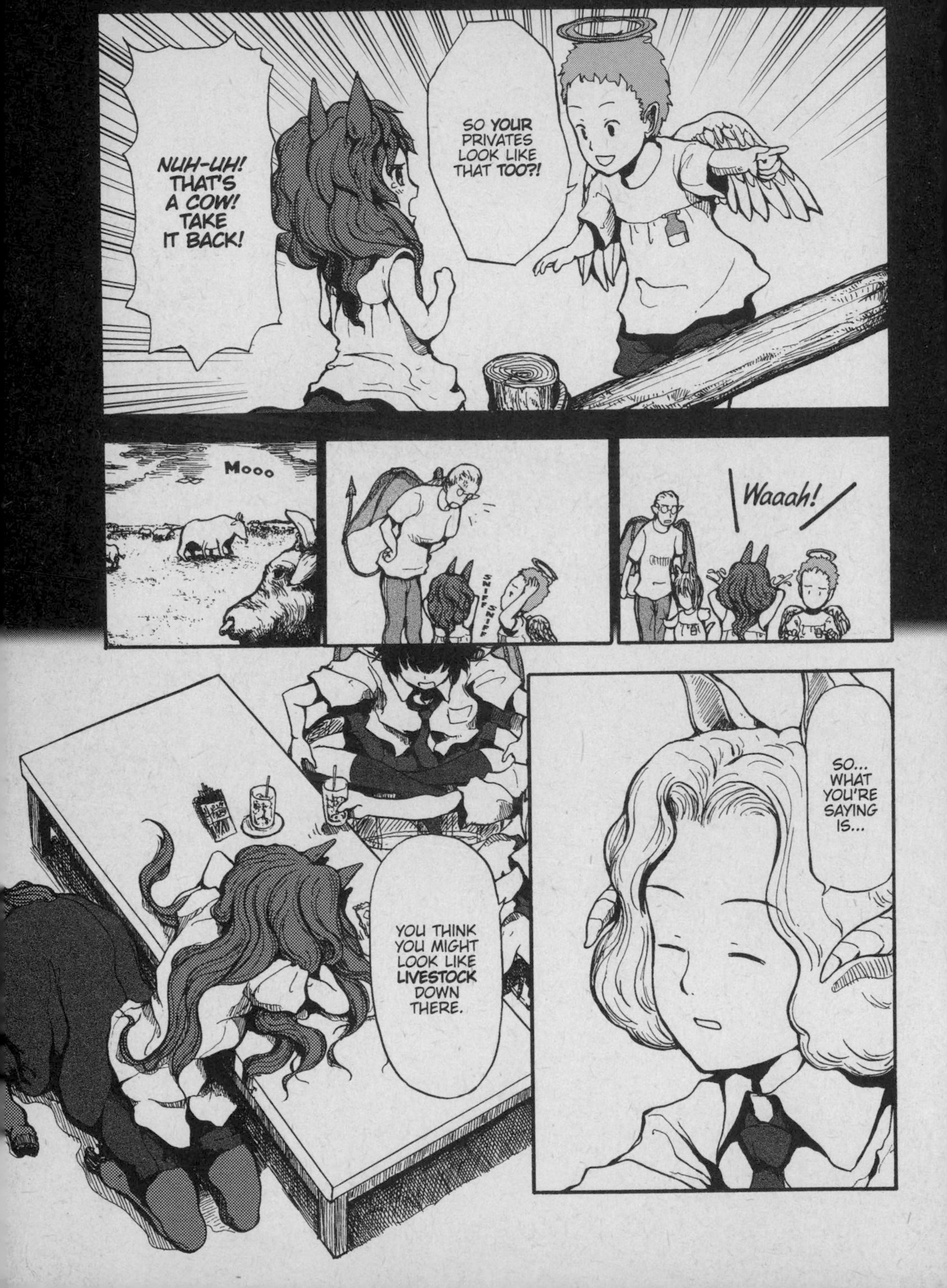
SO YOUR PRIVATES LOOK LIKE THAT TOO?!
NUH-UH! THAT'S A COW! TAKE IT BACK!
Waaah!
SNIFF SNIFF
Mooo
SO... WHAT YOU'RE SAYING IS...
YOU THINK YOU MIGHT LOOK LIKE LIVESTOCK DOWN THERE.

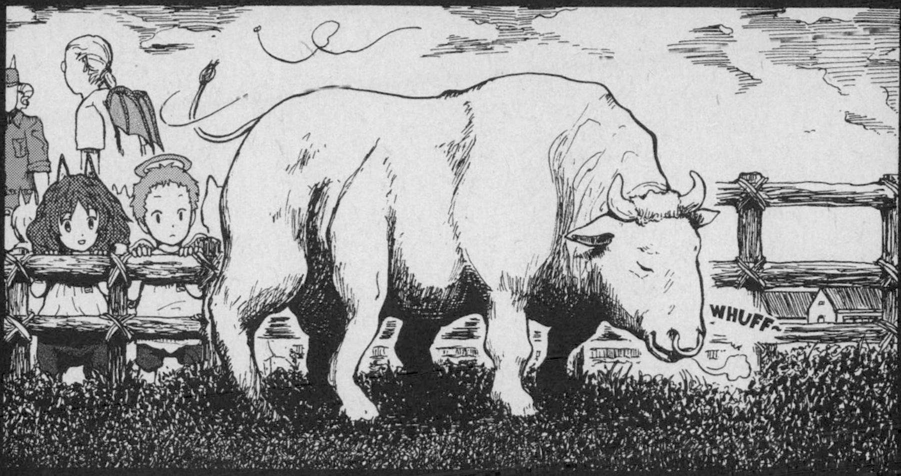
WHUFF
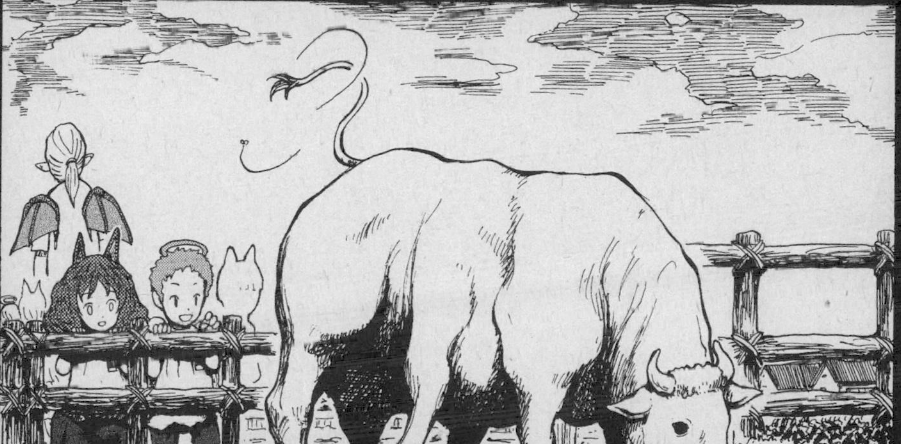
MUNCH
MUNCH
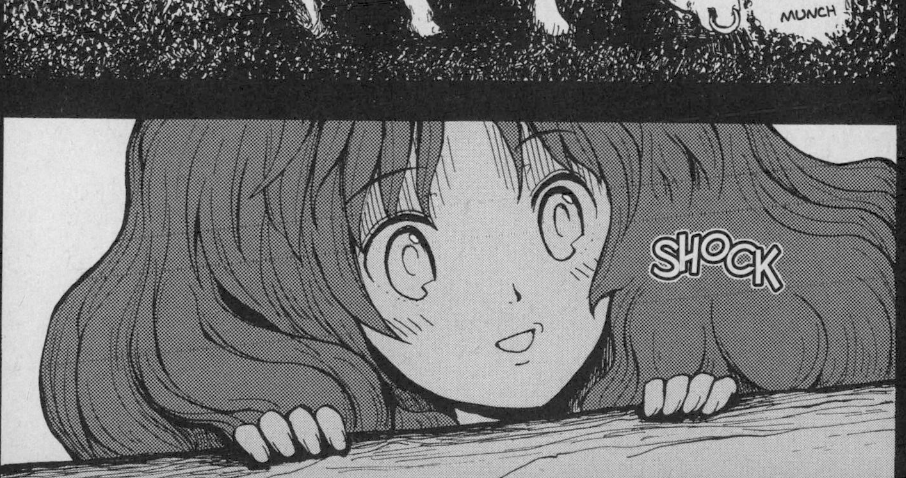
SHOCK

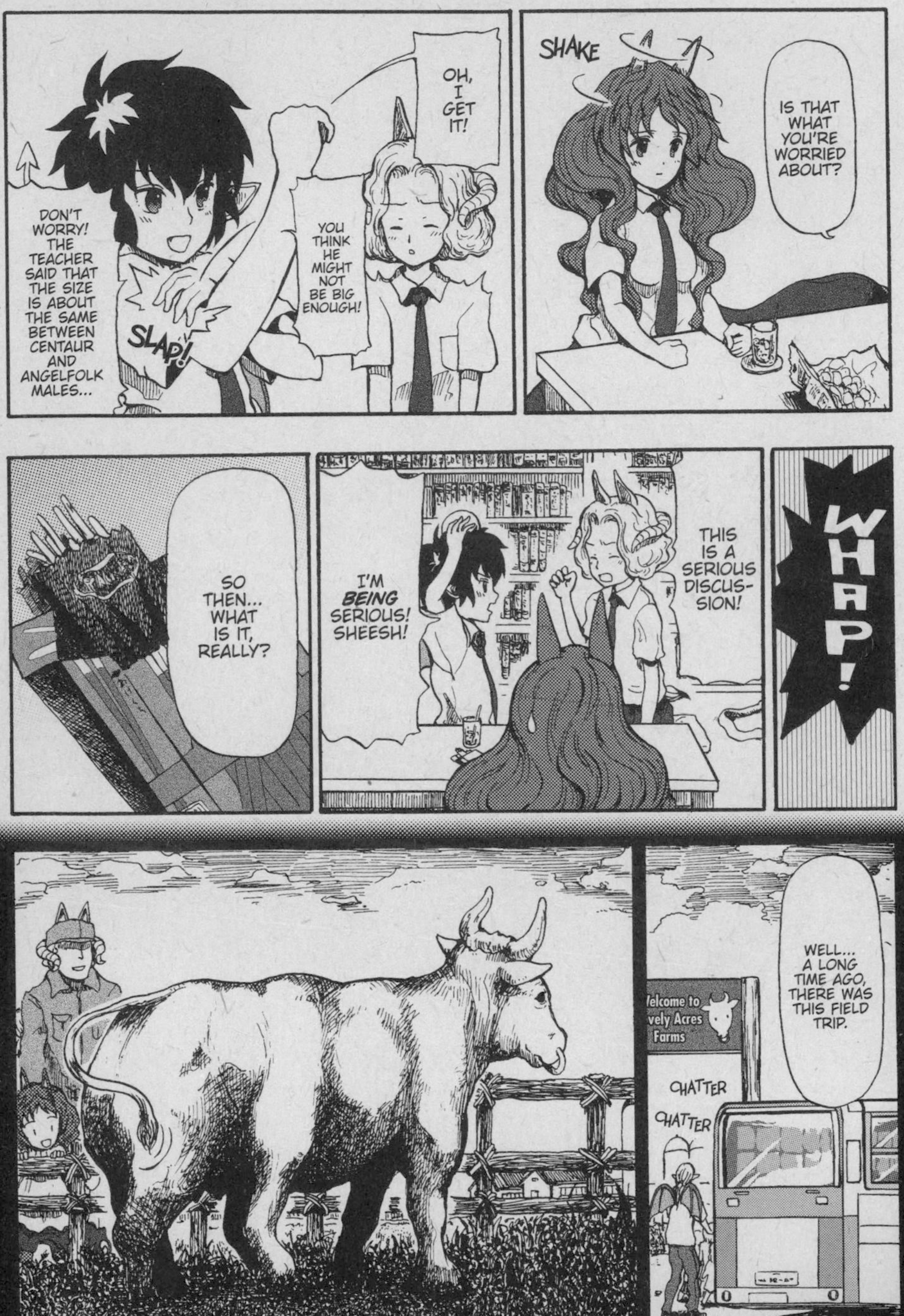
SHAKE
IS THAT WHAT YOU'RE WORRIED ABOUT?
OH, I GET IT!
YOU THINK HE MIGHT NOT BE BIG ENOUGH!
DON'T WORRY! THE TEACHER SAID THAT THE SIZE IS ABOUT THE SAME BETWEEN CENTAUR AND ANGELFOLK MALES...
SLAP!
WHAP!
THIS IS A SERIOUS DISCUSSION!
I'M BEING SERIOUS! SHEESH!
SO THEN... WHAT IS IT, REALLY?
WELL... A LONG TIME AGO, THERE WAS THIS FIELD TRIP.
Welcome to
vely Acres
Farms
CHATTER
CHATTER

THAT'S **NOT** WHAT I'M WORRIED ABOUT!

IS PROBABLY JUST AS INEXPERIENCED.

EVEN WHEN YOU GET THERE, HE...

IT'S TOO EARLY TO WORRY ABOUT THAT!

AT, LEAST, THAT'S WHAT THEY SAID IN CLASS.

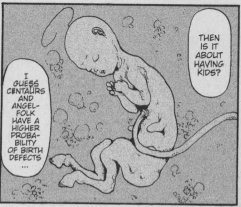

I GUESS CENTAURS AND ANGELFOLK HAVE A HIGHER PROBABILITY OF BIRTH DEFECTS ...

THEN IS IT ABOUT HAVING KIDS?

Government Public Protecting Equality Services for All Citizens

All citizens of any race who hold the empire's royal license for reproduction, as well as all citizens of mixed race and their descendants, are eligible for free access to Medical...

Treatment for comm... reproduction issues... ...if any birth defe... by Medical Serv... ...care for children... ...for monthly find... ...circumstances: Medical... ...by Medical Serv... ...on unsafe and...

...rom Medical Services for... ...n is a serious punishable... ...ees that offspring of... ...access to Medical... ...ompliance with...

GOVERNMENT PUBLIC SERVICES OR SOMETHING, RIGHT?

SINCE THE COUNTRY IMPLEMENTED SAFEGUARDS FOR BIRTH.

BUT EVEN THAT MIGHT BE OKAY...

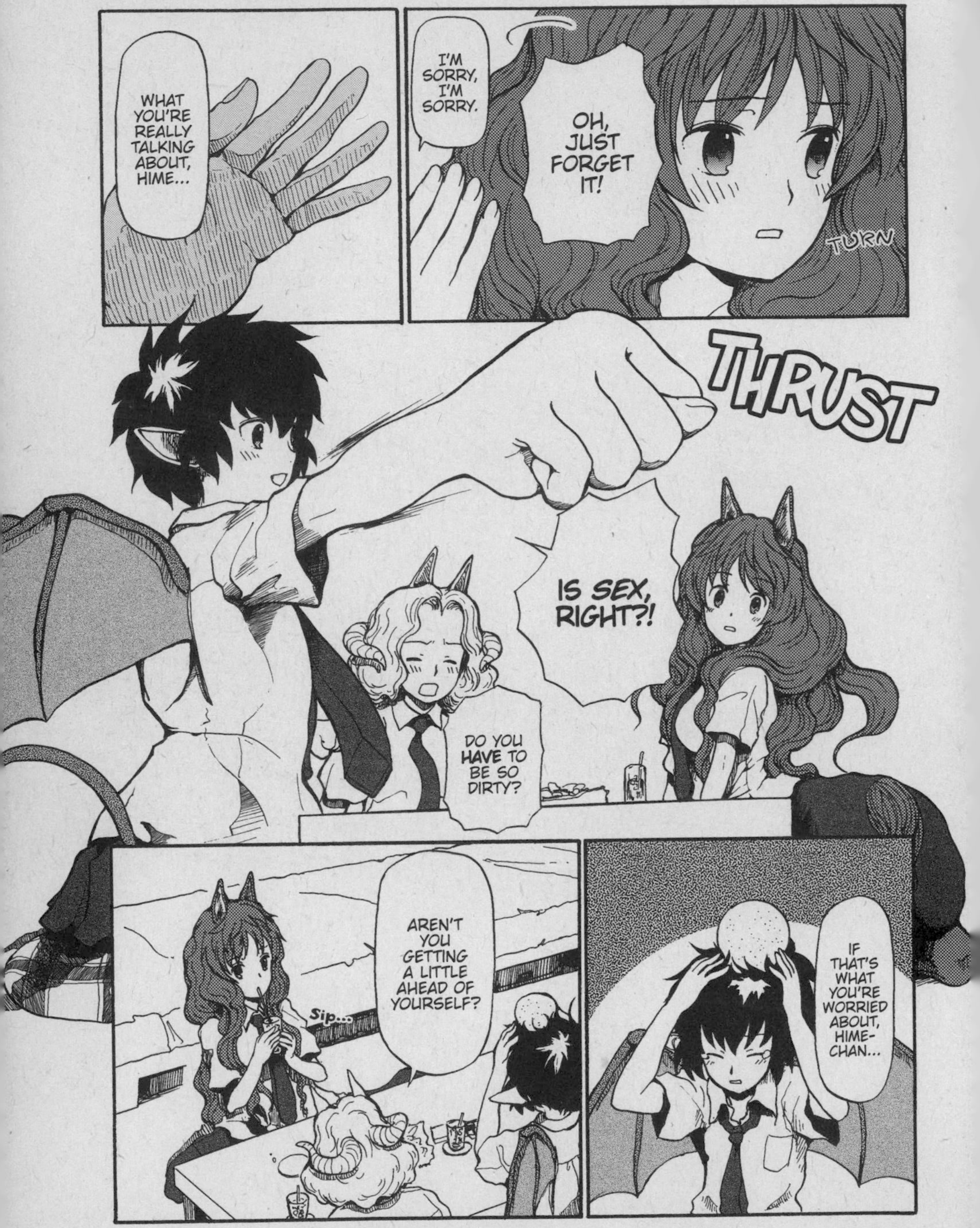
TURN
OH, JUST FORGET IT!
I'M SORRY, I'M SORRY.
WHAT YOU'RE REALLY TALKING ABOUT, HIME...
THRUST
IS SEX, RIGHT?!
DO YOU HAVE TO BE SO DIRTY?
IF THAT'S WHAT YOU'RE WORRIED ABOUT, HIME-CHAN...
AREN'T YOU GETTING A LITTLE AHEAD OF YOURSELF?
Sip...

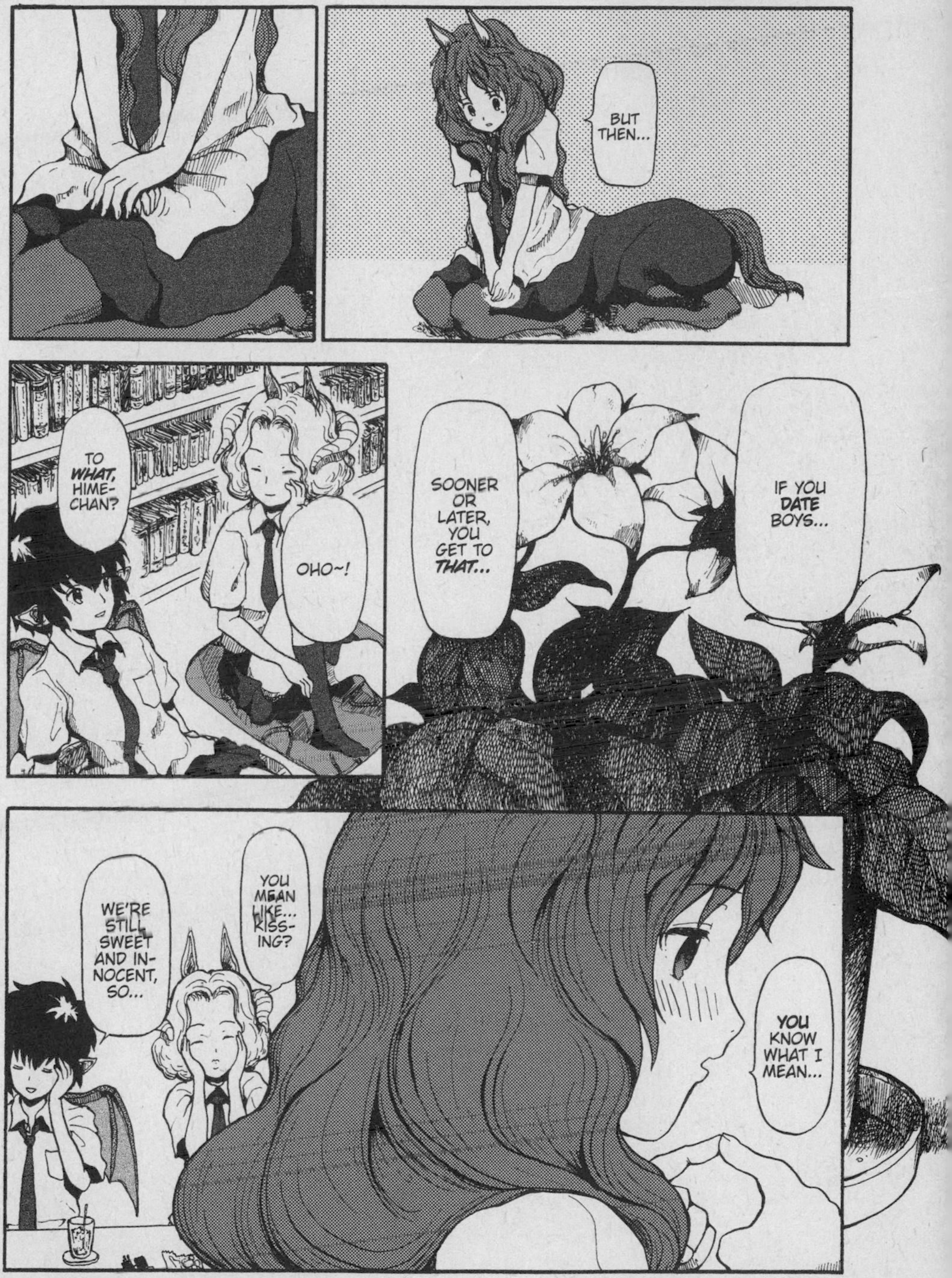

BUT THEN...
IF YOU DATE BOYS...
SOONER OR LATER, YOU GET TO THAT...
OHO~!
TO WHAT, HIME-CHAN?
YOU KNOW WHAT I MEAN...
YOU MEAN LIKE... KISS-ING?
WE'RE STILL SWEET AND IN-NOCENT, SO...

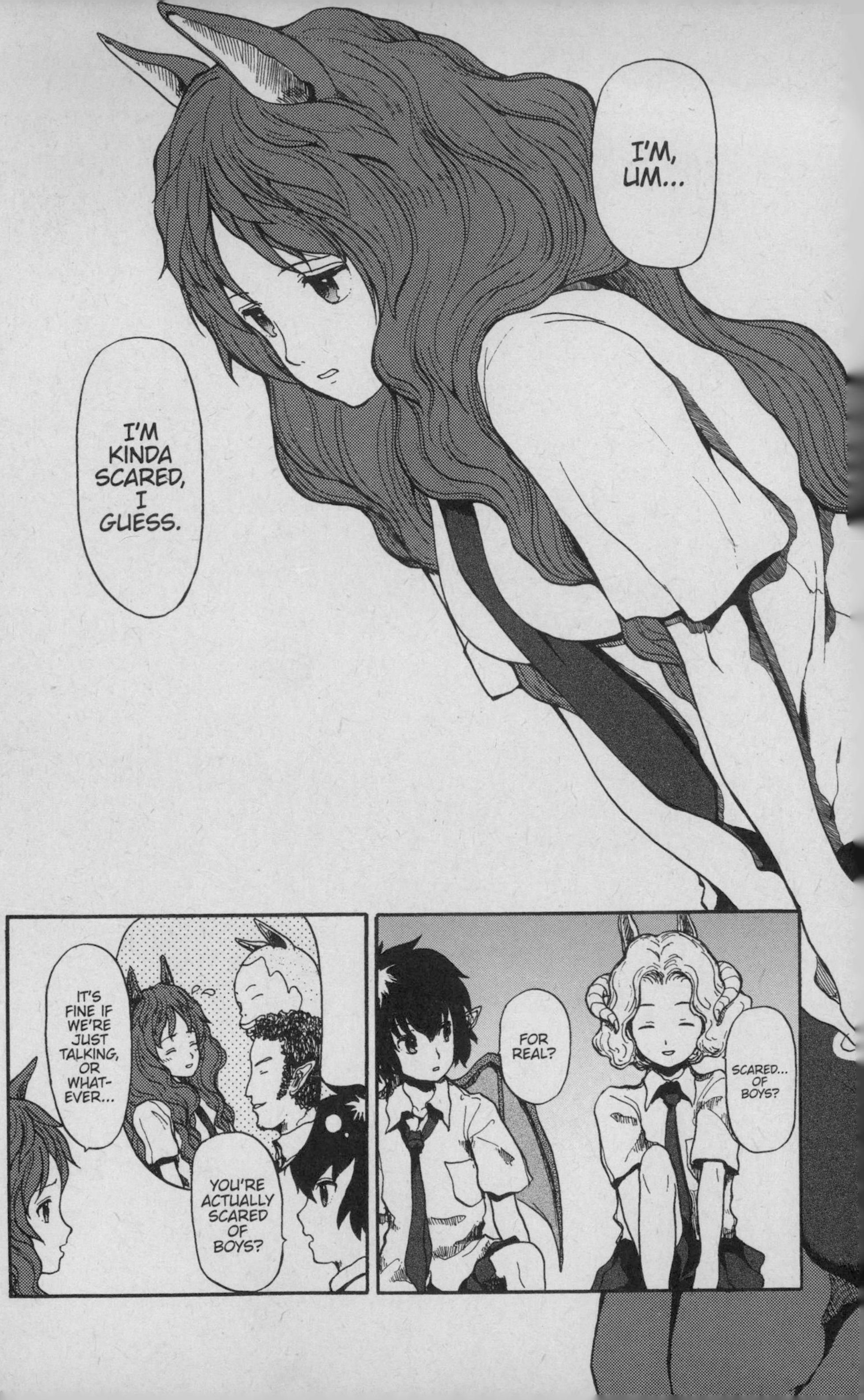
I'M, UM...
I'M KINDA SCARED, I GUESS.
SCARED... OF BOYS?
FOR REAL?
IT'S FINE IF WE'RE JUST TALKING, OR WHATEVER...
YOU'RE ACTUALLY SCARED OF BOYS?

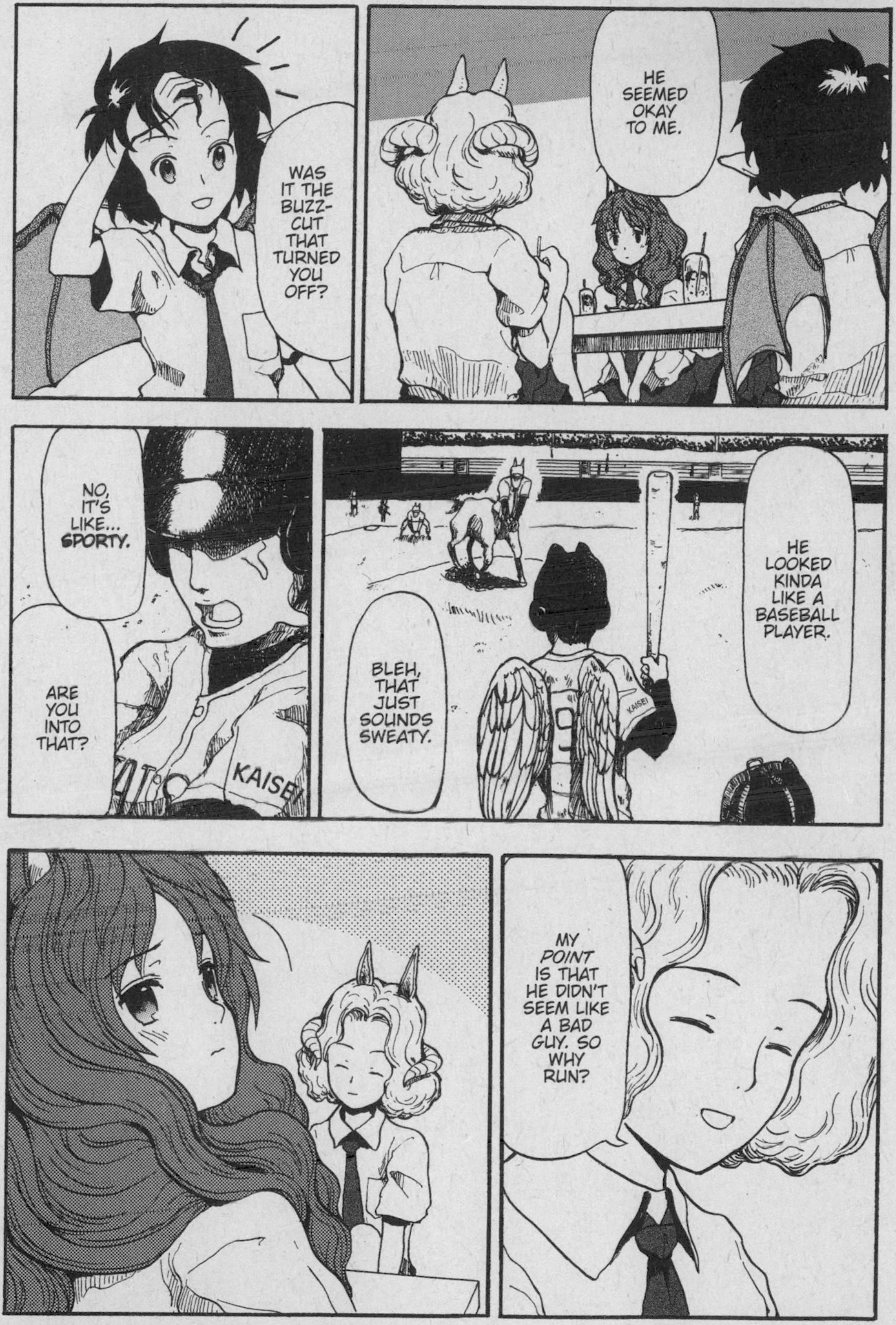
HE SEEMED OKAY TO ME.
WAS IT THE BUZZ-CUT THAT TURNED YOU OFF?
HE LOOKED KINDA LIKE A BASEBALL PLAYER.
KAISEI
BLEH, THAT JUST SOUNDS SWEATY.
NO, IT'S LIKE... **SPORTY.**
ARE YOU INTO THAT?
KAISEI
MY *POINT* IS THAT HE DIDN'T SEEM LIKE A BAD GUY. SO WHY RUN?

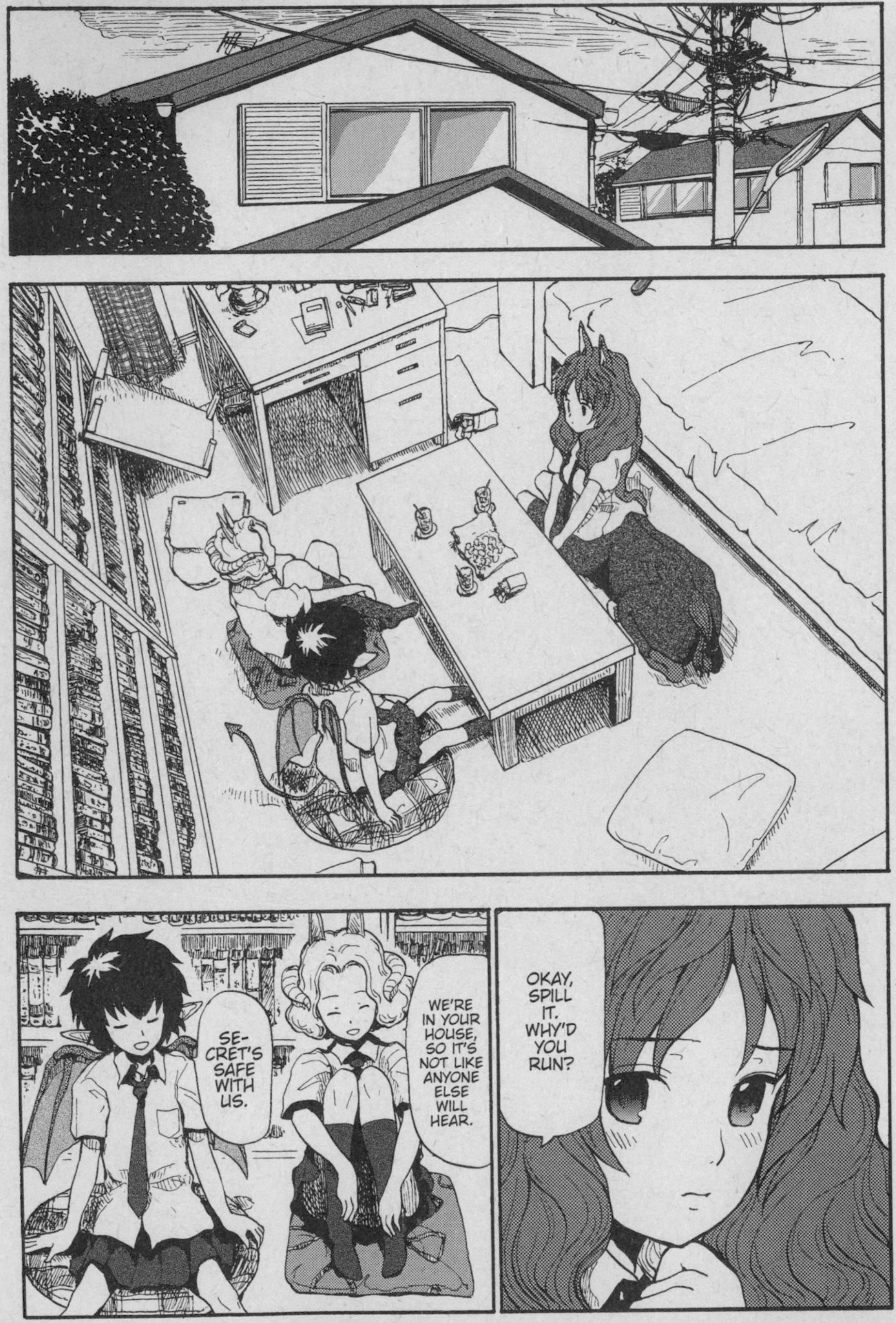
OKAY, SPILL IT. WHY'D YOU RUN?
WE'RE IN YOUR HOUSE, SO IT'S NOT LIKE ANYONE ELSE WILL HEAR.
SE-CRET'S SAFE WITH US.

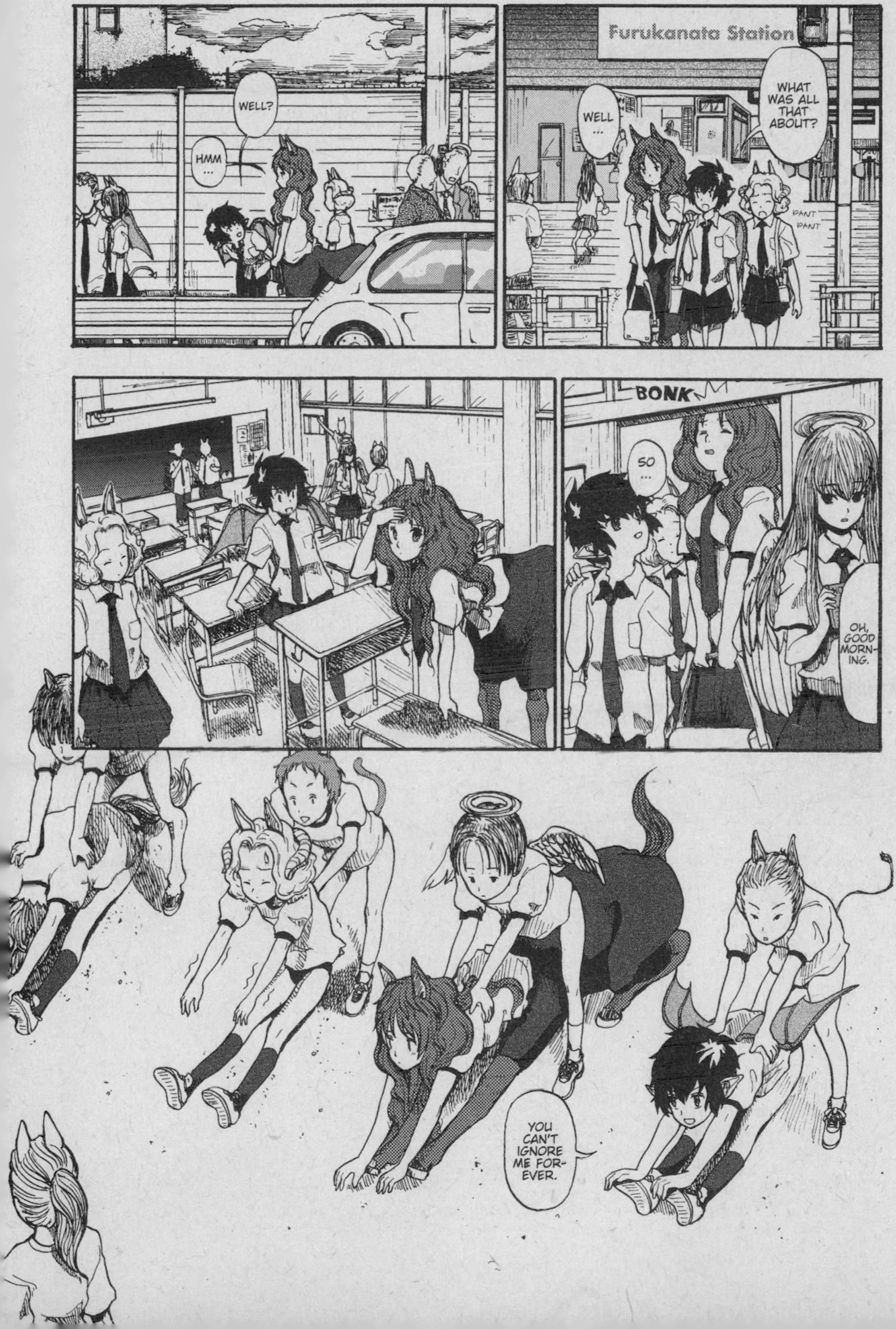
Furukanata Station
WHAT WAS ALL THAT ABOUT?
WELL ...
PANT PANT
WELL?
HMM ...
BONK
SO ...
OH, GOOD MORNING.
YOU CAN'T IGNORE ME FOR-EVER.

PUSH
SHOVE

HIME-
CHAN!

WAIT
UP!

Tickets

PSHH

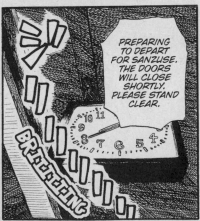

PREPARING
TO DEPART
FOR SANZUSE.
THE DOORS
WILL CLOSE
SHORTLY.
PLEASE STAND
CLEAR.

BRRRRRRING

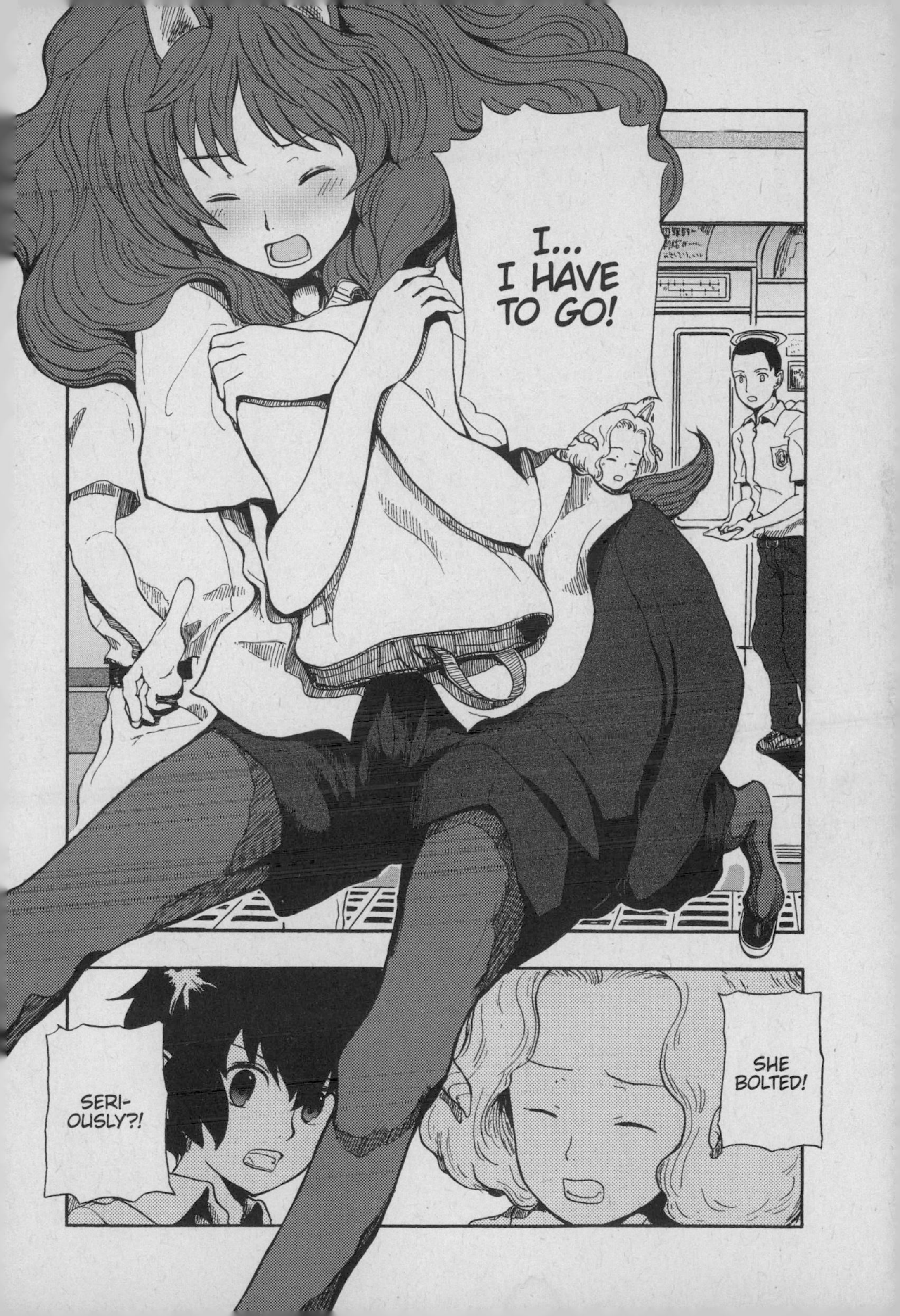
I... I HAVE TO GO!
SHE BOLTED!
SERI-OUSLY?!

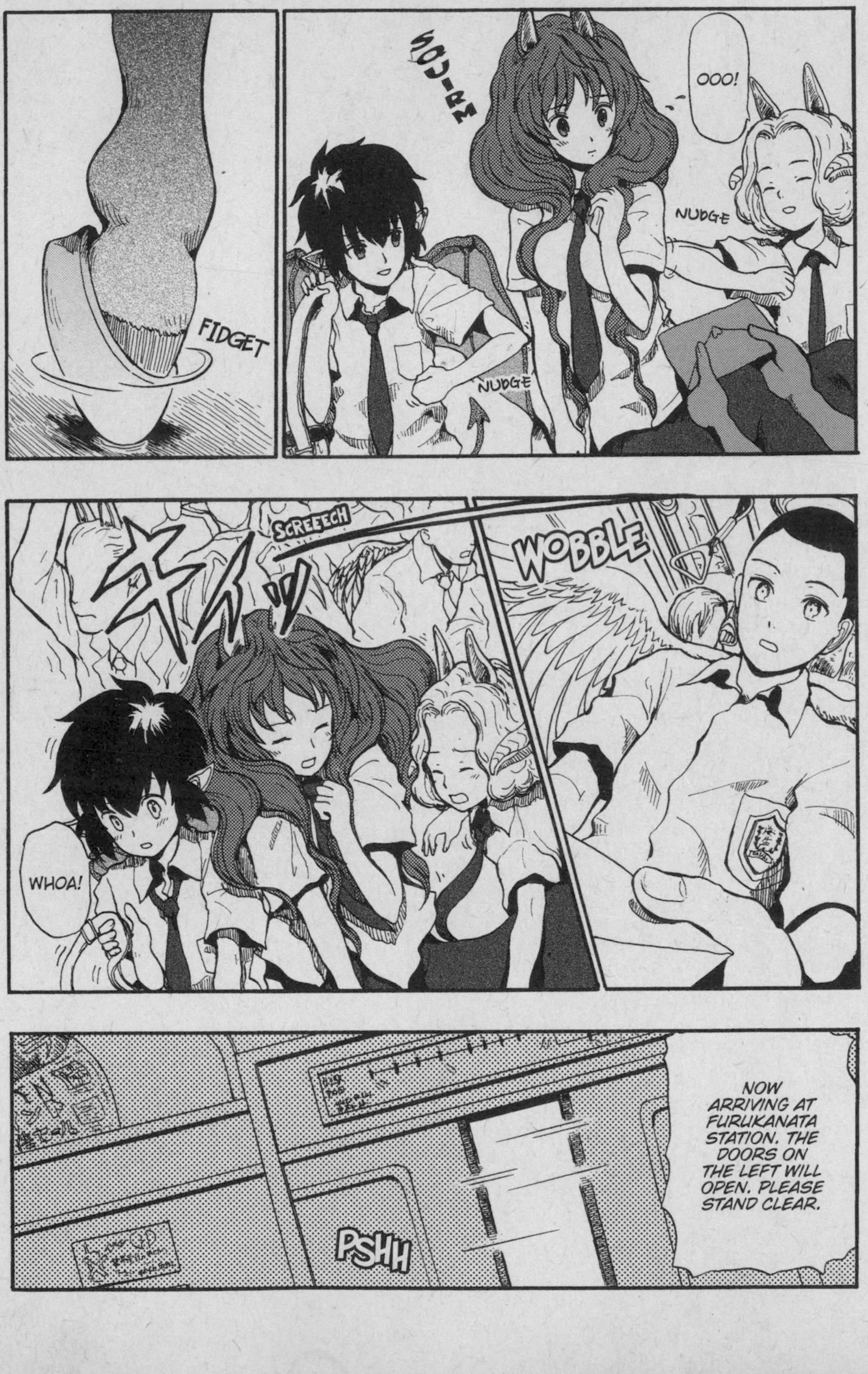
OOO!
SQUIRM
NUDGE
NUDGE
FIDGET
WOBBLE
SCREEECH
WHOA!
NOW ARRIVING AT FURUKANATA STATION. THE DOORS ON THE LEFT WILL OPEN. PLEASE STAND CLEAR.
PSHH

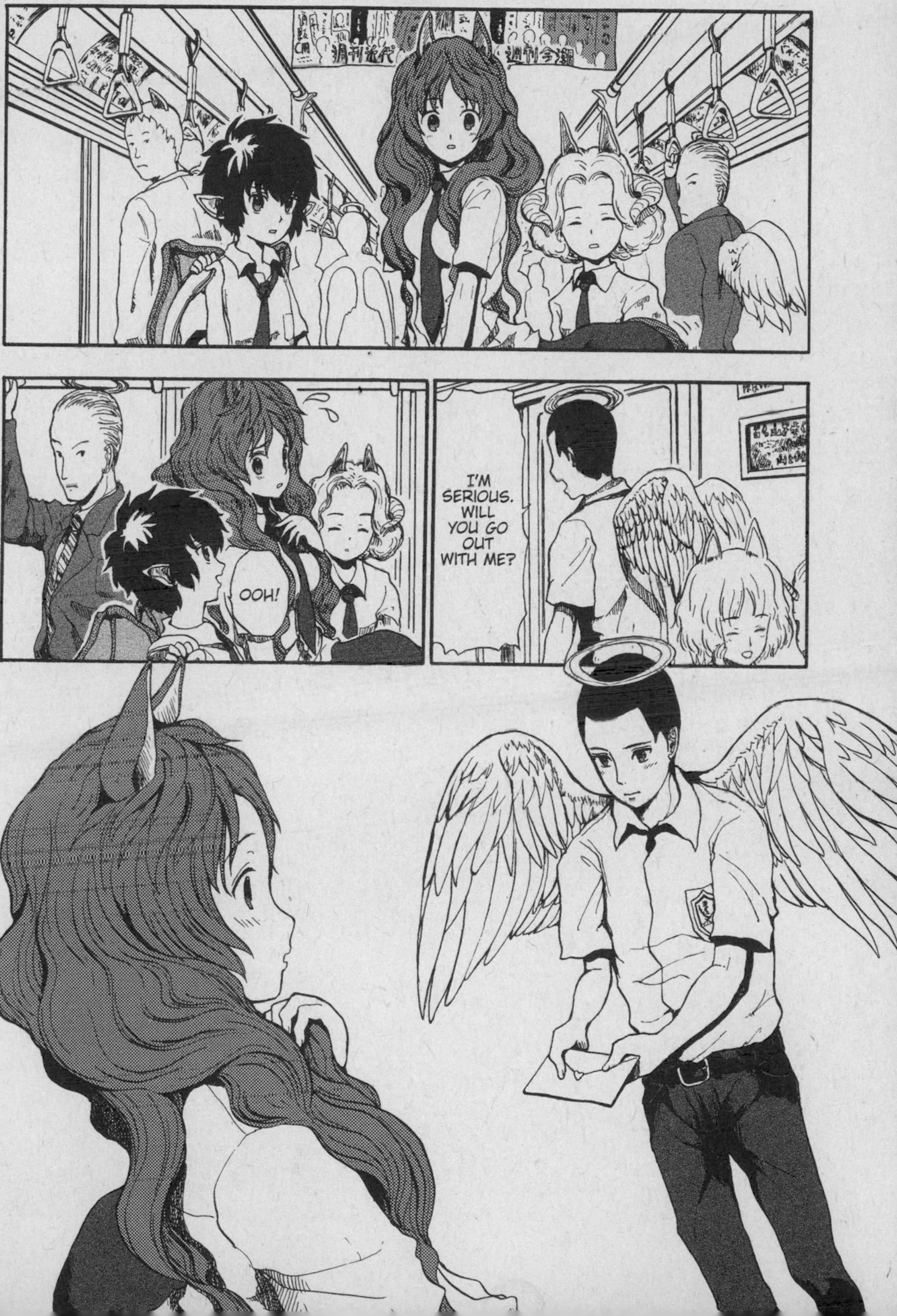
I'M SERIOUS. WILL YOU GO OUT WITH ME?
OOH!

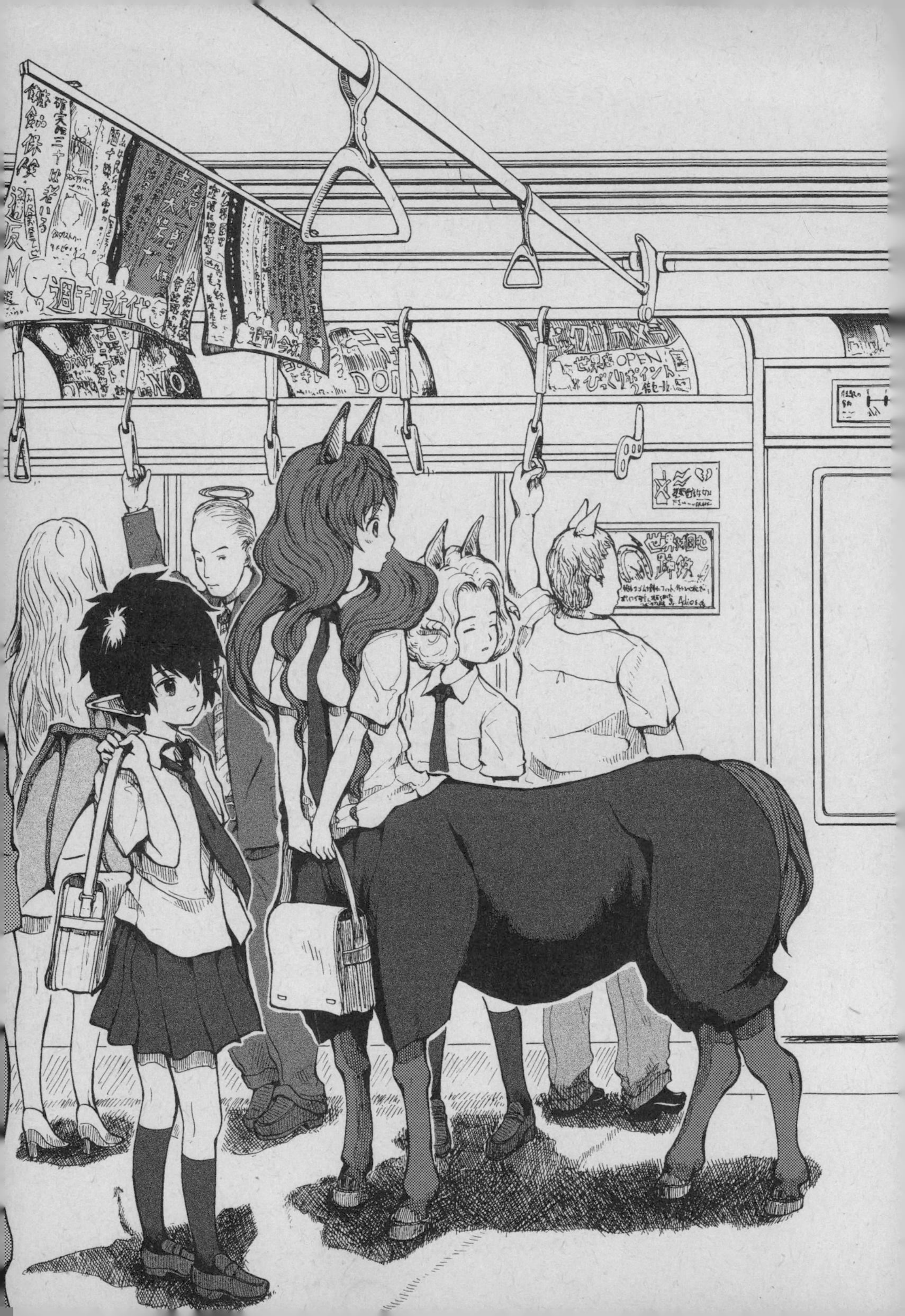
週刊近代
世界店OPEN
DOM

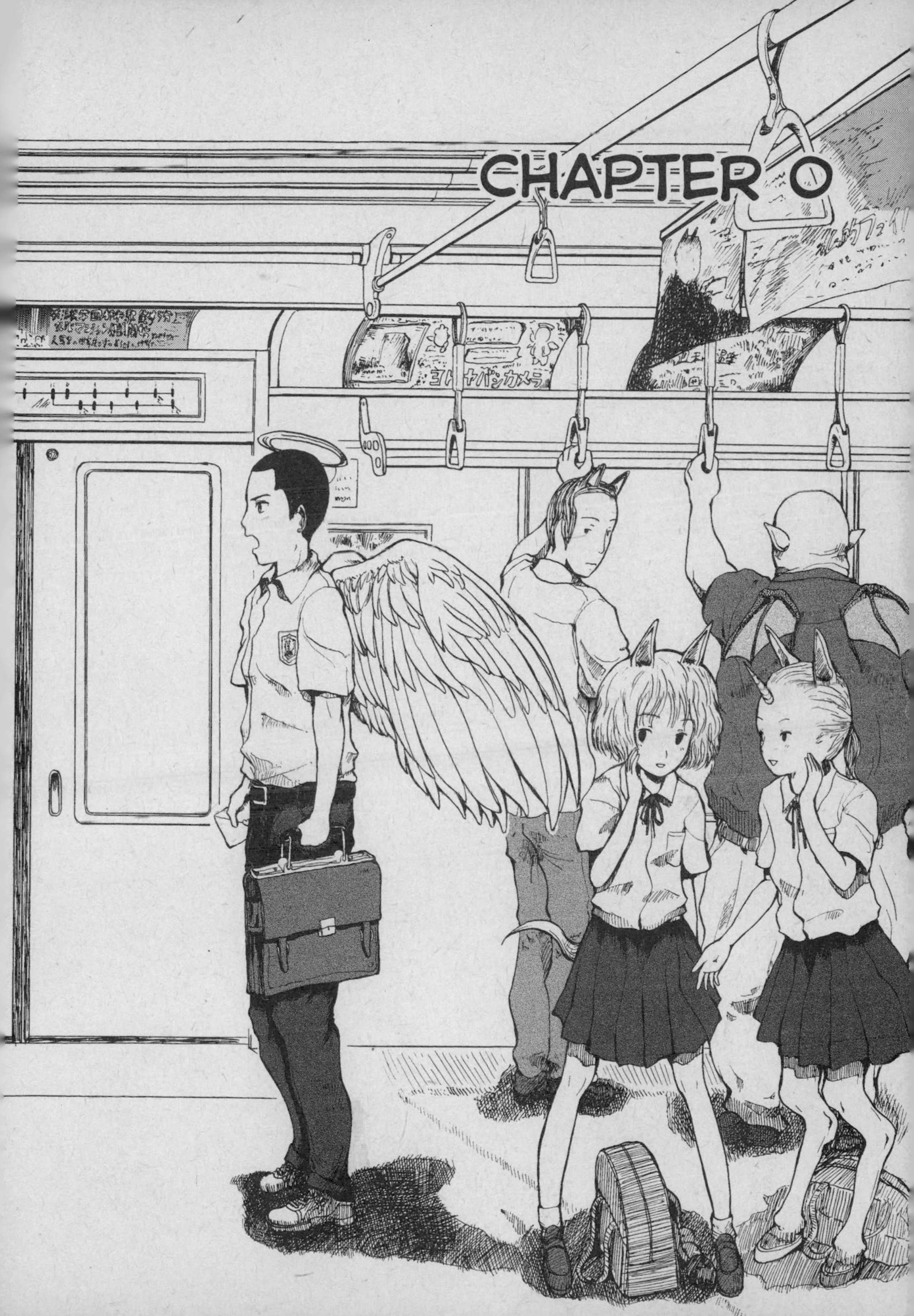
CHAPTER 0

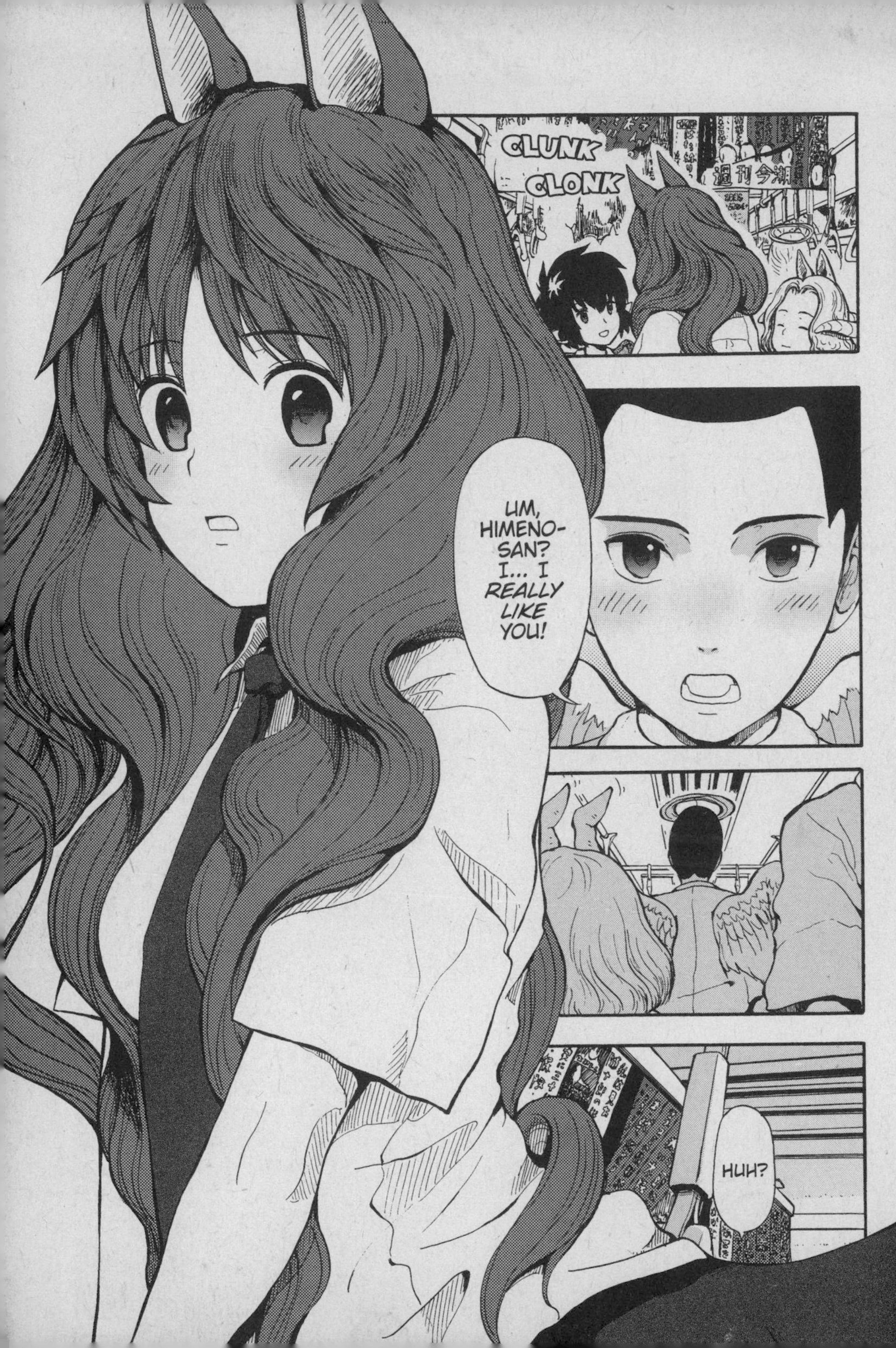
CLUNK
CLONK
UM, HIMENO-SAN? I... I REALLY LIKE YOU!
HUH?

#1

SEVEN SEAS ENTERTAINMENT PRESENTS

A Centaur's Life

story and art by KEI MURAYAMA

VOLUME 1

TRANSLATION
Angela Liu

ADAPTATION
Holly Kolodziejczak

LETTERING AND LAYOUT
Jennifer Skarupa

LOGO DESIGN
Courtney Williams

COVER DESIGN
Nicky Lim

PROOFREADER
Patrick King

MANAGING EDITOR
Adam Arnold

PUBLISHER
Jason DeAngelis

CENTAUR NO NAYAMI VOLUME 1
© KEI MURAYAMA 2011
Originally published in Japan in 2011 by TOKUMA SHOTEN PUBLISHING CO., LTD., Tokyo. English translation rights arranged with TOKUMA SHOTEN PUBLISHING CO., LTD., Tokyo, through TOHAN CORPORATION, Tokyo.

Seven Seas books may be purchased in bulk for educational, business, or promotional use. For information on bulk purchases, please contact Macmillan Corporate & Premium Sales Department at 1-800-221-7945 (ext 5442) or write specialmarkets@macmillan.com.

Seven Seas and the Seven Seas logo are trademarks of Seven Seas Entertainment, LLC. All rights reserved.

ISBN: 978-1-937867-91-1

Printed in Canada

First Printing: November 2013

10 9 8 7 6 5 4 3 2 1

FOLLOW US ONLINE: www.gomanga.com

READING DIRECTIONS

This book reads from *right to left*, Japanese style. If this is your first time reading manga, you start reading from the top right panel on each page and take it from there. If you get lost, just follow the numbered diagram here. It may seem backwards at first, but you□ll get the hang of it! Have fun!!

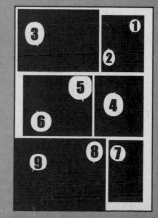

A Centaur's Life

Vol. 1

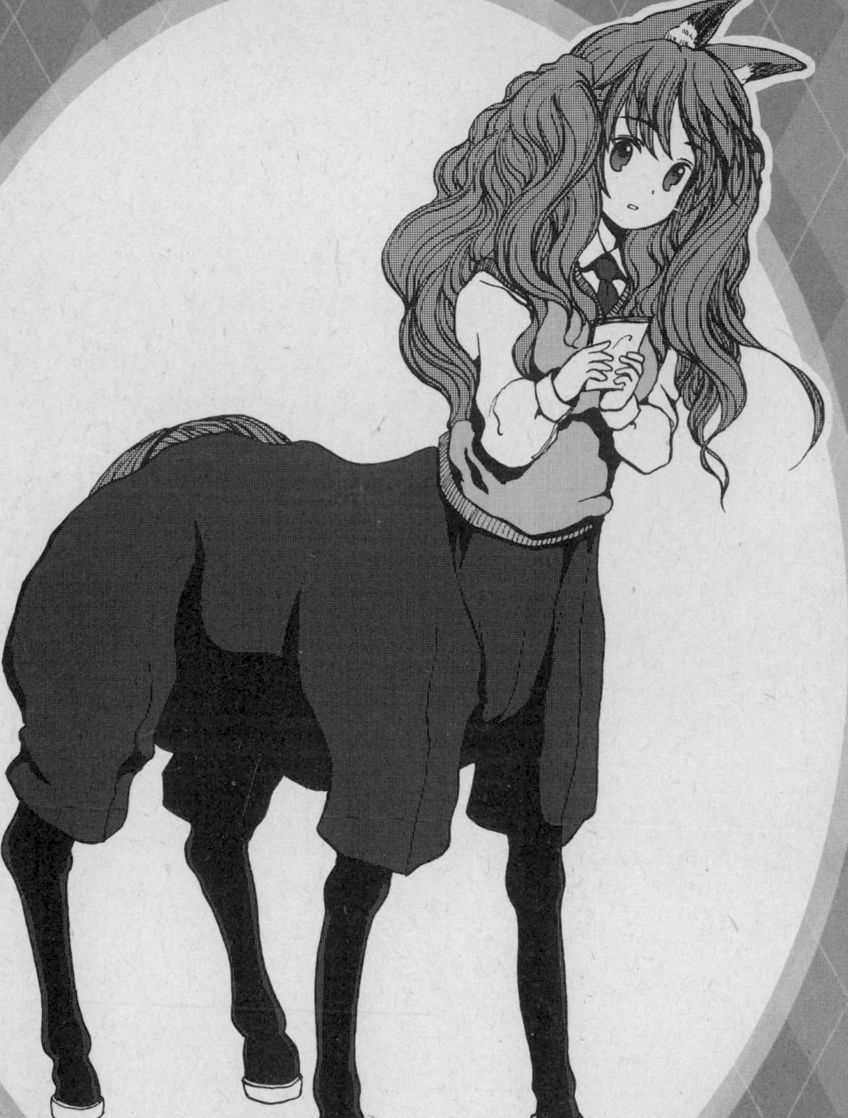

story & art

KEI MURAYAMA